T0302831

THE DERRYDALE PRESS    FOXHUNTERS' LIBRARY

# Foxhunters Speak

## AN ORAL HISTORY
## OF
## AMERICAN FOXHUNTING

*Interviews and Photographs by*

Mary Motley Kalergis

*Drawings by*

*R. E. Lee Gildea Jr.*

THE DERRYDALE PRESS

Lanham • Boulder • New York • London

## THE DERRYDALE PRESS

Published by The Derrydale Press
An imprint of The Rowman & Littlefield Publishing Group, Inc.
4501 Forbes Boulevard, Suite 200, Lanham, Maryland 20706
www.rowman.com

Unit A, Whitacre Mews, 26-34 Stannary Street, London SE11 4AB

Distributed by NATIONAL BOOK NETWORK

British Library Cataloguing in Publication Information available

**Library of Congress Cataloging-in-Publication Data**

Names: Kalergis, Mary Motley. | Gildea, R. E. Lee, Jr., illustrator.
Title: Foxhunters speak : an oral history of American foxhunting / interviews and photographs by Mary Motley Kalergis ; drawings by R.E. Lee Gildea, Jr.
Description: Lanham : The Derrydale Press, [2017] | Includes index.
Identifiers: LCCN 2016043658 (print) | LCCN 2016045056 (ebook) |
ISBN 9781564162151 (hardback) | ISBN 9781564162168 (e-book)
Subjects: LCSH: Fox hunting—United States.
Classification: LCC SK286 K35 2017 (print) | LCC SK286 (ebook) | DDC 799.2/59775—dc23
LC record available at https://lccn.loc.gov/2016043658

♾™ The paper used in this publication meets the minimum requirements of American National Standard for Information Sciences—Permanence of Paper for Printed Library Materials, ANSI/NISO Z39.48-1992.

Printed in the United States of America

*In loving memory of my beloved brother,*
*Hugh Camp Motley*

1955 ~ 2016

# Contents

# Introduction

My brother Hugh Motley, former Master of Foxhounds of the Keswick Hunt Club, often used to say, "If there are fifty people out foxhunting, they are out for fifty different reasons." The first time I heard this adage, I had my doubts, but a quick look around the field showed me its wisdom. From the newcomer to the fourth-generation "hound-man," from the billionaire to the local kid on a borrowed pony, from the champion show rider to the steeplechase jockey, it's fair to say that everyone who comes out foxhunting is there for a different reason. But one thing they all have in common is that no matter how long they have been foxhunting and how knowledgeable about it they may now be, *someone introduced them to the sport and taught them how to participate.* That insight was the seed that sprouted into this oral history of foxhunting in America.

But let's start at the beginning. When I'm not foxhunting with central Virginia's Keswick and Farmington Hunt Clubs, my work over the past thirty-five years has been to travel around the country with camera and tape recorder, creating human interest documentary books on subjects from the birth experience to adoption, from immigration to race relations. The theme that ties my eight previous books together is that they all bring together groups of extraordinarily diverse individuals who share common bonding experiences about something that is very important to them.

Over the decades, my foxhunting friends often asked why I didn't author a book about the subject of horse and hound. But as passionate as I am about foxhunting, I wasn't sure that I had anything new to say about a sport that has been the subject of literary masterworks. The inspiration for this current approach began when my husband David suggested that I do a book about foxhunting that was like the type of book I always do—assemble a collection of faces and stories that inform the reader on a given subject and present them in such a way that they give the subject a distinctive cohesion and narrative structure. And thus was born the idea of an oral history in which foxhunters ranging from the most experienced and respected in America to relative beginners are asked, "Who got you interested in foxhunting, and what did you learn from them?" That simple question formed the basis of these interviews with fifty individuals who collectively embody well over two thousand years of foxhunting experience.

Fortunately, there's not a group of people more adept at storytelling than foxhunters, and so the book began to take shape. From the seventy years of hound breeding experience of the legendary Melvin Poe to the retired grandmother who overcame her fear of horses and got her colors on her seventieth birthday, an oral history began to develop that would ultimately explore the sport through the faces and voices of fifty different people whose lives have been tremendously influenced by foxhunting and who, in turn, have been a tremendous influence on the pursuit.

Hugh Robards describes the foxhunting community as "smaller than a wren's egg," and when talking with foxhunters in these pages, one quickly notices that while they may be spread across the United States from California to Virginia, from Florida to New York, from Colorado to Texas, there's never more than a few degrees of separation in their life stories. Everyone knows someone who knows the someone that the story is about. And although this is an oral history about American foxhunting, many people, such as Hugh Robards, Ben Hardaway, or Marty and Daphne Wood, have been influenced by and have been an influence on foxhunters in the United Kingdom.

There's an old expression: "Some people hunt to ride, and others ride to hunt." That observation certainly holds true in these interviews. Whether it's a young steeplechase jockey riding in back of the field to teach a timber horse to jog a fence or a seasoned huntsman whose hounds have had a basic influence on American foxhound conformation, both are an important part of the whole. Albert Poe's memories of working for the imposing MFH, Mrs. Randolph, during his tenure as huntsman of Piedmont; Andrew Barclay's description of the establishment of the MFHA Professional Development Program; Maureen Britell's embracing of the sidesaddle tradition; or Larry Jenkins' fond memories of his mule King Arthur—all are a delightful part of our hunting traditions. And given that everyone in these pages has been asked to talk about their mentors, there are numerous personal recollections about people who are no longer with us but who have earned their place in foxhunting history.

So these are stories that I hope you agree deserve to be recorded and remembered. If nothing else, anyone who reads them will definitely know a lot more about what happens when hounds are cast in the hunt field. The generations of knowledge that are so generously and colorfully shared in this collection will certainly enhance your experience the next time you ride behind hounds.

We foxhunters know that the stories back at the tailgates after a meet can be as memorable as the cross-country experiences themselves. And once the horses are untacked and the hounds are on the trailer, I'm often amazed at my fellow hunt club members' recollections of the day. Sometimes it's hard to believe we are all talking about the same meet. One person might say it was the best hunt of the year because they jumped thirty coops, while another might lament that it was frustrating because the scent was so poor that the hounds couldn't do much.

For most of us, though, there really is no such thing as a bad day of foxhunting because no two days are ever alike and the anticipation of the chase focuses the mind and makes you grateful to be alive. No matter what is going on in your life outside of the day's meet, once the hounds open up and you're rolling cross country in hot pursuit, all of life's problems fade, and you experience the thrill of being fully present to the task at hand. The sights, sounds, and scents of the experience are a feast for the senses and nourish the soul. You aren't just observing the natural world; you're a part of it.

This is the common bond that unites the people in these pages and provides the underlying counterpoint to my brother's old saying, "If there are fifty people out foxhunting, they are out for fifty different reasons." I hope you enjoy this collection of memories and observations from my chosen fifty.

—Mary Motley Kalergis

# Melvin Poe

BORN IN 1920, HE'S A LEGEND IN THE SPORT—
PROBABLY ONE OF THE MOST WELL RESPECTED
HUNTSMEN IN NORTH AMERICA.

I was born in 1920, five miles down the road from where I live now in Hume, Virginia. There were ten of us in the family—five girls and five boys. My dad worked for a dollar a day. He had hounds when I was a little boy, and as soon as I got big enough to hunt, that was all I wanted to do. I loved to hunt skunks and possum at night when I was a schoolboy. We had no coons in those days. No beavers either. Those skins would have been worth a lot more than skunk or possum. As poor as we were, with so many kids to feed, we took our hounds out every day to catch game. If we carried a gun on foot, dogs would chase rabbit, squirrel, or my favorite, possum, and we'd have it for dinner. Muskrat is one of the best things you can eat. I was a good shot. I got fifteen squirrels in one day with a rifle. You shoot 'em in the head so you don't hurt the meat. If you got on a horse, those same hounds would run a fox and not pay any attention to other game. They were smart and knew what was expected of them. Back in those days, a lot of farmers had their own pack of hounds, and oftentimes on Sundays, they'd join the packs together, and we'd have a big go of foxhunting. On the way to church, the whole community would stop to see this turnout. We called it a turnout because we'd have a fox that we dug out from the last hunt and have the kids hold the hounds while the Sunday school superintendent released the fox. The kids let the dogs go after the fox had a chance to put a good distance between himself and the hounds. Folks showed up on whatever they had to ride, and if they didn't have a horse, they went on foot.

*As huntsman, we're hired to promote good sport for the field, who pays the bills. I say you never count your hounds 'til the dealing's done. It's boring for the field to have to wait while you pick up hounds after a run. Just keep hunting another covert and the strays will catch up. I learned from night hunting that hounds are pretty good at packing themselves up.*

We were fortunate enough in this area to have ponies available to anyone willing to ride. Over at Belle Meade, there were a couple of hundred brood mares, and any kid could take the unbroken babies home for a while. They'd never been handled. They'd herd 'em up in the corral, and we'd catch 'em and put a bridle on. By the time we rode that pony bareback eight or ten miles to the house, he was pretty broke. The next year, we'd return that pony and get another green one. We were ole country boys that came up the hard way and weren't scared of nothing. There were no school buses in those days, and we rode those ponies to school. The families (that were mostly my relatives) got together and built a run-in shed at the school so the kids would have someplace to keep their ponies while they were in class. The teachers drove a buggy, and so did my family.

When I come out of the army in October 1945, I was hired by Old Dominion to be huntsman that November, and there I stayed until I was fired in May of sixty-two. A huntsman never quits because he doesn't want to leave his hounds. Orange County immediately offered me a position, so what at first seemed like a comedown was in fact a step up. I was huntsman there for thirty years. The land is a lot less open nowadays, but it's still a good place to hunt. Like everything else, the rules have changed over the years, and things are different than when I started. Used to be grooms had to ride in the back. Now you'll see five or six professionals right behind the Field Master, and they'll help themselves to the hunt breakfast afterwards. You wouldn't see that back when I got started as huntsman. Ms. Mars does a great job, though. She cracks a big whip and gets things done right.

When I was seventy-seven years old, Jimmy Young told me I had to retire at the end of the season. My wife Peggy and I were in shock. We didn't even know what to think. I stayed on for three more years after that, but they were the worst three years of my life because I was supposed to show the new huntsman the ropes. But two huntsmen is one too many for any hunt club! They wanted to put riders on our jumps when I knew a seven-board coop is always better than a rider, but I was on the way out, so Jimmy Young prevailed, and those riders just rotted up top there with no one ever bothering to take them down. The gate is always a lot quicker than dropping a rail, but if they'd just added a board on top of the jump, we could have still jumped it without having to go through the gate. During that terrible time, Mr. Ohrstrom came to me with an offer to start a little hunt in Bath County, with me as huntsman. I took some hounds that Orange County wasn't hunting on down there. As we drove up that valley, damn if there wasn't a fox just planted on the hillside, like it was waiting for us. I just picked up hounds from other hunts and carried 'em on down there, and we had ourselves a lot of fun hunting in Bath County for twelve or thirteen years. I'd haul the pack back and forth from my place in Hume to Bath County. George Ohrstrom built me a kennel at home as well as enlarging the one in Bath County. I no longer hunt there, but at ninety-three, I still hunt my hounds on Fridays and Sundays from my backyard kennel. I call my pack OPs—other people's. All of my dogs have some little something wrong with 'em—they might be getting old and falling behind, or they follow the horses instead of the pack. My best huntin' hound is a good lookin' son of a bitch—good enough to show. The only fault I can find with him

*Melvin kneeling by his family's foxhounds, with his brother Jim standing in front of a neighbor on horseback in the early 1940s.*

is he's mean, so that's probably the reason I got him. I had a great bitch from Warrington because she had a crooked tail. I got another one that jumped up and licked everyone in the face. Both of them died this past year. They were wonderful hunting dogs despite their faults. When other hunts are dissatisfied with a hound, they'd pass him on to me and most of 'em make it too. I've got a good group that I can rely on.

I wouldn't have an English foxhound. They're not my type of dog. I've always liked an American foxhound because they are so keen to hunt. Sometimes too much so. You never want to excite an American foxhound. You need to hunt them as quietly as you can to keep their minds focused. If you rile 'em up, they'll run crazy. If you kill a fox, you don't make a big to-do over it because it's bad for their minds. It's hard for the English huntsman to understand that because they are used to the English breed, which are much less excitable than the American hounds. If you run a fox to ground, I don't believe in messing with the den. They're scarce, and the huntsman shouldn't let the hounds dig and dig there. If forty hounds are moving all that dirt around, it's too much for a fox to repair. A lot of times, the young fox can get trapped inside. I pick the pack up and move 'em elsewhere. No good can come from letting them scratch up a den. For hundreds of years, we've been breeding dogs that want to chase fox. The breeding is what counts more than praise or punishment.

When I hunt hounds I don't want my whips to call a fox as soon as it jumps covert because a fox will either get killed or go to ground right away if the hounds are close behind. An animal can't run wide open but for so long. If he has enough space between him and the hounds, he'll run all day and have a better chance of surviving to run another day too! As huntsman, we're hired to promote good sport for the field, who pays the bills. You need to give the fox a chance to have enough space so he can sit down and listen and catch his breath. That saves the fox and gives the field a good chase. To me that's a win-win situation. I say you never count your hounds 'til the dealing's done. It's boring for the field to have to wait while you pick up hounds after a run. Just keep hunting another covert, and the strays will catch up. I learned from night hunting that hounds are pretty good at packing themselves up. I love all types of hunting, not just foxhunting. Foxhunting was the only sport that paid me to do what I'd do anyway! Many a day, I'd go deer hunting at dawn, then take the foxhounds out hunting in the morning before I'd take the bird dogs out quail hunting in the afternoon. After supper, I'd put my coon dogs in the truck and go coon hunting. I like to hear hounds run, no matter the quarry, and I can't imagine that changing for me. If you love to hunt like I do, it's just who you are, and I'm too old to change! 🐾

# Charley Matheson

An architect and an artist, he grew up foxhunting with his family and when he had a family of his own began leading the field behind Melvin Poe's pack at Orange County Hunt back in the early 1970s. When illness kept him off horseback, he became a painter of foxhunting landscapes.

Growing up, my father was a foxhunter, and as kids, we were all taught to ride. We had a small farm in Mount Vernon, which is now just a part of the suburban sprawl in Northern Virginia. But as a boy, we were surrounded by other farms, where we could ride out for hours. On the weekends, we'd go to my mother's family farm in Casanova and go foxhunting. I had a terrible Welsh pony who loved to lie down in mud puddles, so that somewhat dampened my enthusiasm for the sport. The old-school method of teaching a kid to hunt was just to say "Follow me," and off we'd go. Even though I got my own children riding lessons, I still think that the best way to learn anything is just to get right in there and do it. Children learn by example.

As a married man and father in my late twenties, the first thing I did when we moved to Virginia from Washington, DC, was buy a horse. We'd had a little weekend place in The Plains, and my first wife was hunting with Orange County. When we were living in DC, I'd see her get up long before daybreak to hunt the hounds, and I got curious as to what was so much fun that she'd get out of bed at such an ungodly hour. She kept her horse at Melvin and Peggy Poe's, and their place was just the most exotic place I could imagine. I fell in love with the atmosphere of the place and the whole way of life that foxhunting offers—beautiful landscape, animals, and people of all

*Our ancestors had to hunt to survive and that human history models our DNA and genetic makeup. When we hear hounds speak, it strikes a very primeval chord, an unconscious memory. For people like me, it's irresistible. To others who don't get it, it can never be explained because it's deeper than logic.*

sorts. By 1970, we were settled in Orange County hunt territory, and I got a horse that really taught me to love the sport. He wasn't a super athlete, but he was always safe and always got the job done. He lived up to his name, Easy Rider. Turned out that he could (carriage) drive, so I started enjoying doing that as well. I can't say I ever had a game plan. I just responded to the opportunities that presented themselves. I didn't want to have both driving horses and hunting horses, so any horse I got to hunt had to also be able to drive. I don't know how I had the time to do both with my horses at the same time I was building my career as an architect in Middleburg and my children were young. Where there's a will, there's a way, I suppose.

Foxhunting is a very absorbing thing to do. It has an almost spiritual quality about it that can't be reproduced anywhere else. For one thing, it's very active and visceral, but to my mind, it's also very serene. The experience is so absorbing; it puts everything else out of your mind. It puts you in the moment with no distractions, or at least you better be, if you don't want to get injured! Even when I'm following the hounds in my car, instead of on horseback, I can get that same sense that this is a special experience. I never take it for granted. I've never been on a bad hunt because of that appreciation. The thing that disturbs that exhilarating atmosphere is chatter in the field. Hunting should be done in utter silence. There is a wonderful book by Simon Schama called *Landscape and Memory*, about our historical origins. Our ancestors had to hunt to survive, and that human history models our DNA and genetic makeup. When we hear hounds speak, it strikes a very primeval chord, an unconscious memory. For people like me, it's irresistible. To others who don't get it, it can never be explained because it's deeper than logic.

I had the good fortune to be able to hunt with a great pack of hounds (Orange County) behind a really great huntsman (Melvin Poe) in wonderful territory. When I started hunting regularly in the late sixties, Charles Turner was the Master, and there were older women in the field who still rode sidesaddle. Turner was older by the time I arrived, and even though his boldest days were behind him, he was a tremendous cross-country leader because he knew how to triangulate. He knew which way the pack was going and the wind was blowing, and he had a way of getting the field in the right place at the right time. It really taught me a lot about how the hounds and the foxes interact. When Cappy Smith arrived on the scene in the early seventies, his horsemanship improved

the quality of the sport in our club. Both the horses and the hounds got faster, and the jumps got larger and more numerous. Because of Cappy's impeccable style, our turnout became much more proper. If it wasn't, you'd hear about it. I bought a couple of horses from him, and both he and they improved my riding a lot. After a few years, Cappy would have me lead the field when he was away in the winter. I started spending more and more time at the kennels, which, of course, got me more deeply invested in the hounds when we were out hunting. Melvin was very good about instructing his Field Masters where to position themselves when he was casting hounds because he really liked to put on a show—not a flamboyant show but a great demonstration of how good the hounds could hunt. He said there's no sense putting on a show if nobody's watching, so he liked his fields as close to him as they could get, long as they were quiet and didn't get between him and the pack. To my mind, Orange County was and is one of the finest hunt clubs in the country.

I went to architecture school before computers, so I knew how to draw and manipulate watercolors long before I started hunting regularly as an adult. My sketching is a second language for my self-expression, a way of sharing my ideas and experience. Drawing commits things to memory like nothing else. It enhances the experience. I had the good fortune to befriend the wonderful equine artist Wally Nall, and he taught me not only a lot about art but also a lot about horses and their conformation.

In the mid-nineties, I was diagnosed with throat cancer and had to go through surgery and radiation, which, needless to say, made doing any physical activity impossible. As a result, I just retreated into my home studio and started painting. I found it very therapeutic and have been doing it ever since. Like foxhunting, painting takes your mind outside of your thoughts and puts you in a landscape outside of yourself. I was surprised how full of color and light my paintings were, under the circumstances. I lost sixty-five pounds and looked like death warmed over when I started hunting again, but I felt like that's exactly what I needed to do to rejoin the living. Both my horses and my art carried me through. Around 2006, I didn't have a horse, so I started following the hunt on foot with a sketchpad. Working on my *Hunting Sketches on the Run* book, I loved making myself invisible in the land-scape and silently observing the hunt unfold. I've had hunted foxes come right next to me and not give me a second look. Both art and foxhunting engage you in the present moment, and it invigorates the mind. My training as an architect taught me to really observe and see how everything's con-nected. Nothing connects you to nature like foxhunting. The sights, sounds, and smells are a dazzling experience. 🦊

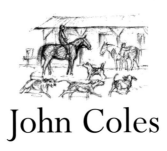

# John Coles

JOHN GREW UP HUNTING BEHIND HIS FATHER BOBBY
COLES, WHO WAS HUNTSMAN AT KESWICK HUNT CLUB.
ONCE HE STARTED TRAINING RACEHORSES FOR GEORGE
OHRSTROM, HE HUNTED BEHIND MELVIN POE'S ORANGE
COUNTY HOUNDS FOR TWENTY YEARS, UNTIL MELVIN
RETIRED AND JOHN BECAME MFH IN 2000.

My dad was hunting hounds since before I was born, and all of us kids just grew up foxhunting at Cloverfields because there wasn't much else to do. My sister Margaret said we rode ponies, then we went and rode ponies some more! Back then, that was our only form of entertainment. We didn't even have a TV. You either went hunting, or you stayed home by yourself while your parents and brothers and sisters were out having fun without you. My early memories of hunting are just as much about getting ready as the actual meets. We'd clean those shaggy ponies the day before. Of course, we had no hot water in the barn, so once it got cold, we'd take the tack up to the kitchen. Why we only had one tack hook for the whole family to use is something we never questioned. It's just the way it was. There were always a few friends spending the night as well. Nobody had a trailer back then, so we just hacked out to wherever we were hunting. Sometimes groups would ride over to our place the night before the meet, and then we'd all ride to the fixture together the next morning.

We didn't stop hunting in the summer months. My dad started the hilltoppings, where families laid out picnic blankets, and we'd turn the hounds out on the mountain in the full-moon evenings. All the kids had a ball chasing the pack through the woods on foot in the moonlight. We always whelped the (Keswick) hunt club bitches at the Cloverfield ken-

*My dad was hunting hounds since before I was born and all of us kids just grew up foxhunting at Cloverfields because there wasn't much else to do. My sister Margaret said we rode ponies, then we went and rode ponies some more! Back then that was our only form of entertainment. We didn't even have a TV. You either went hunting, or you stayed home by yourself while your parents and brothers and sisters were out having fun without you.*

nels, and the Coles kids loved to hunt the puppies before we gave them back to the club.

When I was about six, I started riding alongside my mom in the field. She put me on a white horse named Soapy, and I thought he was huge, though he was probably about fifteen hands. I thought I was a hotshot to be riding a horse instead of a pony. Back in the early sixties, we didn't have deer-proof hounds because deer were just starting to enter our territory and become a problem, kind of like the coyote now.

So since the hounds had never seen deer, when they jumped one up, they took off. The deer runs to water, and for us in Keswick, the closest real water was the Rivanna River, which was quite a ways away. For a kid, to gallop in a straight line for miles and miles was a thrill, though most of the staff probably felt a little differently about the situation. It took at least four or five generations of hounds to breed the inclination to run deer out of them. Now you don't have a puppy even look at a deer, even if it runs though the pack.

When I got a little older, my friends started hunting alongside me, and it was even more fun. Dad passed the Mastership on to Jake Carle when I was about thirteen, and Jake asked me to whip-in, which really got my attention. The camaraderie with your friends along with the responsibility of whipping-in just increased my love of the sport as a teenager. As we became stronger riders, we wanted to run and jump. That walking around on a cold day blowing for hounds is not much fun after a while. My dad had a way of keeping things exciting for the kids, and to this day, Barclay Rives, Hugh Motley, and Jennifer Nesbit are actively involved in the sport. Once it gets in your blood, you're hooked. Dad had an amazing voice. His holla would carry for miles around. He carried a cow horn, which is a sound you never forget.

While I was still in high school, I started riding Mrs. Marion DuPont Scott's racehorses at Montpelier. After graduation, my love of horses brought me to The Plains to ride the Ohrstrom's racehorses. I started on the flat and ended up as a steeplechase jockey. George Ohrstrom liked all his timber horses hunted, so I started whipping-in for Melvin Poe on these wonderful thoroughbreds. It's the best training in the world for them because it teaches them to pay attention. It helps them become more handy over fences. After hunting a couple of days a week for a while, the horse learns a lot. He's a lot less likely to fall down racing because the hunting teaches him to be careful. It slows them down enough to teach them what they need to know to go fast safely. Those years from 1975 to 1990 hunting with Melvin here with Orange County were quite an education for me while I was educating the racehorses. Then Mr. Ohrstrom started the Bath County Hunt for Melvin after he retired from Orange County, and we did that together for another twenty years. So I've hunted with Melvin even longer than I did with my dad. I've been mighty lucky to have those two men in my life. Dad came out of the foot-hunting tradition,

where the hounds pretty much hunted themselves. You just turned them loose, and they ran up into the mountains and did their thing. You dropped the tailgate and

*John with his father Robert at a Keswick horse show in 1972.*

followed them the best you could. Melvin's style of hunting for OCH was much more controlled. The hounds follow the huntsman until they jump a fox, then the huntsman follows the hounds. My dad's hounds came home when they were ready, whereas the Orange County Hounds pack up at the huntsman's command, and it's expected that we'll return to the kennels with all the hounds at the end of a hunt.

In 2000, I became Master of Orange County, and one thing I've always done is support a nonjumping field and a hilltopping field. I think people should be encouraged to enjoy the sport in any way they can. Our hunt is only open to people who own at least fifty acres in our territory, or you can purchase land in a land trust for our club. I think anyone who joins under those conditions should be able to hunt with us even if they don't feel comfortable galloping and jumping. I want older members and young children to be able to hunt with us. Having the landowners out hunting with us makes the whole club operate more smoothly. The three fields give people an opportunity to get started or back off without having to quit hunting. My mother hunted for another thirty years after she stopped jumping. I think people should be able to enjoy the sport for as long as they can.

After all this time, I'm too old to do anything else but foxhunt. It's just been a way of life for as long as I can remember. It really satisfies something deep within my wiring. When the hounds take off and you know they're right, your blood gets up, and it feels good. There is something that makes you really want to be there, even though when the hounds are running, they don't really need you. You need to be there even if they don't need you. I can't explain it, but it's real. 🪶

# Jake Carle

MFH AND HUNTSMAN OF KESWICK HUNT CLUB FOR OVER
TWENTY-FIVE YEARS, JAKE IS ONE OF THE MOST RESPECTED
HOUND JUDGES IN AMERICA TODAY.

My father Ned Carle was such a keen foxhunter that he flunked out of the University of Virginia. He ended up hunting almost every day of the week, often whipping-in or carrying the horn for Julian Morris, KHC Master at the time, so there wasn't much time for academics. Back then, there was a racetrack right across from the Keswick Hunt Club, and he'd ride races there just about every time the horses were running. After he flunked out of college in 1903, he started riding races everywhere and was one of the leading amateur riders in the country. While racing in Morristown, New Jersey, he had a terrible fall that almost killed him. In fact, they left him for dead on a tack trunk in the barn while they looked for next of kin. As the groom was cleaning the aisle, he saw my father's eyelids move. There was a party going on at the farm, and the owner sent down a doctor who was so drunk that the groom and a local vet realized that he'd do my father more harm than good, so they threw the soused doctor out of the barn. Somehow, they were able to get in touch with my uncle in New York City, and someone arranged to have a train stop near the farm, where they loaded my father up in an empty boxcar and took him to a hospital in New York. He'd broken almost every bone in his body and was in the hospital for about a year. As soon as he was released, he was back in the saddle, hunting all the time. He spent a year hunting all over England and Ireland. He bought a pack of harriers to bring back to the Millbrook Hunt Harriers, where he hunted them until World War I broke out. During the war, he ended up on the front lines, being in charge of a horse-drawn ammunition train in France.

He said by the end of the war, he wasn't sure who he hated most—the Germans, who tried to kill him, or the French, who kept eating his horses!

By the time I was born in 1938, Dad had retired from hunting hounds. I think it was my fifth birthday when my parents presented me with what I call "the ten-hand terrorist"—a beautiful little Shetland pony that was mean as a snake. He went from one family to the next and finally ended up with the Rives boys. Old Charlie McCarthy must have been over thirty-five by the time he made his way to the Rives, so he'd probably mellowed by then. My father was a terrible teacher, and the pony didn't instill much confidence, but with my mother's encouragement, I kept at it. The best advice my father ever gave me was, "Hunt thy own hounds. Goddammit!" In 1945, when I was seven years old, he bought a farm in the Keswick Hunt territory, and we moved to Virginia. Charlie McCarthy was still bucking me off all the time, and thank goodness the black groom Charlie Hughes took an interest in me and became my surrogate father. He was my mentor in all things. He taught me to ride, shoot, and fish and shared all his knowledge of foxhunting. He worked for the MFH of Keswick for several years and knew as much about hunting foxhounds as anyone. He also whipped-in to my mother's beagle pack and would sometimes hunt them himself when she was away. Hunting on foot is a great way to really understand hound work. I also whipped-in with my mother's Raynham beagles and learned a lot. Charlie Hughes taught me the skills I needed to hunt my

*Whether a hound is a Penn Marydel, English, or American, they all have to have the same structure, the same running gear. The feet, the shoulders, neck, chest, hind end, and hocks have to be built for speed and soundness. Whoever has the look of eagles about them goes out and wins the championship, no matter what the breed of hound.*

pony Charlie McCarthy, who not only loved to buck me off but would try to kick and bite me on the way down. When the pony would run away with me and I'd be yelling, "Help, help!," Charlie Hughes would encourage me to keep from getting scared: "You ridin' him, boy—good job!" My first horse, appropriately named Troublemaker, was a great summertime horse, but come frost, that son of a bitch would buck until I came off. Thank God, Charlie Hughes was always by my side, to dust me off and put me back on. He taught me to never take myself so seriously that I couldn't laugh at myself, and I've been laughing ever since!

As a boy hunting with Keswick, Andrew Branham was my hero. He was called by some a drunk and a womanizer, but he was a hell of a huntsman. He's been my role model my whole life! He told me, "Boy, if you're a fool and know it, you're much better off than the fool who don't know it!" If I ever write an autobiography, it's going to be titled *A Fool and Know It— Reminisces of a Foxhunter.* His son Sammy and I got in all kinds of trouble as kids while the adults were having cocktails at the hunt club. The only time I ever got sent home from the hunt field was when Sammy and I started racing each other and ended up running right through the pack of hounds. His daddy was so mad he made Sammy sleep in the back of the hound truck for three nights as a punishment, and I was banned from the hunting for two weeks. That was the worst two weeks of my life.

When I was a student at the University of Virginia, I bought from Hi Petter an Appaloosa named El Morocco, who was ugly as homemade sin and used to run away with me all the time. But I didn't mind because you just aimed him in the hound's direction and let him go. You could point him at anything, and he'd jump it. I rode him behind Bobby Coles with Keswick for years. One of the hardest things I ever had to do was put that old horse down, though I went on to have much better horses over the years. That Appie was my first love. I hunted and played polo more than I studied and flunked out after two years. My father was furious, but since he'd done the same thing, he couldn't really make me feel too guilty. I eventually got my degree in English and even got into graduate school. I wasn't very happy there, and the dean asked me what I wanted to do with my life. I said I wanted to go foxhunting, and he said, "Well, go ahead!" so I put the books down and off I went! The following year, in 1964, I was asked to be Joint Master of Keswick. My father was very knowledgeable about hound breeding, whereas old man Coles just bred the best to the best and hoped

John J. Carle II
M.F.H.

1964 Joint Master with Roberts Coles          1966 Elected Master

*Jake as MFH of KHC on his mother's ex-steeplechaser, Pocket Rocket, in 1966.*
GEORGE BARKLEY

for the best. They weren't pack broke, but they were keen American hounds that showed great sport. Joe Collins was whipper-in at the time, and he told me, "Get off your God damned lazy ass and pack break these hounds!" I was able to get a lot of biddable hounds from Farmington when they stopped drag hunting and got rid of a lot of our old hounds. We took the most biddable hounds from our kennel and coupled them up with the Farmington hounds, and they learned pretty quickly.

When Coles resigned from the Mastership a couple of years after I was Joint Master, I got several crossbred hounds from Blue Ridge Hunt that were already pack broke, so that helped a lot. Deep Run got rid of their American hounds, and a couple of those bitches were the foundation of the Keswick pack today. Daylight and Darling, bred by Brandywine, were as fine a pair of hounds as you'll ever find. Albert Poe was hunting the Piedmont hounds then, and I bred to his Render '68—an extraordinary dog who sired some wonderful litters. The Bywaters strain of American hounds used to be all over the country, but now Keswick is one of the few hunts that is bred predominantly from Bywaters stock. They have wonderful noses, cry, and drive. So many of them seem to be born with that intangible fox sense. But the best thing of all is that they are biddable. They want to please their huntsman. It's that desire to please that makes it possible to deer break them as puppies. They take more handling, but if you give them the attention they crave and aren't too heavy-handed, you can't have a better pack of hounds.

Joe Collins hunted the hounds after I became Master, but when he was ready to retire, I started carrying the horn in 1973. Being both MFH and huntsman was what I had always dreamed of. I've always been grateful to be lucky enough to have the opportunity to do exactly what I always imagined doing. My father was right when he said the most important thing a man can do is, "Hunt thy own hounds, Goddammit!" I hired Charlie Brown from Rappahannock to come whip-in for me when I became huntsman, and he gave me one of the best pieces of hunting advice anyone ever gave me: "The best thing you can do with that horn is shove it up your ass!" I didn't take his advice literally, but I did ease off the horn, and hunting improved almost immediately.

My father judged hounds in the show ring for decades and was William Brainard's mentor. I just learned this year that my father judged the first Bryn Mawr Hound Show. When I started judging hound shows in the early seventies, Brainard became my mentor. I'd go up to his kennel at Old Dominion all the time, and we'd talk about confirmation. Whenever he was judging a show, he'd ask me to join him in the ring and ask my opinion on why I liked or didn't like what I saw. He'd tell me his reasons for the choices he made in pinning the hounds. Whether a hound is a Penn Marydel, English, or American, they all have to have the same structure, the same running gear. The feet, the shoulders, neck, chest, hind end, and hocks have to be built for speed and soundness. After you stand them up, you pick the ones you like and have them chase a biscuit to make sure those shoulders and hind legs are in synch. Even though I always preferred hunting American hounds, I don't have a prejudice when it comes to best in show because the best is the best, no matter what the breed. Whoever has the look of eagles about them goes out and wins the championship, no matter what the breed of hound. 🐾

# Hugh Motley

WHIPPING-IN FOR KHC SINCE HE WAS A CHILD,
HE WAS MFH FROM 2000 TO 2005 AND NOW
FOLLOWS THE HOUNDS IN HIS TRUCK.

I wasn't a very good student, so I spent a lot of time in summer school. When I was eight or nine, I was catching up on my studies at Little Keswick School with Bob and Libby Wilson one summer, and they got me on horseback with their kids and the gang over at Cloverfields. Riding in that area with the Wilsons and the Coles meant foxhunting, and back in the mid-sixties, there were masses of children around. Hacking to and from the meets was just as fun as being at the meet when we were young. We'd hack from behind the post office from Little Keswick School all the way down Route 22 past Grace Church to wherever hounds were meeting. I remember falling off a lot. At the time, it was just part of the fun. Once we were hunting, we'd be in the back on shaggy ponies, closing the gates and cantering as fast as we could to catch up. They thought we were being courteous, but we were really looking for an excuse to have a little pony race. John Coles's dad, Bobby Coles, was Master then, and it was a much more casual affair. He'd show up and drop the tailgate, and the pack would fly out of there like a covey of quail in four different directions, but by the time we got up to the power line, they were together on a fox, and off we'd go.

Those early days taught me to love the woods and the weather in a way I didn't appreciate before. After Bobby Coles asked Jake Carle to be Joint Master, I started whipping-in as a young teenager whenever they needed extra help. You'd usually get hollered at in that position if you asked too many questions, so I just pretended I knew what was going on and did what I saw the other whips doing. I so wanted Jake's approval that all he

*If you have fifty people out foxhunting, they're out for fifty different reasons. People are a little more complicated than hounds, who just want to chase their quarry. Some folks are there to see the sights. Some are there to be seen. Some are there to try a horse, while others are out to sell a horse. That being said, I suspect fifty different people love the sport for fifty different reasons.*

had to do was slip those Ray Bans down his nose and look at me in the eye and ask, "Where you been?" and I'd feel terrible about letting the hounds give me the slip. Whipping-in is a tough position because nobody is going to be right all of the time and the huntsman depends on you to keep his hounds accounted for. Back then, Keswick wasn't as proper in their attire as some other hunts. We might not have been looking good, but we were feeling good! When I went off to boarding school, I could only get out over the holidays, but there wasn't anything else I'd rather do.

When Jake Carle took over the Mastership on his own, he began to formalize the hunt to more traditional standards. For a long time, he was my hero. He was always beautifully turned out and well mounted. He was the first person I ever saw who always had a man bring him a second horse halfway through the hunt. He also knew as much about hounds as anyone would need to know. Back then, the Keswick territory was from the Shadwell store to Cobham, on both sides of the road. Now the traffic is so bad, we never cross 22 or 231. When I became Master forty years later, one of the older Coles ladies asked me if we still hunted on both

*Hugh on his beloved Herbie, with the Keswick hounds at Ben Coolyn during early cubbing season, 1999.* WINKIE MOTLEY

sides of the road, and when I told her there was too much traffic now to get near that road, she said, "Have you ever noticed how much faster people drive now that that road is paved?" Now that must have been long before I was even born, but I thought her comment was a great example of the way a true Virginian sees the world.

Hunting Keswick territory forty or fifty years ago was quite a different go. Almost all the farms had someone in the family who hunted with the club, and as a result, the landowners were much more invested in keeping their farms open to the hunt by keeping up coops and gates and keeping trails cleared. The most important thing a Master does is keep good relations with the landowners because without them, there would be no sport. Oftentimes, if there's trash on the side of the road or a gate is left open or a cow aborts, a landowner might think that our hunting through their farm caused these mishaps. It's up to the MFH to smooth things over and make things right. When Jake was ready to retire and asked me to take over the Mastership, I was hugely honored, but I was really anxious that the responsibility might mess up my enjoyment of foxhunting. But that man had shown me a lifetime of good sport, so I really couldn't say no to his request. To tell the truth, I kind of enjoyed dealing with the landowners. There usually wasn't anything a good listen and a bottle of booze couldn't fix. It was the board of directors meetings that I could do without. Now Old Man Coles knew how to handle that situation. When he was called on to give a report on the foxhunting, he'd say, "Those who were out there with us know what it was like, and those that weren't don't really care." Then he'd sit down, and the hunt report was over! Being Master really drives home the point that you can't please all the people all the time. "You're going too fast. You're going too slow. The jumps are too high. The jumps are too low." You learn to do your best and hope for an approval rating of over 50 percent.

My first year as Master got off to a shaky start because our new huntsman Jack Eicher died the week before the staff was supposed to start cub hunting, and I was left with a kennel full of hounds and no huntsman. There were well over a hundred hounds in the kennels—a lot of them were too old or too young to do their job. For thirty-six years, Jake Carle had lived by the adage, "Breed the best to the best and hope for the best." I was lucky if I could even identify half of them at that time, so I had some quick work to do. Talk about a small world—when word got out that Keswick needed a huntsman, Tony Gammell called and said he was available. I remembered meeting him when I hunted in Ireland with Hugh Robards. He shows up the day after our first conversation on the phone, and I show him a kennel full of overweight hounds desperate for exercise. Jake had retired, I'd been in Saratoga all month, and Jack had died. Tony took to the position immediately. He has that magic thread that connects a huntsman to his hounds. It's a mutual love and respect. We were fortunate to be able to both reopen old territory and open new fixtures. In no time, our hunts got faster and our runs got longer. I hugely enjoyed the experience, and I try to live my life by the motto, "The best time to leave a party is when you're still having fun," so I retired about six years later, feeling like I left things better than I found them.

Nowadays, I'd say at least three-quarters of the landowners in our territory are not foxhunters, and they let us hunt through or meet on their property as a generous favor. Another big change for Keswick is that we hunt in five counties now, not just along Route 22 and 231. It's a tremendous amount of land and upkeep. Although the club can afford to have a few more hired staff than we used to, we're still dependent on the volunteerism of active hunting members to keep the operation up and running. Our territory started expanding outside of Albemarle County when Jake Carle traded some territory with Bull Run, and over the years, we added territory in Orange, Madison, and Lousia counties too. Personally, there's nothing I hate like having to stop a pack of hounds when they are running a fox, and fortunately most of our territory is far enough off the road that we don't have to do that very often. The railroad line in Rapidan is worse than the road—those trains come by constantly, and it's a real potential danger to our pack when they have their noses to the ground and are doing what they were bred to do.

As far as the field is concerned—if you have fifty people out foxhunting, they're out for fifty different reasons. People are a little more complicated than hounds, who just want to chase their quarry. Some folks are there to see the sights. Some are there to be seen. Some are there to try a horse, while others are out to sell a horse. Probably most just enjoy the opportunity to get outside and enjoy the countryside. Of course, the effort it takes to get up before dawn and get a fit horse to a meet miles away, with your tack clean and your boots polished—well, it's certainly a lot of work for a trail ride! Most people are out there to run and jump. I'd say only a small percentage of the people know the hounds by name and what they are up to at any given moment. For a lot of us, even if you don't know the hounds by name, once you hear them at full cry, you keep coming back for more. The only way to get to know the hounds individually is to come by the kennels and walk out with them. I used to know the voice of every hound out there when I was whipping-in and later on as MFH because I walked hounds in the summer. But now that I don't do that, I can't begin to tell their voices apart.

I used to get tickled at the hunt breakfast when I'd ask people, "How was your day?" and you'd get answers like, "It was the best day ever. I jumped twenty-seven fences." Now it's never occurred to me to count each fence, but I suppose that's one way of looking at it! Other people the same day would say they never heard the hounds speak, and I'm thinking to myself, "They ran at full cry for an hour and a half, but I guess they just missed it somehow." Sometimes I'd think maybe we weren't at the same fixture—sometimes I'd think we weren't even in the same sport! That being said, I suspect fifty different people love the sport for fifty different reasons. Once it gets in your blood, it draws you in hard and deep. I just follow the hounds in my truck now, but the sound of their voices still puts a smile on my face. 🐾

# Tony Gammell

HE WHIPPED-IN FOR HUGH ROBARDS BACK IN LIMERICK,
IRELAND, AS A LAD AND HAS BEEN HUNTSMAN AT KESWICK
IN VIRGINIA FOR FIFTEEN YEARS. A CONVERT TO AMERICAN
FOXHOUNDS SINCE HE IMMIGRATED TO AMERICA, HE IS NOW
A TRUE BELIEVER OF THE BREED.

Both my father and older brother were horsemen, but I was only interested in the dogs as a kid. I hunted beagles on foot every Sunday and otterhounds in the summertime. I had my own terrier and whippet and hunted every chance I got. By the time I was fifteen or sixteen, I was foxhunting on foot with a subscription pack of harriers. I'd been whipping-in for years by then and eventually started carrying the horn. I'd just half-ass blow horn and run! In Ireland, there were no roads to worry about, and the land was configured so you could hear them from so far away. The harriers were great hounds and didn't need much help. The joy of a foot pack is once they find a fox, there's nobody on horseback to distract them. More fox have been lost to people interfering with the hounds than bad scent. I guarantee it. Limerick also had a mounted foxhunt, the Stonehall Harriers, which I always admired, and I decided I better learn how to ride if I was going to go into hunt service. I certainly couldn't make a living with a foot pack. There was no way I'd ask my big brother to teach me to ride because I knew he'd kill me just for the fun of it.

So I approached Shaun Shaughnessy, and he laughed out loud at my goal, but he did put me to work mucking stalls. I got on as many horses as I could while working there and started hunting with Hugh Robards at Limerick, both on horseback and on foot. My parents were determined that I was going to college, but I had other plans. I wanted to go to a racing and

*Once hounds have been left alone long enough to really get locked into that vector beam of drive and focus, there's no stopping them. But they need time undistracted to get the focus it takes for a great run. If you mess with them too much after they're cast, they'll never know that it's possible to hunt with such focus.*

jumping barn in England to continue to sharpen my riding skills. At first, my parents laughed at the idea, then they got very mad.

*Tony hunting the Keswick hounds at Mt Sharon.*

But off I went, at seventeen. In England, I worked like a dog for Nigel Goddard in exchange for riding lessons. I breezed the racehorses and worked with the jumpers for a year. I was often able to start them hunting too.

After a year there, I learned of a hunt in Wales that was looking for a second horseman. My job was to ride out on a fresh horse halfway through the hunt and exchange it with the huntsman's first ride. The fun part for me was finding him while he was riding with the hounds, then I'd jump off at a trot, holding the reins of both horses, and the huntsman would switch over to the fresh horse while still at a jog, and off he'd go. After a season there, I'd felt like I'd learned how to ride enough to apply for a job as whipper-in back in Ireland with Limerick. Well, I thought I knew how to ride by then, but I still had a lot of falling off to do back at Limerick before I figured things out. I had no clue about the capabilities of a horse, and some of the fences we jumped there were so big that the only other things going over them were birds and planes! Robards had a terrible temper out hunting the hounds, and if I wasn't where he wanted me to be when he wanted me to be there, he'd just rip me a new one. I'd come home some days in tears. It was quite an education. It was tough, but it made me pay attention. After three seasons, I was ready to move on, but I'll always be grateful for the opportunity he gave me to get established in hunt service.

I got a position as first whip at Tauton Vale, and that was a shocker. English fox packs are like a tight little ball, always looking to the huntsman for direction. There are two different schools of hunting. There's the huntsman who helps the hounds hunt the fox, and there's the huntsman who hunts the fox with the help of the hounds. The English tradition is from the second school of thought. Once the hounds are speaking and come to a check, instead of figuring out for themselves how to get back in the scent, they turn to the huntsman, and he'll lead them around until they get back on the line. If you're constantly helping them hunt, they learn to be dependent on you, and that weakens their keenness. It's the same reason I don't like carrying a radio—I like to use my senses to hunt instead of relying on something else.

Eventually, I got an opportunity to be a whip at Leicestershire. Robards had warned me about hunting in the Shires, but I didn't know why until I got there. I figured it out pretty quick during my trial period with them. The huntsman there was such a tyrant, I wasn't allowed to speak unless spoken to first. He'd do things like have me count hounds before loading in the trailer, then remove one while I was in the truck, then have me count again when we got to the meet to see if I'd catch the change. After a while, I was more than done with England, so I applied for a job as kennel huntsman in Scotland with the Jed Forest hounds. They're Hill hounds—a cross between Fell and English. In North Umberland, the territory is so rough, it's almost impossible to ride behind the hounds, so you have to have a pack that can hunt on their own because you'd kill a horse trying to stay with them. It was a breath of fresh air for me to hunt those hounds. I loved it despite the rough terrain and terrible weather. They didn't need my help once they got started on a fox. After two seasons there, they banned foxhunting in Scotland, so I knew I had to go anywhere but England. I decided to come to America even though I didn't have a job there. I made some phone calls and discovered that Jack Eicher died of a heart attack and Keswick was looking for a huntsman down in Virginia. When I came down and met Hugh Motley in September of 2000, we realized we'd met before when he was over in Ireland hunting with Limerick and that we both had the same ideas about foxhunting. When Hugh asked me when I could start, I said right now, and I've been here ever since.

Hunting in America was an eye-opener for many reasons. Even though I didn't approve of the full-scale slaughter of foxes in England, I was a little taken aback here when I was told we're supposed to chase 'em without catching them. I was never down for murdering foxes for the ego trip of getting the highest tally. I always wanted a good chase where the fox had a chance to escape, no matter where I was hunting hounds. The Keswick hounds were mostly crossbred and American, and I told Hugh I wanted to start breeding to English hounds, and he gave the best piece of advice I've ever had. He said, "Give these guys a season, and if you still feel that way after hunting them for a while, we'll talk about drafting some English hounds." By Christmas, my eyes were open. I'd never hunted such a pack. The American foxhounds reminded me of a bred-up Irish harrier. It took me a few seasons to learn how to hunt to their strengths, and I was constantly talking to Hugh and Jake Carle for advice. I'll never forget very early on when the Keswick hounds were chasing a fox out of one covert into another and I started blowing my horn and whooping and hollering. Jake Carle just shook his head and said, "Why were you making so much noise? It just distracts them from doing their job." The Keswick foxhounds were originally bred here in Culpeper, Virginia, where the old-timers let them run through the mountains at night and the lads sat down below and listened to them. They're far smarter than the English hounds that are always looking to the huntsman for direction.

I think a lot of times, we blame bad scent on losing a line, but I think hounds lose their focus and that causes them to lose the scent line. It's like when you're reading a book. If you're repeatedly interrupted, it's hard to keep focused on what you're reading. It's the same thing for a foxhound. If the huntsman pulls them too quickly out of the covert or blows his horn too frequently or the staff or field gets in their way—they are going to lose their focus. Then people say, "Oh they were going great, then the scent changed." Once hounds have been left alone long enough to really get locked into that vector beam of drive and focus, there's no stopping them. But they need time undistracted to get the focus it takes for a great run. In the winter when it snows too much to follow hounds on horseback, we'll hunt them on foot. After a few days of hunting like that, the hounds have really recharged their focus because of no distractions and are really locked down on the scent line when we once again follow on horses.

After I'd been hunting the Keswick hounds for a few seasons, coyote started moving into our territory. Hugh and I talked about what to do and decided that chasing coyote was not what we wanted to do with our American foxhounds. We decided to hunt red fox and only red fox. We wouldn't even chase the odd gray that showed up. Then we purposely started hunting the puppies where there were the most coyotes, so we could break them off that scent. "No" is the simplest thing in the world to teach a dog. When you walk out puppies in the summertime, of course, the pups are going to get excited by the scent of everything—deer, turkey, raccoon, possum, coyote, bear, bobcat, you name it. You want to expose them to as much as possible as soon as possible so they learn what is acceptable to open up on. In our case, that would be red fox. Each pup is different. Some might need a harsh correction and others not much at all. I don't buy that American hounds are more sensitive. I think they're more intelligent. There's no need to overreact. They were bred to hunt pretty much on their own, whereas English hounds are bred to be dependent on the huntsman. It takes a smarter hound to make their own decisions. Even though the hunt club has been around for more than a hundred years, the Keswick hounds weren't really pack broke before the 1960s. Before that time, the huntsman would just drop the tailgate and let them go. Here it's often dry, and the fox are fewer. The American hounds are bred for those conditions. Even though American hounds are faster, so are American red fox. They are so much tougher than fox over in Ireland and England. You hunt a cub over there for twenty minutes, and you're either going to catch him or he goes to ground. Over here, it's not unusual to chase a cub for an hour. Later on when the dog foxes are traveling, we can have a three-hour run on the same fox. That would never happen on the other side of the Atlantic. So I've come to believe that the American tradition of chasing but not killing the fox comes from the fact that the foxes here are as swift and smart as the American hounds. Not only do American hounds have longer legs for speed, but if they do over run the line, they'll often cast themselves again without having to wait for the huntsman. They are the best thing going in the sport of venery. I love the challenge of the red fox, he's a worthy prey, and that's what we'll chase as long as we can. 🐾

# Albert Schreck

HE'S IN HIS EIGHTIES AND STILL FOXHUNTING AS MFH
EMERITUS OF LOS ALTOS HOUNDS AFTER FORTY-FOUR YEARS
AS MFH. AFTER BEING JOINT MASTER AT LIMERICK HOUNDS
IN IRELAND, HE TRANSFORMED THE LOS ALTOS DRAG HUNT
TO LIVE QUARRY FOXHUNTING IN THE MID-1960S.

After Josephine and I got married, we moved to Portola Valley, California, and I noticed that the Los Altos Hunt was nearby. I knew my wife had hunted with Myopia back East and I thought it would be something we would both enjoy. We joined the hunt in 1960, and I eventually became hunt secretary. I was then made Joint Master with Dick Collins in the late sixties. I've now been involved with this hunt for so long that our hunt territory is now owned by the children and grandchildren of the landowners we first established relationships with. I'm hoping that my son Tommy will be able to take over when I retire because he's known all the landowners since he was a little boy. He's had his colors since he was a teenager. Being an MFH of Los Altos for so many years has taught me a lot about getting along with other people. If your hounds go on someone's land where we're not allowed, you quickly learn that when you approach that unhappy landowner, the first thing you do is get off your horse, so you're not talking down to him but instead are looking at him eye to eye with mutual respect

It was my first Joint Master, Dick Collins, who got me going over to Ireland to foxhunt. He started hunting over there when he was stationed in Europe in World War II. He made close friends with people in Limerick, and by the mid-sixties, my wife and I started going over there every year, staying at the Dunraven Arms. Back then, it was still owned by the Dunraven family. Lord Dunraven had been a Master of Limerick. We eventually

*I think the thing that has kept me committed to this time-consuming and dangerous sport is the friends I've made along the way. Our shared passion for horses and hounds, our mutual love of nature, and the experiences we had out hunting together is a tremendous unbreakable bond. We look after each other when we're out hunting in a way that is no longer seen in our modern society. Like soldiers in the battlefield, we watch each other's backs.*

stayed with the close friends we made while hunting there. Of course, the foxhunting in Ireland was first-rate, but it was the people that kept us coming back year after year. Lord Daresbury was hunting the hounds back then, and his first whipper-in was a young Englishman, Hugh Robards. Hugh eventually started carrying the horn, and I became a Joint Master with him. I've never seen a huntsman that had better control of his hounds than Robards when he was hunting the Limerick pack. Even when the pack was in full cry, you could throw a blanket over them. We would ride with our pack right through the main street of Adare. Back then, Limerick hunted a bitch pack one day and a dog pack the next. Daresbury always said the bitch pack was fastest because nothing got caught in the gorse! Over there, we jumped cattle guards, banks, and ditches that we would never even think of going over back in the States. You had to be thinking all the time to stay up front before the footing got too slick, and at the same time, you had to leave the horse alone and let him figure it out.

I'll never forget when Bruce Davidson and some other US Olympic riders came over to hunt with Limerick and they attempted to school their horses at the beginning of the meet. Not a good idea. The Irish way of fox-hunting is just to sit up and stay out of their way! There were and probably still are a lot more spectacular crashes in Ireland than there are over here, but the ground is so soft because of all the rain, so there aren't any more injuries. When I think about it now, I think I'd have to say that the happiest days of my life were when my family and I were over in Ireland hunting. I remember one day hunting in Galway. We were in stonewall territory, and when the hounds struck, we flew over those big jumps every few minutes for over an hour. I couldn't have stopped my horse if I wanted to. My god, what a ride! You don't forget something like that. Every foxhunter has their stories that stay with them always.

After seven years as Master at Limerick, I resigned and put all my energy towards Los Altos. At that time, it was a drag hunt. My wife Jo used to lay the drag, and she was good at it too. She would lift and resettle the line so the hounds would have to recast themselves, just like hunting a live fox. After our time over the years hunting with Limerick, I was determined to switch to live quarry. Trying to convert a drag pack to hunt live fox is problematic. Because the hounds were so used to running from jump to jump, they never really opened in full cry. So we sent one of our bitches to Mr. Hubbard's kennel in Kent County, Delaware, to be covered by a Penn-Marydel dog, which have deep, resonant voices. Our huntsman Patrick Ellis was keen to breed our pack to some of the wonderful English hounds that we hunted in Limerick. So we started breeding our Penn-Marydel crosses with the old English foxhounds from Ireland. When our English and Irish friends would come over to California to hunt with us, they would say (rather judgmentally, I thought), "Well. You have a nice collection." Our pack wasn't perfectly matched in looks, but they could hunt live quarry in full-throated cry. I'm no longer actively involved in our breeding program, but that's how our drag pack converted to hunting live quarry.

Many years ago, we used to import our foxes into the territory, and there weren't as many coyote. Today, the coyote have taken over, and we rarely jump a fox. If hounds jump wild boar, we'll let them run them, and we'll come in with a gun when the hounds have him at bay. There are Samoans who work on these ranches who know how to slow roast them to perfection. Most of our hunting here is really more chasing than hunting. Rarely do our hounds take down a coyote unless it's old or sick.

*Al and his wife Jo in Ireland, 1970.*

Another issue that I had to deal with when we decided to stop drag hunting was that we had to move our kennels father away where there was more acreage. We had to raise our dues too because you need more hunt staff when you hunt live quarry. Any change takes some adjustment, but folks came around to driving longer distances and enjoying the unpredictability of a live hunt. Part of the fun is never knowing what is going to happen. I think anyone who appreciates good hound work would much rather have live quarry. Follow them long enough, and you can't help but appreciate the clever tenacity of a foxhound. Watching them work together is a wonderful thing to behold.

In California, riding with the hounds isn't in the culture like it is back on the East Coast. Even today, our members still feel like they are ambassadors of the sport, and our job is to introduce foxhunting to others. This is still cowboy country in this agricultural part of the state. Even though Los Altos was established as a beagle pack in 1952 and recognized as a foxhound pack since 1960, our members are still met with curiosity when the subject arises. California has a protest group against anything you can imagine. We don't put our fixture locations on our website. Of course, the ranchers want us here because the coyotes are a real problem for their livestock. That and, of course, they like to see the pretty girls in their riding breeches! The ranches out here are twenty, thirty thousand acres of emptiness. As long as we close the gates and don't tear up the crops, we're welcome. The western coyotes will pack up and kill baby calves and foals and play havoc on sheep. Our dogs and cats are always at peril. We've lost some of our own pets to them.

Foxhunting has been a big part of my life for over fifty years now, and I have to attribute that to my wife, who got me started and shared it with me through the years. I would never have made all the wonderful friends both at Limerick and Los Altos unless she had encouraged me along. There are so many connections in the small world of foxhunting. As a teenager, Tony Gammell whipped-in to Hugh Robards while we were Joint Masters at Limerick. Now Tony is huntsman here in America with Keswick, and Hugh is huntsman at Middleburg, after being Joint Master with Sophie Mellon at Rolling Rock. If you stick around long enough, everybody knows everybody else. Once you start judging hound shows, the circle gets even smaller.

When we hunt on Wednesdays, the field is mostly women, so like our old huntsman Dick Collins used to do, I've started calling the weekday field my bitch pack. And any huntsman can tell you, that's a compliment! The ladies know enough about hounds to take it as such and even have hats that say "Los Altos Bitch Pack." I think the thing that has kept me committed to this time-consuming and dangerous sport is the friends I've made along the way. Our shared passion for horses and hounds, our mutual love of nature, and the experiences we've had out hunting together is a tremendous unbreakable bond. It's not a competitive activity, but it's a thrill nonetheless. In fact, if anything, it's a cooperative sport, where people help each other out. We look after each other when we're out hunting in a way that is no longer seen in our modern society. Like soldiers in the battlefield, we watch each other's backs.

# Hugh Robards

MENTORED BY THE STORIED CAPTAIN RONNIE WALLACE OF
HEYTHOP HUNT IN ENGLAND AND LORD DARESBURY OF
LIMERICK HUNT IN IRELAND, HUGH WENT ON TO BE MFH AND
HUNTSMAN OF ROLLING ROCK IN PENNSYLVANIA AND IS NOW
HUNTSMAN OF MIDDLEBURG IN VIRGINIA.

When I was about twelve or thirteen, I was pigeon shooting with my dad when I first saw the Eridge foxhounds at work. I'll never forget the gorgeous voice of Major Field-Marsham. When they put a fox to ground and were digging it out, father led me away because he knew I didn't even want to kill a pigeon. I was really excited about the whole thing, though, and took him up on his offer to follow the hounds the following weekend when they left from the local village. From then on, I never looked back. I was hooked. I'd get in the jeep with the terrier man every opportunity I could get. I'd cycle seven miles to the kennels for the privilege. I realized I wanted to be a hunt servant, so I talked to Tom Cooper, who was kennel huntsman for Eridge, who stated the obvious by reminding me that I needed to learn to ride. I knew mum and dad could never afford lessons, so I went to work in the local livery stable. I'd muck stalls and exercise the horses, figuring things out as I went along. I never once had the opportunity to jump a horse while working there. I had to learn that the hard way—out hunting. When I first started jumping out with Sussex, I'd fly the full length of the stirrup leathers out of the saddle and somehow land on the poor horse's back. Fifty-four years ago when I was first looking for a position in hunt service, I was told that the sport was "finished"—but obviously that obituary was a bit premature!

Major Field-Marshall was both MFH and huntsman at Eridge and a major influence on me. When he retired, the hunt took on a professional

*Even when things seem terrible, over time, I've come to realize that every hunting adventure is just part of a greater story. It's such a wonderful sport. The hunting world is as small as a wren's egg. When you start talking to people who share a love of the sport, you quickly realize that you all have the same friends.*

huntsman, Brian Gupwell, and when a whipper-in position became available, he took a chance on me despite my youth and lack of experience. So against my parent's wishes, at sixteen, I moved into the garden shed with no water, behind the kennels. After a couple of years of being Gupwell's sole whipper-in, I was ready to move on. He taught me a great deal, and I took it with me. Field-Marshall still gave me guidance and suggested I take the second-whip position that was open at Heythrop. That hunt went out five or six days a week, so I knew I'd learn a lot, even though I was going from a first-whip to a second-whip position. Captain Ronnie Wallace was a wonderful man to whip-in to because you were never right, so you learned a lot! He was a brilliant huntsman with a foul temper. I remember one occasion when the hounds divided and I went to stop my lot and was feeling pretty good about stopping them when Captain Wallace comes blazing down the road, cursing me for stopping the hounds. His part of the pack had accounted for their fox, and he wanted to go on to the next quarry without a moment's pause.

There was a second occasion when the same thing happened again. He cursed me out to such an extent that his wife made him apologize. One time, I viewed a fox in a field of Brussels sprouts, and when he rode up to ask the exact location, he insisted I turn my head when I spoke to him, so I did, and the fox slipped away unseen while I was minding my manners! I remember Bill Lander talking about the captain, saying, "There will never be another like him. I do the same things he does, but it doesn't work for me like it does for him!" Like all good huntsmen, it was a pleasure to watch Wallace on a slow day when the hounds were having to work extra hard and he had to nudge them along. That's when I really learned something. On a great day, the huntsman could have just stayed in bed. There isn't a whole lot to do once they are hot on a scent. I stayed at Heythrop for three seasons. It was hard work but an invaluable education. After a while, it was frustrating because the huntsman and the kennel huntsman were allowed two horses a day and I was only allowed one—which meant I was supposed to save my horse and go through the gates. Well, there was an artist named Tom Carr, who used to sketch while following the hunt, and he showed the Master drawings of me going over a gate and falling over a wall, which put me in a bit of hot water. I talked to Charlie Wilkin, the huntsman at Wynnstay, and realized that not only would I be supplied with two horses per hunt but that I would probably hunt the hounds if anything happened to him. So off I went, and I had three wonderful seasons there. Beautiful country, beautiful. When Charlie got concussed, he was true to his word and let me hunt his hounds. I'll always be grateful for that opportunity. I think he could have come back sooner, but he wanted to give me a chance to carry the horn. He was a lovely, lovely man. Of course, I grew restless to get my own position, so with Captain Ronnie Wallace's recommendation, I found myself on a boat headed to Ireland to be a huntsman for Lord Daresbury's Limerick Hounds.

It was a wonderful opportunity. I hunted the dog hounds twice a week, and he hunted the bitches twice a week. I whipped-in to Daresbury when I wasn't hunting the dogs. He was sixty-eight when I arrived at twenty-four, and he said he was going to retire at seventy and I would have the lot—and he kept his word. I'll never forget the look he had in his eyes the first day I hunted his bitches. What an act of hopeful generosity to let a young man hunt your hounds. I was fortunate to have twenty-seven years hunting the Limerick hounds. It was a wonderful life, surpassing my wildest dreams. Of course, there is no such thing as happily ever after, and eventually politics took over in Limerick, just like it does everywhere else.

I'd married the ex-Master's daughter, Caroline, and Al Schreck, who was Joint Master with Lady Melissa Brooke, wanted me to be a Joint Master, which seemed fair enough because I was doing all the hunt accounts, sending out all the cards and in charge of all the hound breeding. Funnily enough, I thought it would make my job more secure, but in fact, it had the opposite effect. MFH is just three little letters, but it's a position more coveted by hunt club members than huntsman. As a result, my days at Limerick sadly came to an end, and I was at a loss what to do.

Once again, I was lucky to have the support of people that believed in me. Al Schreck met Sophie Mellon at an MFHA Hunt Ball in New York, and they discovered that they were both looking for a huntsman. What they came to realize was both Al's Los Altos and Sophie's Rolling Rock had hired the same huntsman! Albert persuaded Sophie to get me over to the States for an interview. Her dream was to build up Rolling Rock back to the glory days of its founder, General Richard Mellon, so it was an exciting opportunity. My original agreement with Rolling Rock was to stay for five seasons, then I agreed to another five years. I started drafting hounds from Los Altos to the Rolling Rock pack because Al had brought those bloodlines over from Lord Daresbury's pack in Limerick. After ten years at Rolling Rock, I had established a great pack of hounds, but my domestic life went off the rails. I was drinking entirely too much, and things became a mess. Alcohol abuse seems to be an occupational hazard in hunt service. Drinking is deeply embedded in the culture, and more than a few of us mess ourselves up with the daily drinking routine. My marriage to Caroline didn't survive, but I've now been sober for seven years and am married to a wonderful woman.

Julie stood by me at times when I probably didn't deserve it. I couldn't get a job in hunt service after Rolling Rock and ended up being a cab driver for a year. At least I drove a Lincoln Town Car, so I hadn't hit rock bottom! Seriously, though, it didn't do me any harm. Those hard times just made me more grateful when I was able to turn my life around. I was still drinking when I took a position at Saxonburg, and it finally dawned on me that I had to quit drinking. So I did—I just stopped because I knew it was what I had to do. I just accept that truth, and it keeps me sober. After four years there, I started thinking about retiring, so I called Mr. Blue at Middleburg to see if he knew of any caretaker's positions. Julie has always wanted to live in this area, so it seemed like a good place to

retire. I learned that Barry Magner was looking for a whipper-in, so I thought that opportunity looked like a good way for us to move to Middleburg. So I *Hugh on Willow, hunting the Limerick bitch pack in 1976. Jim Meade* put my retirement plans on the back burner. When Barry left for Australia, I stepped in as Middleburg huntsman. I love the people here. I've inherited quite a good pack of hounds, and since they are American hounds, I'm inclined to leave them alone a lot more than I would the English hounds. Despite hunting English or crossbred hounds for most of my life, I have to admit these Middleburg hounds have tremendous nose and voice. I think this pack suits this territory very, very well. One thing I learned from Captain Wallace was to keep the field close behind. I want people to see the hounds work so they can really appreciate what's going on out here. He also said that your hounds should be like Labradors. They should come look for you, you shouldn't have to look for them.

I don't use a radio or tracking collars because I like to use my initiative. I expect the same from my whips. I don't tell them to go on the main road. If they need to be there, they will. I use my horn to let people know where I am or where I'm going and what I'm doing with the hounds at any given moment. Our country is wooded, and you can easily slip the field if you don't let them hear you from time to time.

It's a terrific privilege to live a life where you're excited to get out of bed each morning. Of course, at my age, you don't exactly fly out of bed, but I do drag myself out with enthusiasm and gratitude. Through the years, this sport will teach you humility. You can do everything right, and things can go terribly wrong. I was mortified when *Horse and Hound* was out with me to do an article on the famous Limerick hounds and we ran into more hares than I've ever seen and I couldn't stop the hounds from chasing them. They even caught one. I was horrified. Even when things seem terrible, over time, I've come to realize that every hunting adventure is just part of a greater story. It's such a wonderful sport. The hunting world is as small as a wren's egg. When you start talking to people who share a love of the sport, you quickly realize that you all have the same friends. Maybe because it's physically dangerous, we watch out for each other and help each other out. Of course, there can be petty rivalries and politics, but our mutual love of this hunting life also inspires acts of generosity and kindness.

# Ellie Wood Keith Baxter

AT AGE NINETY-FOUR AND LEGALLY BLIND, HER GREATEST
PASSION IS STILL CANTERING CROSS COUNTRY AND LISTENING
TO HOUNDS IN FULL CRY. HER MOTHER, BIG ELLIE WOOD,
TAUGHT GENERATIONS TO FOXHUNT AND COMPETE IN HORSE
SHOWS. HER DAUGHTER WAS HER STAR PROTÉGÉE—AN
EQUESTRIAN LEGEND IN NUMEROUS HALLS OF FAME.

I was born in 1921, and my earliest memories of foxhunting are with my mother, "Big" Ellie Wood, with Farmington Hunt Club. Ever since I was a baby, I just loved ponies and riding. My favorite toy before I got my first beautiful spotted pony was a stuffed horse that my mother used to pull down the sidewalk. She just loved the sport of foxhunting, and I just naturally fell in behind what she did. Of course, back then, no one was taking photographs like they do today, so the first picture I have of me on horseback was one taken at Keswick Horse Show when I was five years old. By the time I was eight or nine, Farmington became a recognized hunt, and I remember being thrilled when the Virginia Foxhound Club came to Charlottesville in 1929 and mother brought me along to the event. Lots of people from other hunts were there for the joint meet, and I was swept up in the excitement. One of my early memories is being impressed that so many would come from so far to foxhunt. How all those people got their horses and hounds here back then, I have no idea. I suspect they came by train. Of course, I was just a little girl at the time and wasn't concerned about anything but being on my pony!

By the time I was school aged, my mother took me hunting practically every weekend. When drag hunting was offered on Saturdays, of course, as a child, I loved it because it guaranteed the opportunity to run

*Fifty years ago, everyone who hunted spent a lot more time in the saddle. More families owned farms and had horses on the place with plenty of room to ride out. Kids today spend maybe an hour in the ring for a lesson and don't have as much opportunity to ride cross country unless they are foxhunting.*

and jump. I only got to hunt live fox on school holidays like Thanksgiving and Christmas. Either drag or live hunts were just such a pleasure that I was just happy to be there. I just loved keeping up with the hounds however it was offered. The Rineharts ran the drag pack, and the Joneses ran the live hunt pack. Mother would never go to the hunt club board meetings because she said the two factions were always arguing. Mother's love was teaching children to ride and introducing them to competition and foxhunting. She never cared much for hunt club politics, and neither do I. Horse-crazy local kids and UVA students found their way to mother's barn, and from there she'd get them out hunting with Farmington. Mother always had children out in the hunt field. It would have been unusual to be out on a Saturday or holiday and not have children jumping right next to the adults. Her students rode wherever they wanted to ride, unlike today, when kids tend to line up behind their instructor and stay there. When I questioned the wisdom of that approach, I was told, "It's so much easier to keep an eye on them." Now that may be, but I don't think you can acquire much heart (courage) if you don't get used to making your own decisions as you go along. Very few children today have the opportunity to get up on a pony and just go. They're not taught to gallop and control their horse. Back in my day, there was never a gate anywhere near the coops, and everyone was expected to jump. Fifty years ago, everyone who hunted spent a lot more time in the saddle. More families owned farms and had horses on the place with plenty of room to ride out. We hacked out from our place, Keithwood, to both meets and horse shows. That would add many hours of riding to whatever activity you were pursuing. Kids today spend maybe an hour in the ring for a lesson and don't have as much opportunity to ride cross country unless they are foxhunting.

Everyone who rode out from mother's stable learned by her example. She upheld the tradition of turnout and behavior, and we did as she did. She never sat me down and gave me a lecture; she just announced, "We're going hunting Ellie Wood," and I just followed along. I raised my son Charlie the same way—by example. Like me, he loved to both compete and hunt. I was never the best turned out with my horses, but they were always good looking, and that helped a lot. Of course, how you sit up on a horse is as important in appearance as grooming. Anything I ever rode, you better believe it was a nice horse—and I'm not just talking about his looks!

*Ellie Wood jumping in a horse show back in the day when the fences were four board and helmets were optional.*

Back then, I loved to compete in horse shows as well as hunt, but there really wasn't any conflict there because the horse show season ended about the time of opening day of foxhunting. Now the horse show season goes on all through the winter, so you don't see as many show riders out hunting as you used to.

One tradition that survives stronger than ever is the hunt breakfast. Today, it's just expected that there will be a tailgate hunt breakfast at the end of the meet. Back in the early days of Farmington, we didn't expect to have food after the hunt. Everyone had a long hack back to their barns and had to get going. We'd occasionally have a pig roast at the hunt club, but it was a special event. Mrs. Wyatt would make her caramel cake, and we'd have a feast. One big difference I've noticed in the foxhunting community today is that people who hunt together don't necessarily socialize together outside of hunting. Back in Mother and Daddy's day, and when I was a young mother, we tended to spend time with the same people both on and off the hunt field.

Back in my younger days, those drag hunts were fast and furious. I don't think many people want to ride like that nowadays. No drag hunt can beat a good live hunt, though I have to admit it can get a little boring standing around waiting for the huntsman to pick up hounds. Once our countryside started getting so cut up by development, the staff has to pick up hounds between each cast, and that can be tedious and time consuming. I appreciate why they have to do it, but it doesn't mean I like it! To add to the congestion of development are the watershed requirements that cause streams and creeks to be wired off from livestock. The obstacles to follow a good running fox continue to add up, but the love of the sport carries on.

# Tom Bishop

HE WAS FIELD MASTER FOR THIRTY YEARS AND NOW
WHIPS-IN FOR FARMINGTON HUNT. EVERYONE LOOKS TO HIM
FOR SARTORIAL ADVICE.

G rowing up in the San Francisco area, I rode in a stock saddle as a
kid. I spent the summers at my uncle's ranch riding around the
countryside all day long, living a cowboy fantasy. It wasn't until I
went to boarding school that I sat in an English saddle, and at first, I wasn't
so sure that I was crazy about the tack or the fancy clothes you had to wear.
But the first time I jumped a jump was the biggest adrenaline rush I ever
had until I kissed a girl. I was hooked for life. You could have dressed me
up in a clown costume, and I'd get out there to jump a course! The Pebble
Beach barn where our school rode housed the United States Equestrian
Three Day Team in the early sixties, and that's where I was introduced to
both eventing and foxhunting. Los Altos Hunt was a drag pack back then,
which was fun for a teenager because there was a lot of running and jumping. When I got interested in what the hounds were doing, it didn't take me
long to figure out that they were just running from one jump to the next
because they knew how the drag was laid. When I graduated from high
school in 1964, the California college system was a bit too radical for my
politics and inclinations. I applied to the University of Virginia, which at
the time was all men who wore coats and ties to class, just like back in the
day when it was Mr. Jefferson's university.

Before classes even started, I signed up for ROTC, where during
my interview a marine colonel told me about a stable just a five-minute
walk from the first-year dorms. I walked to Ellie Wood Keith's barn the
next day and met a thirteen-year-old girl named Claiborne, who would
eventually become my wife of now forty-five years. I had my Connemara

*My first pair of custom French wax calf boots came with a deer shin in the box. It was just assumed you'd know what to do with it. After you rub beeswax on the leather, you use a heated spoon to melt it on the boot before you scrape it with off the shin bone. The results give a mirrorlike surface you could use to shave with if you had to!*

thoroughbred cross shipped to the stable and was introduced to live foxhunting with Farmington Hunt Club. I even arranged my schedule for only afternoon classes so I could get out cubbing. After I joined Farmington in the fall of 1964, I got my first thoroughbred, Squire O'Leary, and together we won the Virginia Field Hunter Championship in the early seventies. Our hounds were really rattled by the introduction of deer to Albemarle County. It was a tough period for the hunt club. Some of the older Bywater hounds were just incorrigible, and we had to get rid of them. The sharp crack of a whip eventually dampened the deer enthusiasm of the rest. Once we got four or five hounds we could really trust, we had a program we could build on. Over the years of vigilant breeding and training, you can get yourself a pretty deer-proof pack, though now we've been having the same problem with coyote. Like deer, it's a fixable problem, as long as the fox population is not run out of the territory by the coyote. Our fox population thinned for a while but now seems to have stabilized and is thriving again. I've had a long run with Farmington. I was Field Master from 1977 to 2006 and have been whipping-in for the past nine years. Jack Eicher was our huntsman when I began leading the field, and he was a wonderful mentor. He taught me so much about hound work. Walking out the hounds on the days when we weren't hunting gave me the best opportunity to get to know the hounds by name and know which ones were the ones to take seriously. Being hands-on at the kennels really deepened my appreciation of the sport.

The more you know, the more you can enjoy yourself. It was good to get into the kennels and learn the hounds' personalities up close and personal. When John Tejbatchka became huntsman in the early nineties, I'd had twenty-plus years' staff experience with the Farmington hounds, and we worked really well together. By that time, we had radios because now that the hounds were deer broke, coyotes were getting to be a problem. We were always able to work in synch, adapting to the situation. When he left for Green Spring Valley Hounds, we got an English huntsman, Daron Beeney, and it was a very different kind of hunting—more measured and controlled—and in time, I was ready to pass on the responsibility of Field Master and take on whipping-in, which I'm still doing today. Being Field Master can be tricky because you want to keep the thrusters happy without it looking like Napoleon's retreat from Moscow, with dead bodies and horses turned over everywhere! Once we got a middle flight, the job got a lot easier. Horses and riders could go along at their appropriate pace, and our casualty rate dropped tremendously.

When I was on active duty in the navy, I obviously didn't get in much hunting, but I did learn how to do a boot polish, and it has held me in good stead since. The spooning and candling technique is something I learned in the military, and I still do to this day if my wax calf boots dry out. My first pair of boots made of French wax calf, heavy leather turned rough grain side out, came with a deer shin in the box. It was just assumed you'd know what to do with it. About an ounce of beeswax is applied to each boot, then heated with a spoon warmed by a candle flame, melting the wax, which soaks into the rough leather. The wax provides waterproofing and, after rubbing down thoroughly with the deer shin in a process aptly known as "boning down," leaves the once-coarse leather smooth. Later, you can use the bone to touch up the surface or erase scars and scrapes from the leather. I bone my boots after every use but rarely use the hot spoon, as the heat dries out the leather. In the thirty years I've owned my present boots, I've only hot waxed them four or five times. You want to use a paste polish on wax calf. I apply it with a soft cloth and again use the deer bone to smooth it all out. After I've applied a coat of paste, I lightly dampen a soft shoe brush and brush the polish. After brushing, I use a soft cloth to buff. I wrap the material around three fingers, and once again, using a just small amount of water on the cloth, I rub the boot in a circular motion until no polish comes off. The results give a mirrorlike surface you could use to shave if you had to! Don't put beeswax on the colored tops of boots but use a neutral polish. They will naturally darken over time. If you have patent leather tops, go over them with a cloth lightly dampened with spray furniture polish, then buff. I may have been a bootblack in a former life!

Every aspect of hunting attire is there for a practical reason. The clothes make a lot more sense than they might look to an outsider. We've done away with the great butterfly flair britches now that stretch fabrics are available. That voluminous design helped take up the slack in your knee and leg when in the saddle. The tall boots obviously protect your legs from briars and branches. At one time, the boot tops rolled over the knees for extra protection on the thighs. Now the tops are just a nod to the old-style military boots. Modern boots still have the tab at the top that used to be used as boot pulls. Boot garters are still considered appropriate for formal attire, even though boots are now stiff enough that they won't roll down without them. Frock coats should cover your saddle as well as your back-sides. The stock tie not only keeps your neck warm, but it also can be used as a sling or a bandage or to tie a splint if necessary. The pin on the stock tie not only keeps it from blowing out of your coat at a gallop but can be used to secure it as a bandage.

Some of the gear gives a visual clue as to who's who on the hunt field. Back in the day, only Masters, farmers, and staff wore velvet hunt caps, and everyone else in the field wore a top hat or a bowler. Ladies didn't ride astride until the 1920s. Married ladies wore a top hat and unmarried ladies a bowler. Professional huntsmen and staff used to wear five-button coats, honorary staff and Masters four buttons, and field members three. Today, as hunt caps and helmets have become universal and head wear no longer distinguishes position, many Masters and staff members have gone over to five-button coats as well. Only professional hunt staff have their rib-bons down in the back of their hat. The rest of us should have our ribbon tabs sewn up. Most people today wear a hard hat with a harness, but my bespoke Patey (hat) fits so beautifully on my head that it stays put with-out a strap. Traditionally, only men wore scarlet coats when they got their

*Tom whipping-in to the Farmington hounds.*
CATHY SUMMERS

colors, and women wore black or dark blue coats with their hunt club colors on their collar. Today, however, some hunts permit women to wear scarlet as well. The expression "a pink coat" probably comes from the fact that the red was an imperfect dye that would fade in the elements over time and age to a pinkish patina. A bright red coat would peg you as a neophyte. Old gear becomes a badge of honor.

# John and Mary Scott Birdsall

MARY SCOTT'S FATHER, EVERNGHIM BLAKE, IS A LEGEND AT
FARMINGTON HUNT CLUB, AND JB'S INVOLVEMENT WITH THE
PIEDMONT ENVIRONMENTAL COUNCIL HAS HELPED PRESERVE
OVER NINETY-SEVEN THOUSAND ACRES OF ALBEMARLE
COUNTY LAND IN PERPETUITY.

**Mary Scott:** My father had a modest position in the State Department, and before our post in Ireland, we were in Germany, where both my father and I learned to ride. No matter where we lived, we always found a place in the country to live. It seems like we never had trouble finding horses to ride. I think Ireland had a huge influence on my father's personality. He fell in love with foxhunting and its way of life. He was passionate about his newfound sport and didn't let the hours in the day stand in the way. After he bought his first horse, he hunted with every pack of hounds along the Irish coastline since his diplomatic assignment there was to examine all the Irish ports. It was a tough job, but someone had to do it! When we moved back to the States and bought a farm in Virginia in 1950, our young nanny, who was quite a good rider, gave me my first lessons, and that made a big difference in my confidence. Before then, I was always just trying to keep up with my father. And as anyone who has ever ridden behind him will tell you—that was no easy task!

We'd always hack to the meet when I was a child, so a day of foxhunting was a full day. From the very beginning, hunting was more to me than just riding my pony. I always knew we were looking for something, even if as a very young child I wasn't sure what it was. As soon as the hounds made their amazing music, we were off and running. I was often a little further up front than I should have been because my pony Little Fellow just took off when the hounds were in full cry. Billy Jones would usually rescue me

*My father left me a legacy of loving not only the sport but the landscape that sustains it. I fell in love with the access to horizon as a small girl foxhunting in Ireland, and that love of wide-open spaces is something that will always stay with me. Land preservation is something that both JB and I care about very much. Open space is an irreplaceable treasure. Once it's gone, it's gone forever.*

and return me to the rest of the field. The sound of the hounds opening is so exciting, such a jolt of joy, that I didn't think about my own safety or the safety of the fox. I think when you're introduced to the sport when you're really young, you just accept it for the thrill it is. The Catholic Church says, "Give me a child before seven years of age, and we'll have her for life." My childhood at Schelford centered around fields and woods, ponies and horses, and weekend events at the hunt club. Mother always followed the hunt by car, along with other family members of the field. She took some riding lessons, but my father wasn't very encouraging. I think he thought of her as a fragile flower, more suited to prepare a tailgate breakfast than gallop cross country. His enthusiasm for the sport and the land we rode over was one of the biggest influences of my childhood. By the time I was in college and met JB, one of the first things I did was bring him out to the farm.

**JB:** I didn't know anything about riding, much less foxhunting, when Mary Scott and I met doing theater with The Virginia Players. When she took me to meet her father, Evernghim Blake, over Thanksgiving vacation my second year of college, of course, the first thing we did was go for a ride, even though my only previous experience on horseback was once at a birthday party pony ride in Florida. Apparently, Evernghim had lost his whip out hunting, so the plan was the three of us would ride out cross country and try to find it. They decided I should ride this high-withered beast named Bold Fellow. Life on the farm was rather discombobulated at that time, with her father camping out in the dairy barn and the tack room a disorganized mess. I remember Mary Scott saying, "Well, I'm going to ride bareback. You don't need a saddle, *do* you?" I didn't even know enough to say that a saddle might be helpful. I just said, "Oh, no. Bareback is fine." So off I go on Bold Fellow of the high withers, holding on to the mane for dear life. We were out for hours and it was quite cold and began to snow. By the time we get back to the stables, it's obvious there's no way I could drive my MG back into town, so I spent the night on the floor of the barn. There's only one bed in the place, and her father's in it. That cold, hard floor was no friend to my sore muscles, and by the next day, I could hardly walk. The silver lining of this story is the next day, when I went to play rehearsal, the director was thrilled when I walked like an old man. My character's walk was something I couldn't accomplish until my first visit to Schelford Farm! I hobbled out onstage to deliver my lines, and the director said, "That's it! That's it!"

Soon after, Mary Scott gave me a few riding lessons, and we started hacking out together when we could. The following year, she took me foxhunting, and from the first, I just loved it. I always joked that it was the only way to court Mary Scott and I'd do whatever it takes, but the truth is I just fell in love with the sport as well as the girl. It was just so damn much fun. By my senior year in college, I was working my class schedule around Farmington's Tuesday, Thursday, and Saturday hunting days. Growing up in South Florida, I had no exposure at all to foxhunting outside of English hunt prints, but I had grown up hunting and fishing, so I loved outdoor sports. Funnily enough, Mary Scott has no interest in any other outdoor sport except foxhunting.

**Mary Scott:** I think we got married under false pretenses because I don't hook things and I don't shoot things. I think for me, the horse and hounds are an important part of the equation.

**JB:** And you taught me to feel the same way, though after college my work took us to Palm Beach, away from foxhunting, for twenty years. We got ponies for our daughters and would occasionally ride, but there wasn't much enthusiasm without a pack of hounds to follow. When Evernghim died in 1984, we moved back to Schelford, and Mary Scott got right back into hunting with her father's horse, Bypass. I don't think I was able to really start hunting regularly again until I was able to live there full-time a few years later.

**Mary Scott:** Once we had grandchildren, I started stepping back from hunting while JB started going out more than ever. He's definitely the dominant horse person in the family now. Now that I'm not hunting, I realize in retrospect that the most compelling aspect of the sport is how it demands your attention. You have to focus with such intensity, really be present. The sounds, sights, and smells all merge into a visceral experience. I do think of getting back out there. Once it's in your blood, it never goes away. It may go dormant, but it's always there.

My father liked to acquire land whenever he had the opportunity. He often rode a horse he couldn't really control, and the FHC Master didn't take very kindly to his Irish style of riding. One day when Farmington was hunting on some of his newly acquired property and his horse was behaving badly, the Master rode up to him and said, "Evernghim, I'm afraid I'm going to have to ask you to go home." He pulled himself up in the saddle as straight and tall as his small stature would allow and said, with as much dignity as he could muster, "Madame, I *am* home!"

**JB:** Her father was a tough bird. I'll never forget when he was crushed between his horse and a tree, and he looks up at me from the ground, still holding his reins, and says, "JB, would you give me a leg up?" We hacked back to Schelford, and I drove him to the hospital, where X-rays revealed numerous broken ribs. The doctor told us that at one time or another, he'd broken every rib in his body.

**Mary Scott:** My father left me a legacy of loving not only the sport but the landscape that sustains it. I fell in love with the access to horizon as a small girl foxhunting in Ireland, and that love of wide-open spaces is something that will always stay with me. Land preservation is something that

*Mary Scott with her father Evernghim Blake in Germany in 1947.*

both JB and I care about very much. Open space is an irreplaceable treasure. Once it's gone, it's gone forever. JB has been really strategic about land preservation from the time we bought our first property near Schelford thirty years ago. From the beginning, we thought about easements and contiguous property.

**JB:** When we donated a conservation easement on that first parcel back in 1984, it was only the third one in Albemarle County, and the total acreage of those three pieces was under a thousand acres. Today, in early 2016, there are over ninety-seven thousand. We've come a long way, but it wasn't easy in the beginning. When I first started talking to my neighbors about the program, they were extremely skeptical and understandably reluctant to consider permanent restrictions on their land. The tax benefit was limited to an income tax deduction, similar to any other charitable gift, so one needed a hefty income to take advantage of the benefit. But in 2000, the Commonwealth of Virginia created preservation tax credits that allowed folks to sell these credits. The combination of the Piedmont Environmental Council's actively promoting the program and the state's encouragement through tax credits has resulted in the permanent protection of open land—much of which is in Farmington and Keswick hunt territory. Of course, this program is not just here in central Virginia. If you look at the map of Fauquier County, which has over one hundred thousand protected acres, you'll see the largest block of privately preserved land in the entire country. Mary Scott and I have been purchasing property and putting it in easement before we resell it, knowing the land will be preserved forever. It's a wonderful legacy to know that your children's children and their grandchildren will be able to enjoy the countryside. 🐾

# Marty and Daphne Wood

They founded Live Oak Hounds almost forty-five years ago. As Joint Masters, Daphne whipped-in to Marty. Both have become respected judges at hound shows in the United States, Canada, and England.

**Daphne:** I whipped-in to Marty for thirty-three seasons, and I always knew what he was going to do next because I was so tuned in to the way he hunted the hounds. To me, it's the mental challenge of foxhunting that is the biggest attraction. I don't care what is going on in your life outside the hunt field; when you're out following the hounds, you are only thinking about the task at hand. Things are happening so fast all the time, and you stay in the moment as each new situation presents itself. If hounds split, you have such a small window to decide which pack the huntsman will want to go with. If they start running in the opposite directions, they are doubling the distance between themselves, and you've only got a moment to decide which hounds should be encouraged and which hounds should be turned around. It takes the decisiveness of intuition and experience.

**Marty:** What I would usually do in that situation was pick the pack of hounds that was headed to the best line of country. I feel that your job as huntsman is to provide sport to those following the hounds, so you make enough noise as you follow the pack headed in the right direction to pick up the others that were going the other way. As Master, I always felt like it's my job to show the field the best possible sport with the pack of hounds on the day that the good Lord gave me. That being said, once the hounds were in full cry, it was the field's responsibility to stay up with me. My greatest thrill in life has been to have my pack of hounds get away fairly

*To me, it's the mental challenge of foxhunting that is the biggest attraction. I don't care what is going on in your life outside the hunt field; when you're out following the hounds, you are only thinking about the task at hand. Things are happening so fast all the time, and you stay in the moment as each new situation presents itself. It takes the decisiveness of intuition and experience.*

on their quarry and be riding a thoroughbred horse who can gallop easily within himself as we fly cross country.

**Daphne:** He would always ride to their flank or sides because you don't ride up the back end of the tail hounds because, on a fast run, you'll end up with hounds behind the huntsman. Some of your best hounds might be a little bit back when they first start running, so you want to give them plenty of room to catch up with the lead hounds.

**Marty:** If you look at a pack when they first open up, they are spread all over the place with their noses on the ground. Once the lead hounds open up and are running with their noses on the ground, they won't be running as fast as the tail hounds who are just running to catch up and honor their cry. They look like filings to a magnet, then they're away as a pack. To me, watching the hounds work is the most brilliant part of the sport. I've bred my hounds to be biddable and to account for their game. We hunt in an area where landowners really want us to account for our quarry. The foxes, wild pigs, and coyote are considered mortal enemies of the farmers around here.

**Daphne:** Your hounds have to have enough confidence to draw and run over deer lines and not stop every time they smell a scent they are not supposed to run. Once we get our hounds steady on deer, we get out of their way and let them hunt. We've got the countryside to let them run. One of the reasons we like a strongly English pack is because they are so biddable. We think they add a necessary ingredient to the American hound for a good crossbred hound. I think American hounds have a better cry and a colder nose, but the English hound has a keenness and biddability that is hard to beat. The Potomac and Bywater hounds have been an important part of our breeding program as well as a tiny amount of Penn-Marydel and even Walker hounds, but the English hound has been the constant in the Live Oak pack.

**Marty:** I like my crossbreds to be 80 percent or more English. I don't like to breed crossbreds to crossbreds—the results are too unpredictable. I love to judge foxhounds because good confirmation allows a hound to run farther and faster than poor confirmation. It doesn't do anything for his nose or cry, but if a well-built hound has those as well, he's going to be an asset to your pack, which is the lovely science of bloodlines. You want a pack with similar confirmation so they can all run together as a pack and not get all strung out.

**Daphne:** When coyotes first started showing up in the early eighties, we had to decide whether to cull from the front or the back because our pack was getting so strung out by the faster speed. We don't have the mountains and paved roads that would make chasing coyote problematic, so we cull from the back to increase the speed of our pack. Another characteristic that has to be similar in a good pack of hounds is similar sensitivity. You can't hunt a hound that needs a whip and rat shot for a correction next to one that puts his tail between his legs if you speak his name sharply.

**Marty:** From the beginning, there was no question that we were going to account for our game. At first, our hounds would chase and bay coyotes but didn't want to take them down. When Captain Ronnie Wallace gave us the dog Landseer '90, that great hound was the foundation of our coyote hunting pack. My father died in 1987, and Ronnie became a father figure to me. Even though he lived in England, we talked often on the phone.

Daphne and I started going over to England to visit his kennels and hunt with him. He shared all his knowledge with me.

**Daphne:** A very valuable bloodline in our pack is Landseer. He's the hound in our oil painting in our library for a reason.

**Marty:** Breeding foxhounds fascinates me. Daphne wrote an article about the rule of seven. When you breed two hounds, you never want to line breed closer than in the third and fourth generations. It takes a lifetime commitment to get a pack of hounds that have the speed, stamina, voice, and biddability that works for your country. My advice to young Masters and huntsmen is to stay out of breeding decisions until you are darn sure you're going to be around with that pack for the long haul because it takes at least seven years to begin to get any consistent positive effect. One responsibility I take quite seriously as Master is to never enter a hound in a show if it's not a good hunting hound. If their hunting ability isn't at least as good as their looks, you'd be doing a terrible disservice to the sport if you win a championship and everyone wants one of the puppies.

**Daphne:** While Marty was in graduate school at UVA, I hunted with Farmington three days a week and was so fortunate to have their Master, Jill Summers, share her knowledge of hounds with me. Before her influence, foxhunting was a galloping cocktail party. Jill taught me what the hounds were up to, and that deepened my love for the sport to a lifelong commitment. When Marty and I moved to Thomasville, Florida, I felt like I was buried alive. I missed hunting so much I couldn't stand it. I started hunting with Ben Hardaway's Midland Hounds and gave Marty a horse for Christmas in hopes that he would want to join me. Well, by May, he was showing and winning at the Atlanta Hunter Jumper Classic. Once he started hunting, he was off and running wherever the chase would lead. Jill Summers gave us a draft from Farmington. Hardaway gave us some Midland hounds, and Jake Carle gave us a Keswick hound. That was the beginning of the Live Oaks pack in 1974.

**Marty:** I know it sounds ridiculously ambitious to start hunting your own pack of hounds, but back then, it took over four hours to get to Midlands. I remember the night I made the decision. We pulled back in to our barn

*Marty and Ronnie Wallace judging Canadian Hound Show in 1986. The beginning of a lifelong friendship.*

at 1:30 in the morning, and I had to get up at 5:00 to get to work. I knew something had to change, and quitting hunting or working was not an option. When Daphne and I purchased this property, we built the kennels and stable before we built the house. I love hunting a mixed pack. When a coyote starts following a deer to throw hounds off their scent, I can trust the experienced nose and keen intelligence of my old bitches to unravel the scent line and get back on the true trail. At the same time, I can trust my dog hounds to keep the pressure on.

**Daphne:** I thought starting our own pack was a great idea from the beginning, but, of course, I had no idea what we were getting into. I always loved whipping-in for Marty, but as we got older, we ended up having to go to marriage counseling to get Marty to understand that I wasn't going to kill myself to get in front of the pack to protect and turn hounds as I had done for decades. I was going to ride at a pace that I felt like I could survive but still enjoy my hunting.

**Marty:** It was hard for me to accept that we were no longer at our physical peak, even though I'd had neurosurgeons tell me I couldn't afford another head injury. I had a deep-brain bleed that was almost the end of me. I continued to hunt despite the doctor's warnings until both of my knees wore out and I was in such pain that I would find myself avoiding covert where we might jump a coyote. I knew it was time to accept the fact that I had to retire from carrying the horn. As past Master and huntsman, it would be very difficult for me to hilltop. I feel more in the thick of things in my Tahoe—which we affectionately refer to as the steel stallion—with my radio, tracking collars, and horn, following their flank. I go places God and General Motors never intended four wheels to go. Even though I've had to hang up my spurs, following my hounds is still my biggest passion. 🐾

# Tony Leahy

HE'S BEEN HUNTSMAN OF FOX RIVER VALLEY HUNT IN
ILLINOIS FOR OVER TWENTY-FIVE YEARS AND MFH SINCE
THE MID-1990S. THEY ESTABLISHED A WINTER KENNEL IN
GEORGIA EIGHTEEN YEARS AGO.

G rowing up in Ireland, all my family foxhunted. I can't even really remember being introduced to the sport. It was just what we did. There are so many hunts over there, and we hunted all over. Growing up, we lived at the next farm over from a kennel. I knew great Masters and huntsmen since I was a kid. My father was very involved with the hunt and always loved the hounds as much as the horses and was interested in their breeding. I just kind of fell into being a huntsman. I was show jumping and got an opportunity to come work in America when I was about seventeen. I went back to Ireland to finish school, then came back to Wellington, Florida, in the mid-eighties to compete again. I had an injury and was laid up for a while, so I went to a friend of my brother's in Pennsylvania to recover. While I was there, a hunt club down the way needed some help, so I started pitching in. I really admired the huntsman Tommy Kneipp at Deep Run, so I went down to Virginia to whip for him. He taught me a lot about foxhunting and gave me time to work with my horses. To this day, I still use a lot of what he taught me about staggering hound pedigrees and creating lines that can be crossed from different angles.

In 1990, I met the Master of Fox River Valley Hunt outside of Chicago, Illinois, and took over as huntsman there and have been there ever since. I met a wonderful girl, and that kept me there. Mr. McGinley also had me riding his show jumpers as well as hunting his hounds, so the job really suited me. It was a very smooth transition for me. I became great friends with the Masters Bill McGinley and Mrs. Fitch, becoming a Master

*This life grabs you like an obsession. It's completely addicting. It's such a joy to be excited to get out of bed in the morning. The work is a pleasure because it's all foxhunting. Schooling the horses, cleaning the tack and kennels, walking out the hounds—every step of the way is part of a life I love.*

myself in the mid-nineties. Tommy Kneipp let me take some Deep Run hounds to Fox River Valley, and that line, crossed with Midland hounds from Georgia, is the backbone of our kennel today. Even though I was a professional rider before I became a huntsman, I think today I spend more time thinking about the hounds than I do the horses. Their bloodlines tickle in my head and keep me awake at night. After I became a Master, I joined the MFHA and became involved with the work they do there, joining the board. It's a solid group of people who really care about the sport and want to see it continue and held to a high standard.

Before we started hunting in southwestern Georgia, I'd only hunted on fox. Fox River Valley was based in a far western suburb of Chicago. Both Mrs. Fitch and I wanted to hunt wilder country, so we partnered with Cornwall Hounds, which are now Masbach Hounds. They had a lovely rolling country out along the Mississippi River in Elizabeth, Illinois. I bought a farm out there and brought the hounds with me, but the winters in Illinois really started to frustrate me because so many days were lost to the weather. It was pretty much impossible to hunt past mid-December, which should be the best time for our sport. I was working so hard shoveling manure in the snow, and horse sales came to a standstill every midwinter. I started packing up the hounds and heading south when I could. I started looking for a winter home for the hounds where there was plenty of diverse land and mild weather. I love the combination of 50 to 60 percent open fields with thick covert for game in the rest. One thing that I also love about the Deep South, besides the weather and the rural landscape, is the people. The folks here are fantastic—super kind to me. It's a pleasure to be a member of the community because the landowners here are so nice. I consider them friends. The acreage where we built the kennels in Morgan, Georgia, is about ten by seven miles, and we have much larger fixtures in our hunt territory that are contiguous except for natural barriers like swamps and rivers. Ben Hardaway of Midlands Hounds has been fantastic to me in every way, supporting my efforts to get established down fairly near to his own hunt territory. I consider him one of my best friends. He's hard on me, but I always feel like he's got my best interest at heart. We'll have such intense conversations about technical aspects of the genetics of hound breeding. He really gets my mind racing.

Being situated in the winter between Hardaway's Midlands Hounds and the Wood's Live Oak Hounds has been a real privilege. I love hunting with those packs. There's always so much to learn. It's hard to believe I've been in Georgia every winter for nineteen years now. When Fox River Valley first started coming down here for the winter season, we rented four eighteen-wheelers and transported our horses, hounds, tack, and household goods. Once we got here, we used the containers as our lodge and kennels. We just fenced off the area in front of the semiboxes for the dog yard. We rented the crappiest little house in the village, and my wife didn't even want to take a shower because the open drain was so disgusting. We just rented the containers and tried to clean them out the best we could when it was time to return them. We used a lot of bleach, then drove out of there as fast as we could after we dropped them off! At first, we leased land, but over the years, were able to purchase land and build permanent structures. Once we owned the property, we got right to work and got the buildings and fencing done in quick order. I'd build coops by using old fencing lumber from other farms.

Now Fox River Valley has a regular routine, where we begin cubbing in late summer and opening meet is the third week in September. We'll carry on three days a week until the weather shuts us down some time in December, then we'll usually be up and running down here in

TONY LEAHY    69

Georgia right after Christmas. This year, I brought twenty-nine horses with me because I sell hunters and jumpers when I'm not hunting hounds. The horse side of it gives us an opportunity to hunt quite a lot because I always have a lot of horses that need to get out. This week, we went out six days in a row because my friends who are snowed out up North like to come down here to hunt. We usually hunt at least four days a week during the winter. We've got enough territory that it doesn't put too much pressure on the game.

Even though it's a subscription hunt, the membership is so small given the rural location that there's really no need for a clubhouse. We just spend time in each other's homes. If you're located in an area where the game and land are plentiful, you're in a remote area away from much population. We're never going to see large numbers of people out hunting like you do in areas near large cities. I love it here because of the closeness of the people who do foxhunt. It's more like the old days, when there weren't as many distractions.

Because I'm an amateur huntsman and Master, I can decide when and where to hunt more freely than professional hunt staff. If you're a huntsman, it's more than a day job whether you're paid for the work or not. It's an all-encompassing way of life. Some of the people that I admire most are professional huntsmen. They are the backbone of the sport. Their influence can't be overestimated, and everyone who loves this sport is in their debt. I'm very much involved with the MFHA development program. Mason Lampton started it and convinced me to come on board. It's an effort to expose young huntsmen to more experienced professionals. Even though there's written materials in the yearlong workshop, this sport is still taught mostly by mentors who share their experience. We send the applicants to work side by side with seasoned huntsmen. It hopefully will let the younger enthusiast see huntsman or whipper-in as a career choice. Like land and quarry, professional hunt staff is key for the future of the sport. Andrew Barclay is fantastic at running the program, and we consider this program as a way to give back to the sport that has given us so much.

One of my greatest joys in life is hunting with my daughter Caitlin. Her bravery and enthusiasm inspire me. When she was about eight years old, I told her if she could catch a baby wild pig, she could keep it, and darn if she didn't jump off her horse and grab one. Now she's telling me she thinks I'm getting a little old for this job, and she wants to take our

professional whip's place and have our first whip Ashley take over as huntsman. I don't think I'll be like *Tony hunting the Fox River Valley hounds in 2013.* Melvin Poe, but at forty-five, I think I still have a few good years left!

I used to have a very traditional view of when we started cubbing and when we started young hounds. Now I have come to like starting my young entry at the end instead of the beginning of the season. As the season wanes, from the end of February to the end of March is, in my mind, the best time to introduce young hounds because the coverts aren't as thick and the crops aren't planted, so we can keep an eye on them and see what's what. You can see who's running deer or who's running mute. It's great if we can jump a gray fox instead of a coyote because the young ones will have a better chance of staying with it. It's good for the older hounds as well. If they can run a gray fox well, they can run a coyote better because it hones that communal capacity to be accurate and persevere on the intricacies of a gray, which zigs and zags much more than a coyote. It's almost like a light switch that turns on the whole pack to cooperate instead of compete. That communal effort is what I'm always working towards with our pack. I'm more interested in their cooperation and accuracy than I am speed. The fact that we're able to get out about a hundred and twenty days a season makes the hounds really sharp. You get into a rhythm and a flow that builds on itself as the season progresses. By late winter, we're in a rhythm of hunting, eating, and sleeping. Mentally, I'm more aware of all the dynamics at play in the pack when

I'm in that flow of late-season hunting. This life grabs you like an obsession. It's completely addicting. There's always the next covert, the next hour, the next day, week, and season. For me, it's the cycle of life. It's such a joy to be excited to get out of bed in the morning. The work is a pleasure because it's all foxhunting. Schooling the horses, cleaning the tack and kennels, walking out the hounds—every step of the way is part of a life I love. 🐾

# Ben Hardaway

WITH OVER SEVENTY YEARS OF FOXHUNTING
AND HOUND BREEDING EXPERIENCE, HIS INFLUENCE
CAN BE FELT ALL OVER HUNTS IN THE UNITED STATES
AND THE UNITED KINGDOM.

I'll never forget the first time I heard foxhounds in full cry. They came running down our creek at night, and it made all the hair stand up on the back of my neck. As a boy, I'd been huntin' rabbits and coons, but the roar of those July hounds on a red fox was something that I knew I'd have to pursue for the rest of my life. The very next morning, I went over to Mr. Eddie's place and traded my coonhounds for foxhounds. Now a lot of the neighbors hunted hounds at night on foot, so folks were used to that, but when I started following my pack on horseback, they'd say, "Here comes that Hardaway boy on one of his hoppin' horses!" When I started building coops over the fences, they thought I was building houses for the fox. And you know, it wasn't that uncommon to jump a gray out from under the coop. The first thing my daddy gave me was a pony, and because I rode cross country alone, he had me ride on a blanket with a girth because he was worried I might hang a foot in a stirrup if I fell off on a saddle. My grandmother saw how devoted I was to my hounds and gave me a book called *The Life of John Mytton*, which became a source of great inspiration. Even though he was a crazy drunk and an incorrigible gambler who was always in debt, he was a rabid foxhunter. He was probably not such a good role model for an eleven-year-old boy! At about that age, our neighbor Mr. Garrett came over to see my fledgling pack of July foxhounds. I took him to the kennels, and he said he wasn't too impressed with the look of things, but I knew my hounds could hunt like the dickens. When I got back from World War II, I took right back up where I left off and registered

my pack in 1950. We continued to hunt around Columbus, Georgia, until the mid-sixties. When twelve thousand acres became available in Fitzpatrick, Alabama, we started bringing the hounds over there on Saturdays to hunt. To this day, we make the same trip back and forth.

As long as the red fox were around, I'd pull my hounds off a coyote. But once the mange wiped them out, the coyote were really able to take over because this far south, once mange is established in the fox population, they won't return to that area for twenty years because the mites live in the dens and reinfect the young ones. Of course, by then, the territory was thick with coyote. By the seventies, there was nothing to run but coyote. I remember the day well when

*Over my ninety-five years, I've drunk enough liquor to have two or three heart attacks, and now that my assistant Beverly is driving me cross country to follow the hounds, I should have had three or four more—but I feel like blowing the hunt horn for all those years has cleaned out my arteries and kept me healthy. To this day, hounds in full cry wipe my soul clean and make me glad to be alive.*

I saw one slinking across the field and first encouraged the pack to get on the line. They were off and running, and we've never looked back.

If the whitetail deer wasn't dumped in our Georgia and Alabama hunt territory in the late fifties, early sixties, I'd probably still be hunting July hounds. It wasn't any particular dream of mine to develop a crossbred hound, but it was necessary to get my dogs to stop running deer. My old Julys were such keen hunters that they'd chase a deer twenty-seven miles before I could get them back. I knew their determination was such that I just didn't have the heart to beat it out of them. Their nature is very much like mine, and I knew I'd have to break their spirit to keep them from running deer. I was determined to keep that thrilling cry and drive and speed that thrills me like no other hound, but I knew I had to cross them with hounds that were more biddable. I knew a good ole boy that would break his July hounds off deer by putting them in a fifty-five-gallon oil drum with a hole in the top and bottom. He'd spray their face with a flit gun filled with deer scent, and as soon as he atomized the hounds' face with scent, he'd get another fella to poke 'em in the butt with a cattle prod. He said it'd deer break 80 percent of 'em and you'd never get any of them back in a barrel again! I got a more humane idea of rubbing deer scent under the puppies' nose right as I was giving them their Parvo shot, so they associated an unpleasant sting with deer scent. Sometimes I'd buy a mousetrap and set it with a cotton ball saturated with deer scent, and, of course, those curious puppies learned pretty quick to stay away from that smell. Just like a human, they've got to learn while they're young for the best results.

I started breeding my hounds with the Golden's Bridge hounds, who were easy to break off deer. They gave me an old dog named Bounder with a deep voice and a nose that wouldn't quit. I bred him to the most biddable bitch I had, named Silver, and she had two dogs and two bitches, Sligo, Step, Star, and Stella. They were the beginning of my Midland pack that still had speed and voice but were more biddable. I started reading Mendel's book on crossbreeding corn and books on cow breeding and got excited about the possibilities of crossbreeding hounds for specific hunting purposes. I bred a pure July (Silver) to a pure Penn-Marydel (Bounder) with good results, but I didn't want to keep doing the same thing over and over again. I wanted to continue improving the line for what traits our hounds needed for our particular conditions. Like corn and cows, hounds need three different strains to get a strong result. Although the Irish ST (Striker) line can be a mean dog fighter, a little bit of that blood adds speed and determination, so the Midland hound still carries a diluted drop of that Irish line. My son-in-law, Mason, keeps this breeding going today. It's been going on for enough generations that you can breed your own hounds without fear of inbreeding, but I believe that it's always good to get hybrid vigor by bringing in a fresh line that has desirable characteristics. You need to take your crossbred to a purebred line to begin a dependable breeding program. Today, Midland kennel keeps about twelve different lines in both our bitches and dogs.

In the early sixties, I got the opportunity to hunt in Ireland with my friend Elebash. He went to Groton and Yale and made a career of becoming close to very rich people. Through the years, that inclination of his opened a lot of doors for me in sport. He was the type of guy the Irish really appreciated because he would entertain you around the dinner table. I loved that guy, though I would have hated to have to write his pedigree!

He was such a wild man that my wife Sarah said he was a good friend for me because he made me look well behaved! The worse behaved we got, the more the Irish loved us. While over there, I met Evan Williams, who'd won the Grand National when he was seventeen years old. He was one of the best foxhunters there ever was. He became an important trainer, then was Master of the Tipperary. He introduced me to Ikey Bell, the first breeder to begin mixing the old English hounds with Welsh and Fell hounds. He was considered an outlaw and outcast by traditional English foxhound breeders of the time. Elsie Morgan was hunting the Bell crossbreds at the West Waterford Pack, and when I saw her hunt those hounds, I knew that's the type of dog I needed. She gave me Gladstone, and I shipped him to my kennels in Columbus, Georgia. It just so happened that Star (half July, half Penn-Marydel) was in the heat pen, so I said, "You old Irish son of a bitch, you might be dead when I wake up in the morning, but you're going to breed this bitch for me tonight." Those puppies didn't disappoint. Over the years, I started shipping my get back across the ocean.

You'll find my hounds an important part of the breeding program all through England, Ireland, Scotland, Canada, Australia, and New Zealand. The Midland hound formula became a quarter July, five-eighths Fell, and an eighth Penn-Marydel. Without losing any voice or enthusiasm, about 80 percent of the puppies are both biddable and keen. That's basically the hound we're still hunting today.

Of course, hound breeding is not an exact science. When I went over to Ireland to judge the Northern Irish Harriers, I was amazed how similar they looked to my original July hounds. I realized that the pack I fell in love with when I was an eleven-year-old boy were from the Irish Harrier line. When I heard their cry, there was no doubt. I brought a dog back with me, and today some of the best hounds we have in the Midland Kennels go back to that Irish Harrier line. Years ago, there were two collie/July mix dogs from a neighbor's farm that used to join my pack and hunted better than anything in my kennel, so I took them in. Despite their unusual lineage, they looked just like July and hunted even better. I would have bred the bitch, but she was spayed and the dog was a bit common looking, so I didn't breed him either. I'd probably have ended up with four collies, so it's just as well, I suppose. Maybe I should have regrets! To this day, I've never seen two hounds that were so dependable. They were smarter than any foxhound I've ever known. Now good looks won't guarantee good hunting ability, but I'd much rather go behind a good-looking dog that knows his business than an ugly one. Same thing goes with a woman! The chest and the shoulder are important for endurance and speed, but the heart and guts inside where you can't see are just as important if you want a good huntin' hound. I judge a hound in competition like Ikey Bell taught me years ago. I run my hand down his front legs and make sure his legs touch my hand when I run it down between his front legs. If the front legs are too wide apart, he'll never have the speed I'm looking for. I want a leg and foot that has a springy pastern.

*Oil painting of Hardaway in his prime.*
Henry Nordhausen

In 1993, my horse hung his hind leg going over a jump, and he flipped me into a tree. I had a subdural hematoma on both sides of my brain. They slapped me in the hospital and drilled two holes in each side of my head to drain the bleeding. After I got home from the hospital, my wife Sarah sat me down and said that I'd had more and more falls in the past few years and she wasn't looking forward to taking care of a paraplegic. I had to agree with her, that after fifty years of putting up with me, she deserved better than that. So I quit for her and was glad to do it. I realized that the future of the Midland Fox Hounds lay with my son-in-law, Mason Lampton. He had been whipping-in with me for years. His grandfather, Mason Houghland, was a great foxhunter, and I was glad that I could see the future for a pack of hounds that I'd dedicated my life to.

Over my ninety-five years, I've drunk enough liquor to have two or three heart attacks, and now that my assistant Beverly is driving me cross country to follow the hounds, I should have had three or four more—but I feel like blowing the hunt horn for all those years has cleaned out my arteries and kept me healthy. To this day, hounds in full cry wipe my soul clean and make me glad to be alive. 🐾

# Tot Goodwin

He whipped-in for Ben Hardaway for over twenty years, then in 1989 became huntsman of Green Creek Hounds in South Carolina. He's the only black MFH in America.

My granddaddy and dad always hunted dogs, and I started hunting the beagles every weekend when I was about eight years old. Now my granddaddy was a horseman. He used to break and train horses right outside of Columbus, Georgia. He died before I was old enough to really ride, so as a kid, I never had the opportunity to ride any nice horses. My parents had mules that plowed the farm. As a little boy, I never heard of mounted foxhunting. We hunted coons, rabbit, and deer on foot and ate everything we caught. There were sixteen kids in my family, so we never wasted any food. I was born in 1944. One of my older brothers worked for Ben Hardaway, and I used to like to hunt on foot with him. When two of his July hounds ran out in the road chasing a fox, I was able to get ahead and stop a tractor-trailer before it ran over them. I think he really appreciated that, and he gave me a job grooming his horses. I can still remember Sparkle and Sanction, especially Sparkle, with her curly hair— she looked just like a white collie. She was a heck of a foxhunter. After I'd been his groom for a while, he asked me if I wanted to learn how to ride, and I jumped at the chance. He asked his trainer, Ann, to give me lessons. Well, the way she gave me lessons was by putting me on top of the young horses to get them saddle broke. She'd lunge 'em for a while, then put me on and let us go. I got bucked off many a time, but I did learn how to ride. To this day, I'm not too crazy about Connemara/thoroughbred cross. They put me on the ground too often!

*Just the other day, a group of us from Green Creek were having breakfast together before the meet, and someone came up and asked me, "Do they let you hunt too?" I could say, "Well, since I'm huntsman and Master, if I don't go, they don't go" but I don't go that route. I just say, "Yes, I go too" and leave it at that. I learned a long time ago to just keep my head down and be polite.*

By the time I was in my early twenties, I was a pretty good rider and started whipping-in for Hardaway. Back then, there was very little traffic on the roads, and when it got dark, we'd just ride on back to the barn, knowing the hounds would get back to the kennel to get fed in the morning. Once he started hunting in Ireland, he started packing up his hounds and expecting them to be more biddable. Elsie and Tom Morgan came over from Ireland to hunt with us and taught us a lot about their ways of pack huntin'. Back in those days, we had a lot of foxes everywhere. We just expected to catch one every time we went out. Nowadays, the coyote have run the fox just about clear off, and so now foxhounds around here hunt coyote instead of fox.

Back when I was whipping-in for Hardaway, a hound hardly ever got away from me. I'd just push 'em on to the rest of the pack if they weren't where they were supposed to be. When the pack would split, it was my job to figure out what hounds weren't running with the huntsman and get them back to the hunted pack. Heck, a lot of times I don't even think he'd know they'd split. Back when I started hunting, if you got after something, you could go. In 1965, landowners didn't mind so much if you hunted through their property, and there wasn't nearly so many roads and traffic.

I was fortunate to get the opportunity to hunt all over the world with Mr. Hardaway, and I picked up a lot of helpful knowledge along the way. I'm probably the first black person to ever foxhunt in Ireland. I'd whip for Elsie Morgan when I was over there, and she was so well regarded that no one ever bothered me. Times have changed quite a bit, but in the foxhunting world, not so much. I'm the only black MFH in America right now. Just the other day, a group of us from Green Creek were having breakfast together before the meet, and someone came up and asked me, "Do they let you hunt too?" I could say, "Well, since I'm huntsman and Master, if I don't go, they don't go," but I don't go that route. I just say, "Yes, I go too" and leave it at that. I learned a long time ago to just keep my head down and be polite. Back at Midland, when I used to get the Hardaway horses ready before the meet, I'd be in my overalls as the barn help. Then I'd be in my hunt staff riding clothes out whipping-in, and I swear I don't think a lot of folks who saw me in the barn beforehand even realized I was the same person out hunting. Most folks just see what they expect to see.

I think my family was proud of all the opportunities that foxhunting gave me. Before I started traveling with Hardaway, no one in my family had ever traveled much. When we weren't in England and Ireland, we spent a lot of time traveling around the country, especially with the Virginia hunts. Every October, we'd go stay up there a solid month and hunt around everywhere. Melvin Poe and Buster Chadwell were two of my greatest inspirations. I learned a lot watching those two men hunt hounds. We went up to Essex to get Chadwell to help us deer-proof our hounds, and that pack he had back in the sixties was one of the best I ever did see. I had all kinds of crazy adventures working for Hardaway. One time, he sent me to Texas to pick up a load of fox and bring 'em back to Georgia. Now, of course, it was just as illegal then as it is now, and no one would do it now, but everybody had to do it back then because the mange and rabies had pretty much wiped out our fox population and the coyote hadn't shown up yet. Dealers selling young fox sprang up out West to meet the demand. Those dealers dealt in a little bit of everything—rattlesnakes, bear, boar, you name it—and they'd sell it to ya. Well, I was driving through Mississippi with another black fella named Leroy, and we had about thirty fox in cages in the back of the van. We got pulled over by the police, and when they asked us what we were carrying in the van, Leroy spoke right up and said, "Corgi puppies." The cop even shown his flashlight back at the cages, but I guess he believed us because they just let us drive on.

I worked for Mr. Hardaway for over twenty years, but after a while, I think he felt dissatisfied with me. I think there comes a time when a young man has to move out on his own. Once you taught them everything you know, it's time for them to go, but I was so tore up when he first fired me. I didn't know if I wanted to hunt anymore, even though I got several job offers right away. I went in the logging business with my brother for a few years until Dick and Peg Secor asked me to help start a fox pack in 1989, which we named Green Creek Hounds. I agreed to come up for four weeks, and I'm still here. The territory in this part of North Carolina felt like home. John Burgess was also a Joint Master along with the Secors, and I just loved working with them. Peg had some Piedmont American hounds, and I had some Midland-bred Julys, and that was the formation of the Green Creek pack. I'm not much interested in a drag hunt. Foxhunting to me is all about jumping live quarry, but I will lay a drag of fox urine and oil to train the puppies before the season begins. Meanwhile, I'll pick up any dead fox or coyote I find on the road and keep it in the freezer until I'm drag hunting the puppies. Then I'll thaw out the carcass and place it where they can find it at the end of the run. It'll really make 'em keen.

Now, with radios, my whips are always calling me and telling me they have two couple over here or three couple over there. Well, I don't need to hear that—I just need them to get those hounds packed up with me. It's not the huntsman's job to pick up what he's doing and go running after hounds spread all over. That's the whipper-in's job. The Green Creek Hounds are probably a tougher pack than I really need, but they are the type of hounds I really like. They've been bred for their keenness more than their biddability. When they get rolling, you can't really stay with them. A horse can't get through the woods as fast as a hound. We only hunt two days a week and these hounds need to hunt, so I usually take the whole pack of thirty couple out every time we go out. Trouble is, my whips have a hard time pulling them up if they are running on something. A lot of people whipping-in today have never hunted without a radio, so they don't know how to use their ears like we used to do when we had to rely on our own instincts.

When I got to Green Creek twenty-five years ago, you could do some serious hunting without bothering anybody or putting your hounds in danger of getting run over. No matter when or where I'm hunting, I always prefer

*Oil painting of Tot on Shenandoah hunting the Green Creek Hounds.* Joan MacIntyre

a bitch to a dog hound. The females are always the keenest hunters. But a good dog hound pulls his weight and when the pack really gets to rolling, you want a mixture of voices to ring out through the hills. Seems like the females are best at chasing, but the dogs do most of the catchin'. The females absolutely hate a male fox and when they get on one, they'll run him to death. Now I suspect that a dog fox probably leaves a stronger scent. I know a pregnant fox is hard to chase. Hounds won't half run it and if they do get on her trail, she'll usually just jump in a hole. I suspect they don't have much scent at all. Once the fox vixens are bred, I've heard they will run to a dog fox and he'll lead the hounds away from her. If that happens, I guarantee ya he'll take you on a chase out of the country! It seems like when fox are chased, it's like they enjoy it. They know they have the advantage over the hounds, who have to run with their noses on the ground.

Now because coyote are pack animals, they'll pull a trick or two on ya. I've seen a coyote lie down flat in the grass when they get tired and a fresh one jump up and lead the hounds away from the original hunted coyote.

I guess because of all the years traveling with Hardaway, I still love to travel to other hunts every chance I get. I'm going to Belle Meade in a few days to hunt with Ep Wilson. He used to hunt with Hardaway's Midland hounds a lot when I was a young man. I go to a lot of hunts and help them get problems straightened out. I did that last week down in Low Country. I like going in somewhere and helping someone out. It's a challenge and gratifying when you can help out. I guess if you do something all your life, you learn a thing or two along the way. I always appreciated it when folks helped me out, and I like to do the same thing for other folks.

I've been lucky to live a life where every morning when I get out of bed, I'm looking forward to my day. Training and hunting hounds is my life's satisfaction. The more time you spend with your hounds, the better pack they are. One thing I love most about my wife, Colleen, is she loves my hounds, and they love her too. I trust an animal's instincts about people. They know who to trust. 🐾

# Mason and Mary Lu Lampton

BOTH ARE THE CHILDREN OF LEGENDARY HUNTSMEN. MASON'S
FATHER WAS DINWIDDIE LAMPTON AND HIS GRANDFATHER,
FARLEY MASON HOUGHLAND, WAS AUTHOR OF THE CLASSIC
*GONE AWAY*. MARY LOU'S FATHER, BEN HARDAWAY, PASSED
THE MIDLAND HUNT HORN TO MASON WHEN HE HUNG UP HIS
SPURS, AND MARY LU IS FIELD MASTER.

**Mason:** I've been carrying the horn for Midland for about eighteen years, but I've been foxhunting since I was a young boy. My father, Dinwiddie, had hounds, and my grandfather, Farley Mason Houghland, did too. He started the Hillsborough Hounds and wrote the book *Gone Away*. I grew up in Louisville, Kentucky, and my grandfather lived in Nashville, Tennessee. We used to foxhunt one place or the other every weekend when I was a boy. Both my parents taught me to love the sport. My mother was very elegant riding sidesaddle, and my father taught me to love the hounds. By the time I went in the army, I had my own farm pack and was hunting all the time. I was stationed at Fort Benning, Georgia, and friends contacted Ben Hardaway and asked him to invite me out with his pack. He was in his prime and hunting hard. That was when I first met his daughter Mary Lu, and that was the beginning of the rest of my life.

**Mary Lu:** Growing up hunting with Papa was sometimes tough, but the physical challenges made us kids feel proud of ourselves. I hunted with him often until I went off to boarding school. Of course, hunting when I was at Foxcroft was entirely different because the young girls always had to ride at the back of the field. At home, I got to ride up front where the action is. After I graduated from the University of Georgia, I went home to Columbia County, Georgia, and started hunting regularly with my dad again. I

*Like wolves, they are very pack oriented, and when a hunted coyote gets exhausted, they'll tag team, and the tired quarry will squat low and still, and a fresh coyote will come in and lead the hounds away from the first coyote. How they communicate their timing, I have no idea, but we've seen it happen time and time again. Like scent, it's a mystery—one we've enjoyed our entire lives.*

never whipped for him because I didn't want to be in his line of fire when he was hunting his hounds. He'd get so wound up, I was afraid he'd hurt my feelings! That's when Mason started hunting with us.

**Mason:** We got married about a year after we met and moved to Kentucky, where we stayed for about six years. It was a hoot, hunting with my brother and best friends in my twenties. When Mary Lu and I were down visiting her father on a hunting trip, we discussed my moving back to Georgia to run the family business. Ben was in his late fifties, still young enough to be at the height of his powers. His horses were fit, his hounds were swift and their cry fantastic, the country was open, and the jumps were stiff but inviting. It was brilliant hunting then and still is today. I think there's something about accounting for the game that really keeps your pack sharp. When Ben was seventy-five, he had a head injury and passed the hunting horn to me, but twenty years later, he's still actively involved in all aspects of hunting hounds. At ninety-five, he still knows the hounds and their bloodlines. He follows the hunt in his jeep and enjoys the chase.

**Mary Lu:** The big change for Midland Fox Hounds is that the fox are gone and we hunt coyote. The speed and distances are greater than with fox. You need the staff to carry radios to communicate. Because coyote are pack animals, you usually get into a cluster, and they'll split, and you need to get the hounds back together on one line. It takes quick communication at that point to keep the pack from splitting. We first started using radios when the coyote drove the fox away, and many people thought that was unsportsmanlike, but it really makes a lot of sense for the safety of both the hounds and the people in the field.

**Mason:** I think the fox uses his guile to hide his scent. He runs on top of a log or goes through a thick spot where hounds can't maneuver. He can't outrun a foxhound, so he uses his brain. A coyote might start a run that way, but if he feels the hounds are really latched on to his scent, he uses the power of those four long legs. Your whips are really important with such fast quarry. Robert Miller has been whipping-in for twenty-five years, and when the hounds are in full cry, he says over the radio, "They are locked on!" Because of the busy roads, you've got to really know what you're doing if you need to stop them. The staff carries pistols to fire in the air to get their attention. You need to make some noise. That type of run isn't for everyone. It really weeds out someone who wants to come out for just an hour or two because in no time, you're many miles from the trailers.

**Mary Lu:** Now we've started having a first, second, and third flight, so people can get out at their own comfort level. We've got a field that truly hilltops, watching the action from hill to hill, then a field that doesn't want to jump but wants to keep up and then the first flight, who really does whatever it takes to keep up with the hounds. That's really helped us because people feel like they have options.

**Mason:** It's really cut down on injuries because you aren't as likely to be overfaced when you're out there. My son has five children, and they can all get out hunting because of the different flights.

We also hunt wild pig and bobcat as well as coyote. A bobcat will use his wiles like a fox. He'll climb up the tree, then jump back down on his scent line a ways out from the trunk and run heel on his own line for a while, then take a sharp right or left and disappear. Many times, my hounds would be marking the hell out of a tree, and there's no bobcat to be seen up in its branches. Once I figured out his escape plan, I followed his line back away from the tree, and the hounds could pick up his sharp turn, and away we'd go again. Unlike a fox or coyote, a bobcat will wind around the same area, usually a very thick overgrown spot, foiling his scent with hound scent. You have to be very patient and let your pack work it out. It might take them some time to get back on a clear line again.

Now with a coyote, I try to cast forward aggressively because I know he's moving forward at great speed. If you see an old hound you believe in is feathering with his or her nose on the ground, you push the rest of the pack in that direction. You'll have the pack almost running silent on the road, and as soon as they hit the woods where the scent holds strong, they'll explode in full cry. It's brilliant to watch, absolutely thrilling. Unlike a bobcat, the coyote isn't going to twist and turn in the thicket. He's going to flat-out run as far and fast as his long legs will let him.

**Mary Lu:** I lead the second flight, and I'm always thinking about the fastest and safest way to get everyone as close as possible to where the hounds are working. I have to keep up without getting in the way.

*Mason's mentor and grandfather, Farley Mason Houghland, hunting his Hillsborough Hounds in Brentwood, Tennessee.*

**Mason:** You're sensitive.

**Mary Lu:** And you're not!

**Mason:** She has a lot more patience than I do, that's for sure. You don't want people out there riding to the hounds because they want to wear the clothes. You have to know how to ride to go at full speed cross country. And this pack flies. I rode steeplechase races for about fifteen years, so the horsemanship is an important part of the sport for me, even if I am out there to hunt the hounds. Now Mary Lu can ride with the best of them, but she's being nice and pacing herself so everyone out hunting can enjoy themselves safely.

**Mary Lu:** Like most huntsman, Mason's empathy level goes way down when his hounds are working. My job is to help people enjoy the sport like Mason and I do. Our country is so big that people don't understand it's no place for an unfit horse or rider. After a few hours, they'll say they've got to pull up and hack back to the trailers, and they don't realize that we may be so many miles from when we started that it's impossible to find your way back unless you spent years riding through the territory.

**Mason:** I think a lot of hunts have folks that like to show up for an hour or two, but that's not us. By opening day, we'll usually be out for at least four hours. We try to draw the line at five for our hounds' and horses' sakes as well as our own.

These coyote are an amazing quarry. They hunt by scent, so they know how to run according to the conditions. If you put a lot of pressure on him, he's going to go fast as his legs can carry him. During breeding season, the visiting dogs can lead you on a chase for hours. Once he runs out of gas, he has to rely on his wits more than his speed. When he starts circling tight, you know he's winding down.

**Mary Lu:** Like wolves, they are very pack oriented, and when a hunted coyote gets exhausted, they'll tag team, and the tired quarry will squat low and still, and a fresh coyote will come in and lead the hounds away from the first coyote. You'll be running a brown one for a while, and the next thing you know, you're running a red. How they communicate their timing, I have no idea, but we've seen it happen time and time again. Like scent, it's a mystery—one we've enjoyed our entire lives. 🐾

# G. Marvin Beeman

AT TEN YEARS OLD, HE BEGAN WHIPPING-IN FOR HIS
FATHER, WHO WAS HUNTSMAN FOR ARAPAHOE HUNT.
MARVIN BECAME JOINT MASTER THERE WITH ELSIE PHIPPS
IN 1991 AND JUST COMPLETED HIS SEVENTIETH YEAR
OF BEING ON THE HUNT STAFF.

My father was working as a whipper-in for the Arapahoe Hunt in Colorado when I was born in 1933. It was the private farm pack of Elsie Phipps Jr. that was started in 1929 and became a recognized pack in 1934. That year, my father became the huntsman of Arapahoe, and the family moved to the Phipps ranch, and I was there until I went away to college. I can clearly remember the first time I went foxhunting. I was four years old on a little bay mare. By the time I was six, I was exercising the hounds regularly. Every morning when it was time to get to the one-room schoolhouse a mile and a half away, my parents and I would mount up and ride the hounds out to the school yard, and then they'd lead my horse back home with them, and I'd go to class. Once I got a few years older and my sister started school, the two of us would ride together and put the horses in the school barn while school was in session. In 1941 after the war started, there were very few men left to hunt. I was a gate boy for the hunt, and my job was to open and close all the gates. I was also exercising hounds regularly with my father. In February of 1942, my father's horse fell, and he broke his shoulder, so he was not eligible to be drafted into the military. But my two uncles, my mother and father's younger brothers, who whipped-in for my father, were both drafted. I started whipping-in, wearing my uncle's scarlet coat and boots, in 1943. Luckily, he was small because I was only ten years old—the youngest recognized whipper-in in MFHA. When I ended the season a month ago, it was the end of my seventieth season of being on the Arapahoe Hunt staff. I became Joint Master with Elsie Phipps the third in 1991.

One day when I was a kid, it was unusually cold, and my dad and I were watching four coyotes playing king of the mountain on a tall straw pile about two miles away from the kennels. My dad started wondering what the scent would be like when it was two degrees, so we turned out fifty couple of hounds, and off they ran on that scent—a straight line for five miles. I mean we were flat-out galloping as fast as our horses could carry us. It was a very foolish thing to do because if one of us had had a fall, there was no one else with us to

*I whipped-in for my dad for forty two-years, and now I've been huntsman for twenty-eight years. My love of the sport is much more meaningful to me than a recreation. It's really a way of life.*

go after the hounds, and if we left a person on the ground, they would have frozen in no time. My mother was furious at our carelessness. She met us in the car as we were making the long ride back to the kennels with our tired horses and hounds. I'll never forget her jumping out of the car and putting her hands on her hips and saying, "George, if you want that boy to be a dummy, that's your business, but I'm taking Bunny (my sister) to school." By the time we got back to the barn, my dad says, "Well, you're already this late, you might as well help me exercise the horses." So that's what I did before I finally made it to school. My father told the teacher not to blame me for being late, that it wasn't my fault. But I was the only kid in my grade and was on top of my studies, so the teacher didn't mind at all. My father decided to take advantage of this state of affairs and told her I wouldn't be able to get to class on Wednesday mornings because I'd be working with him back at the farm. Of course, I was just fine with that arrangement! By the time I got to high school, I wanted to play football, which my dad thought was a waste of time. But he agreed to let me play if I promised to grab a horse by the hind leg every time he needed grabbing! I said, "You're on!" and my dad never missed a game. After the games on Friday night, the kids went out and did whatever it is teenagers do on Friday night—but not me because I had to get up on Saturday morning at 4:00 a.m. to go cubbing. And I never objected a bit.

I can remember the day when I decided I wanted to be a veterinarian. My father and I had been out visiting a couple of ranchers, and on the way home, we started talking about whether I wanted to farm when I grew up. Now we had a vet that I just adored, and when I thought about it that day, I realized I wanted to be a vet too. I could show you the spot today where I made that decision, and I never did change my mind. My dad liked that idea a lot, and that just reinforced my determination.

At Colorado State, I met Eunie, who would become my wife. If my father got injured, I'd go back home to hunt the hounds. Eunie used to tease me about my pay as huntsman, which was a tank of gas to get there and back. That routine continued through vet school as well. When I graduated with a DVM, I was able to get a job seven miles from where I grew up. By then, Eunie and I were married, and she started hunting regularly with Arapahoe. When I wasn't building my practice, I was hunting in the fall and winter and playing polo in the summer. When the kids came along, the children would help us get the polo ponies fit so I could play on the weekends when I had a day off. Of course, all the kids hunted too. Mr. Phipps was, of course, the Master, as it was his private pack. There was a subscription for membership, but he footed all the bills. Both my father and I were so lucky to be involved with such a fine operation. We both felt that even if we had millions of dollars, we'd be doing exactly what we were doing. My father asked Eunie to start whipping-in with me, and she continued to do so when I became huntsman. My father had a unique ability to make everyone out hunting with him feel very necessary. He got both of our children so keen to hunt that they didn't even ski like the rest of the kids in that part of the country. They became whipper-ins for Arapahoe as well. I whipped-in for my dad for forty-two years, and now I've been huntsman for twenty-nine years.

My love of the sport is much more meaningful to me than a recreation. It's really a way of life. When my father passed his horn down to me in 1986, Eunie and I talked a lot about what it would mean for my veterinary practice, which I loved as much as I did hunting the hounds. We knew it wouldn't be easy to do both, but I'm so glad that we decided to do what it takes to keep both concerns going because it's been so worth the effort. I have so loved being huntsman. As a whipper-in, you are really the hound's adversary because you're always having to tell them what not to do. As huntsman, you're really the alpha hound, the leader who gets to hunt alongside and encourage instead of just calling them off.

Working with the hounds and riding the horses has really augmented my ability as a veterinarian. Riding a horse gives you another way of assessing soundness that you can't get from just watching them jog. You have a sensitivity to the owners as well, being a horse owner yourself. My experience in the kennels and the stables gives me a unique vantage point to practice veterinary medicine. We used to call my dad the resident pathologist because he knew so much about equine disease and injuries from cutting up the dead horses to feed the hounds. He'd always go by the clinic and tell the docs what he found. He never called us by our first names at the clinic. He always called us "doctor."

Hunting English hounds all my life, I can't tell you how many times I've been told they don't give tongue or they're not fast enough, and I start to feel defensive. But then, I realize that the best breed of hound is the one that works best for the geography of your hunting territory. Since our territory is so open, our hounds' voice and speed is just right for our needs. Our hounds have been hunting this cold, dry country for generations, and they know what they're doing. A coyote will run as hard as you press him, and we want a long chase instead of a rapid kill. We account for our quarry about 10 percent of the time. We don't get a close start because there's no thick covert where we can surprise him. It's not unusual for the pack to be a half a mile away from the quarry when we pick up the scent line. One reason I like the biddability of the English hounds is because when someone sees a coyote, you have to pick those hounds up and go as fast and quietly as you can to where he was viewed. A coyote can put a lot of distance between you in that wide-open country. It's dry and windy, so you don't have a lot of time before the scent disperses. We don't need radios because we can communicate with our hunt caps since we can see each other from great distances. In that wide-open country, a good hound soon learns that when he sees another hound feathering his stern and opening up, he needs to catch up quick to get to running.

Our hunt territory is twenty-one thousand acres without roads or development. It's a utopian place to hunt. The Colorado plains have very few trees, so we can always see our quarry. The geography is nothing like

*Marvin hunting the Arapahoe hounds.*
Zina Balash

the east of the Mississippi. We have five-thousand-acre pastures, so your hounds better do a good job because everybody can see every damn thing they do! The field sees the coyotes 95 percent of the time we're out hunting. When people first hunt our territory, it's hard to understand why we cast the hounds where we do because it all looks the same. There isn't any covert like there is back East or in Europe. Our hounds stay with me until I give them the sign. They quickly spread out, and it doesn't take long to jump a coyote. I'm sure there are some folks around here who look at us in our white britches and scarlet coats and think, "What kind of deal is this?" This is cowboy country, and I grew up being teased all the time about my little itty bitty saddle and funny pants, but once you put them in that English saddle, you earn their respect. You ride a lot more saddle when you ride western, and you ride a lot more horse when you ride English. When Mr. Phipps started this pack eighty-five years ago, he and my dad always wanted the ranchers to feel welcome. We have always welcomed them to join us, and after about three goes in their western gear, they change their minds and want to give English tack a try. I made a promise to myself, as both a huntsman and a vet, that if I am asked to do something that will help hounds or horses, I will do it. Being the president of the MFHA was never one of my goals, like being a vet or huntsman, but I feel like I owe it to the sport to give back whatever I can so our traditions can endure for the next generations. In my mind, even as much as I love horses, the hub of the foxhunting wheel is the hounds. The horses are the spokes and the rims the social part, but the thing that ties it all together is the integrity of the hounds. 🐾

# Albert Poe

HE IS EIGHTY-FOUR YEARS OLD. HIS TWENTY-YEAR TENURE

AS HUNTSMAN FOR THE FORMIDABLE MRS. RANDOLPH,

MFH OF PIEDMONT HUNT, WAS THE STUFF OF LEGEND.

EVEN FORTY YEARS AFTER THEY PARTED WAYS, ALBERT'S

INFLUENCE ON THE BREEDING OF AMERICAN FOXHOUNDS IS

FELT IN KENNELS ALL OVER AMERICA.

Because I was growing up during World War II, all the young men were in the military. By the time a boy was twelve or thirteen, he was doing a man's job. I was driving a pair of horses and filling silo for my daddy and uncles and neighbors by the time I was thirteen. My whole family rode every day. We had no tractor, and it was our transportation to work and school. I had to feed the cattle before I caught the school bus, so I was always running late. I'd jump on my daddy's horse and gallop to the bus stop, then pat him on the butt and send him home after I got there.

I was huntsman for Piedmont for twenty years and Mrs. Randolph's farm manager as well. When I came on board at twenty-three, I was the youngest professional huntsman in the country at the time. To this day, she was the best Master that I've ever seen. If I saw one of our neighbors in need of hay for their animals, I'd ask Mrs. Randolph to give them some, and it gave Piedmont a good reputation in the community. We'd send some of her workers over if a landowner needed extra help getting in corn. Mrs. Randolph never questioned me if I said someone needed our help. She knew it was important to have good landowner relations.

When I first got to Piedmont in the mid-fifties, there were only thirty-two hounds in the kennels. In fact, most of their hounds had gray faces when I first showed up, and none of the bitches were bred, so one of the first things I had to do was start a breeding program. Mrs. Randolph brought both her husband and her daddy down to check out the kennel after I'd been huntsman for about a year. When they saw how many new puppies I had coming along, Dr. Randolph asked me if I bred every bitch that comes in heat, and I said, "No, doctor, I only breed the ones I like." And he said, "Looks like to me you like 'em all!" I believe it takes ninety hounds to have what you need to have a fully operational pack. It took me about ten years to get the hounds with the qualities I wanted. To this day, I still think you should whelp out twenty puppies every season and start

*The groundhog is the fox's best friend because he digs the den, and then their babies are good to eat. Groundhogs not only build the fox's shelter, they supply the meat. They will even come back in and clean up after the baby foxes when they move out. The best fox dens are old groundhog dens.*

twenty new entry every year so that your pack always has sixty that are four, five, or six years old. That's a hound's peak, and you want them to all run together at that age. That's how you get a tight pack that doesn't get spread out.

I kept a pack of beagles that I would turn out early in the morning on hunting days so I could see what the scent was like. The rabbit never wanted to cross Beaver Dam Creek, so he'd always turn on to the road at that point, and if my beagles could follow the scent on the road, I knew it was a good scenting day, but if they couldn't find his line on the road, I knew the scent was bad, and that would help me decide what hounds I was going to hunt that morning.

Now my sons couldn't hunt their ponies with the Piedmont Hunt because we only went out on the weekdays, so I took those beagles and invited all the kids in the neighborhood to join me and my boys on their ponies to hunt rabbits on the weekend. Mrs. Randolph, of course, heard what I was up to and said she wanted to go with us on Saturdays, and I said she could come hunt rabbits with the beagles if she was Field Master, and she agreed. My beagles were good hunters, and I'd cut off a rabbit foot after a kill and give it to the kids that kept up with the pack. Mrs. Randolph was uncomfortable with all the bloodshed and said we'd have to quit passing out those paws to the children, so I said we'd start hunting foxes with the old hounds and puppies that I hunted on Wednesday. Though they hardly ever caught a fox, they were pretty good at chasing them. She said she didn't think the children were old enough to keep up with foxhounds, and I told her she didn't have to worry about the kids. Well, the first day we gave it a try, every kid kept up really well, jumping every obstacle in front of them. We had a ball—so much so that now all their parents wanted to join us on Saturdays. Now we're hunting Tuesday, Wednesday, Friday, and Saturday instead of the two days a week we were going out when I first arrived.

In the sixties, there was a terrible rabies epidemic, and our fox population was very fragile. It started with the grays and crossed over to the red fox population. They were practically trapped out of existence because the state paid a bounty to get rid of the rabies and all the farmers were afraid of gettin' bit. We had to really nurture every fox to help reestablish the population. To help get the new foxes established, we started raising the young fox in cornfields, where there's shade and grain. To make it even more attractive to the fox, we'd put three chickens in a cage with three birds free to roam around in the corn. As soon as the fox ate the outside ones, I'd let the caged ones out and put three more in the cage. Early cubbing season was perfect to train the hound puppies because the foxes just want to run around the cornfield until they found a groundhog hole. Now the groundhog is the fox's best friend because he digs the den, and then their babies are good to eat. Groundhogs not only build the fox's shelter, they supply the meat. They will even come back in and clean up after the baby foxes when they move out. The best fox dens are old groundhog dens.

Now, of course, every huntsman has their own ideas about a breeding program, but one thing my brother Melvin and I have always done, which is a little unusual, is keep our dogs and bitches together in the kennel. It makes them a lot more biddable when you take them out to hunt because the dogs don't have to waste a lot of time sniffing over each other when you let them out to hunt together. Since a bitch comes into heat five days before she can breed, you just keep an eye on things and make sure you separate her before she's receptive, so you can control if she's bred and who she's bred to. Also, if you keep them together, they earn respect for each other. I never have to hunt them separated by sex because they've settled all their squabbles back at the kennel. A mixed-sex pack also works a lot better because their voices are like a choir. They blend together in a way that makes the woods come alive.

During my career as huntsman, I worked for eight different Masters, and not a one of them told me who to breed or how many hounds I could have in the kennel. At Fairfax, we only went out two days a week, so I didn't need ninety hounds like I did at Piedmont and Middleburg, where we hunted four and three days a week. On the days when the field wasn't out, I'd take all ninety hounds out by myself and was able to get back to the kennels with all but maybe three or four, who'd stay at the den a little longer. I'd let them run a fox until they ran him to ground, then I'd pick 'em up and gallop back to the kennels so they wouldn't get distracted. The few that stayed behind to dig and mark would come on after soon enough.

Most knowledgeable huntsmen know if you breed a crossbred to a crossbred, you never know what you're going to get, but purebred to crossbred is much more predictable. Dallas Leith at Elkridge–Hartford really had a great crossbred breeding program going because he really understood that it takes many years to get your crossbred hounds to breed true. Now at first, Mrs. Randolph didn't like crossbred hounds at all. She wanted only American foxhounds, but over the years, she came to understand that you can breed crossbred with American to great results.

It was the racehorses that made us have a parting of the ways. Before I came on board, she was very successful and involved in horse racing. She was steeplechase horsewoman of the year and had a horse that was three times steeplechase champion of the year. But after that horse retired, she didn't really have any other big-stakes winners coming along. Just as she was slowing down, I was speeding up. The 1974 steeplechase book showed that I won six thousand dollars with one horse, while Mrs. Randolph won ninety dollars with two horses. Well, she didn't like her name being under mine in purse earnings. She told me she wanted me to get out of racing so I wouldn't be distracted from hunting the hounds and managing her farms. I tried to explain to her

*Albert with the Piedmont hounds in early 1970s.*

that I'd already leased a barn away from her farms and that my wife and my two sons would take care of things while I took care of my business with Piedmont Hunt and her farm, Oakley. But she had made up her mind—so I did too. I told her I had no intention of selling my racehorses, and she said if I walked out that door, I wasn't coming back—so I walked out and never came back. I don't think she really believed I'd call her bluff and leave the Piedmont hounds. She sent everybody to ask me to come back, but I said she had to ask me herself and say I could keep my horses. She couldn't bring herself to do it, so that was the end of a great partnership. I got fully invested in running racehorses. Mr. Randy Rauss said I could run all the horses I wanted if I would hunt the Fairfax hounds. After four years there without a raise, I signed a contract with Middleburg and was huntsman there for many years. Their hounds were horrible—completely out of control. It took me about ten years of culling and breeding to get a good pack.

While I was huntsman at Middleburg, Mrs. Randolph arrived by herself at my barn and asked to see a couple of field hunters that I had for sale. I walked out the first horse, and she said she'd take it. Same thing with the second one. I asked her if she wanted to get them vetted or know how much they cost, and she said, "No, I trust you. I made a mistake when I gave you an ultimatum." Then I knew why she drove alone (which she never did)—she didn't want anyone else to hear her apologize. In my lifetime of working with hounds and horses, I've made friends and enemies along the way. But at the end of the day, I always felt like I had more friends than enemies. 🐾

# Bart Poole

HE GREW UP HUNTING GAME WITH HOUNDS FOR FOOD
AND NOW CARRIES THE HORN FOR ESSEX HUNT.

**M**y grandfather always hunted hounds. His beagle pack was our gun dogs. We'd shoot the rabbits for food. My father and grandfather both hunted with a farm pack of foxhounds, and I started whipping-in for them when I was a boy. Because my grandfather was a feed salesman, he knew all the landowners, and that's how we got the foxhunting connection. At Mayberry Hunt Club, I just kinda got thrown in the deep end. I had an unbroken pony and had never had a riding lesson, but that didn't bother me. I just followed my old man around and did what he did. By the time I was about thirteen, that little mare was one of the best field hunters out there. When I got to high school, I fell away from foxhunting because I wrestled and played football. I got a wrestling scholarship to West Virginia University, but when I injured my shoulder, I had to drop out because I could no longer afford the tuition. I went home at twenty and started working with my dad as a welder.

I became a professional huntsman by pure dumb luck. I never even knew you could make a living foxhunting until Mr. George Mahoney, Master of Green Spring Valley, called me and offered me a job as a professional whip. I grew up with his barn manager, and I guess that's how Mr. Mahoney got my name. When he called me about the job, I told him I hadn't been on a horse in seven or eight years, but he was more interested in my experience with hounds and hired me anyway. Once they saw me on a horse, though, they immediately set me up with riding lessons. Green Spring Valley barn manager, Sarah Stein, took me under her wing and gave me lessons three days a week for my first year whipping-in there. She was tough, but as a high school and college athlete, I was used to that type of

*You can sit around and listen to stories about the good old days, and you can either feel sorry for yourself that those days are gone, or you can let the nostalgia inspire you to make things as good, if not better, than they were before.*

rough coaching. I had never ridden such nice horses, and I loved working with her. I didn't know what a distance was, but these horses knew their job and took me everywhere I needed to go.

Now that I've been a huntsman myself for three seasons, I can more appreciate how a good ole boy who grew up hunting in the woods with hounds his whole life can really be valuable as a whipper-in. Still, I don't know that I would ever hire a whip that was as clueless about horses as I was. I'll always be grateful Green Spring gave me the chance to learn. Ignorance is bliss, I suppose. I'm lucky I didn't kill myself out jumping those line fences my first year working there. One of Green Spring Valley huntsman Sam Clifton's favorite stories is how he was so mad with me, he just wanted to get as far away from me as possible. So he jumped over the biggest four-board fence he could find, and the next thing he knows, here comes this big-eared dope right behind him saying, "What ya want me to do now, boss?" That's when he realized I was much more concerned about keeping up than I was about saving my neck.

My instinct with horses is the same as with hounds—I never harshly force them to do anything. I work with them like it's team-work or even their idea. That attitude helps you get along with people too. I had some great people at Green Spring who taught me so much. Andrew Barclay, who used to be their huntsman, taught me tons about whipping-in, and their present huntsman, Sam Clifton, was a good role model. Before I started carrying the horn myself, I didn't understand why Sam would get so mad at me. Now I certainly do! The way I learn is by failing, by making mistakes. That's what inspires me to get things right, but I'm sure that's sometimes hard on the people I'm working with when I'm figuring things out.

After two seasons at Green Spring, I got offered a job as a whip at Essex, and once I got the position as barn manager, as well as whip, I made more money and had a nicer place to live. After four years here, I was offered the job as huntsman. John Gilbert was leaving, and I knew I better take the job while I had the chance because that kind of opportunity doesn't come around often. I was really getting to know the territory, and the more I learned about Essex's past, the more I wanted to be involved in being a part of building a program for the future. I just finished my third year here as huntsman, and I already feel like the pack has a keen-ness they didn't have when I got here. They are hunting maniacs. In early cubbing, we hunt in soybeans, and last Saturday they ran so fast and hard, they had heat exhaustion. After they marked the hole like hell, I got them down to water. As I was loading them in the hound truck in the courtyard surrounded by a four-foot stone wall, they took one look at the trailer and one look at the wall—and the next thing I knew, they were over the wall running another fox in the soybeans. They are nuts—the best kind of nuts—ready to go hunting. In late summer, we take 'em out five days a week at 6:00 in the morning. Essex has twenty-five and a half couple, and I try to hunt at least twenty-two and a half couple every time we go out so the pack is fit and ready to go come fall. There's nothing like second- and third-season hounds to raise your game. They are ON it.

To me, the hounds are my family. They come first for me, and they know it. I love them, and they love me back. Now my relationships with other people might suffer as a result, but that's just the way it is. If it's hot and my young hounds are wearing down, I'll take 'em in, even if the field wants to stay out longer. The pack is my number one concern. If they're pretty, that's great—you can take 'em to a hound show and get a ribbon. But my number one priority is I want 'em to want to hunt. Nose and drive are my biggest concerns when it comes to breeding. The brain and the heart are what gives a hound the drive I'm looking for. The Essex bitches are second to none, and I bred them to some great dogs this spring. Our brood bitches are something else. These three this season had between eight and eleven puppies and raised them all. They are tough. They are twice as roughed up as the dogs after a day of hunting because they are relentless. I laugh and say to the dogs, "It's pretty obvious who is doing all the real work around here!" Now the boys are better at finding, but when it comes to actually driving a fox to the earth, that's where the bitches come through.

Unlike a lot of huntsmen, I own all my horses. And a couple of my whips' horses too. I want to make sure I'm on a good horse, and bringing them along myself is the best way to do that. I have the same kind of rela-tionship with my horses that I do with my hounds—we trust each other. I can think stuff, and they do it. It's so much more fun to hunt hounds when you're on a horse that you trust and trusts you. I want to be an exceptional huntsman, and to do that, I think you have to be a good horseman as well as good with hounds.

I really love this place. There's more game here than anyone could ever want. Even though there's plenty of coyotes, there are still tons of fox

too. I prefer chasing a fox, but since these hounds have always been allowed to chase coyote too, I think it would be terribly demoralizing to them to be too hard on them about it. When they do get on a coyote line, they usually catch it because they just run straight instead of all the weaving and dodging through livestock foil, the running on top of logs and down creek beds, that a fox will do. He's got a whole bag of tricks to keep the hounds guessing. That's why he's my favorite quarry. He'll really put a pack of hounds to the test. That being said, getting on a flat-out running coyote can be a thrilling chase. And, needless to say, the farmers are glad when we do because they can put a hurt on their animals. Coyotes around here have been breeding with wolves, and they are big and hunt in packs—not something you want around your livestock.

I always have a five-year plan for everything. Right now, I'm breeding for nose and drive more than hound show confirmation, and I'm also working on getting our hunt country expanded. North and west of our territory is still pretty undeveloped. After learning about Essex in its glory days, that's my goal—to bring it back to what it was in the days of Buster Chadwell. I love hearing the stories of the old-timers, and I'd like to make some new ones. These older foxhunters are my go-to guys about trails and landowners. I learn a lot listening to how both Buster and his son Roddy Chadwell hunted the hounds in this territory. I consider these older men my best friends. It's a great well of information that I can go to anytime. Apparently, I remind them of Roddy, and they have shown me nothing but support since I got here. You can sit around and listen to stories about the good old days, and you can either feel sorry for yourself that those days are gone, or you can let the nostalgia inspire you to make things as good, if not better, than they were before. Don't get me wrong, we're in New Jersey—of course, development has screwed up a lot of our old hunt country, but there's always other places to open up and even preserve. There's still plenty of land north and west of here that is full of game and would be great hunt territory. Essex is also lucky to have patrons like the Murphys and the Johnsons that are buying land and protecting it from development. I'm not a big one for stopping hounds once they are locked on and rolling with their quarry. Sometimes we end up running through land that we weren't planning on going to, but instead of the landowners getting angry, for the most part, they are glad to see us. They'll say, "Oh my gosh. You guys used to come through here all the time. It's so great to see you again." Of course, sometimes landowners aren't so welcoming. But I find most things can be sorted out with a bottle of whiskey or champagne. I find that if you approach things with a positive attitude, it helps to get things done. I'm not overly intelligent or overly ambitious—I'm just happy that I get to live a life doing what I love to do.

# Sandy Dixon

SHE FOUNDED THE BRAZOS VALLEY HOUNDS IN PARADISE,
TEXAS, IN 1994, AND HER COWBOY HUSBAND IS HER FIRST
WHIP AND KENNELMAN.

I'm originally from the East Coast and started foxhunting as a child with my father at the Wicomico Hunt, on the Eastern Shore of Maryland. I grew up riding with the Zimmermans and showing in the hunters. Although I started foxhunting to ride my horse, it didn't take me too long to realize that the hound work was really cool, an important part of the action. When I went to college, I hunted with Deep Run whenever someone had a horse to spare. When I started my career as a cardiovascular sonographer at a hospital in Texas, I stopped riding for a while. It was there that I met my husband Bobby. He was a bull rider and saddle bronc rider—a real cowboy who rode racehorses as a kid and managed a large thoroughbred breeding operation before we met. He's a farrier as well, which does have its advantages! One day after we were married, he was shoeing at a barn and heard people talking about a hunt in the area. He knew how much I loved and missed foxhunting, so he helped me find a horse off the track, and that got me riding again. In 1982, I started hunting with Hickory Creek and began whipping-in for them. Although my husband had only ridden western saddle and found English hunt clothes ridiculous, he started hunting with me and was whipping-in soon after because he's such an accomplished horseman. When their huntsman retired in the early nineties, they asked me to hunt the hounds. I'm not a professional huntsman. I do it because I love it. I still work five days a week at the hospital, then on Friday I clean my horse up and off we go every Saturday morning.

After I was huntsman for a while at Hickory Creek, there were a bunch of us who thought we could do things better, and we decided to

*Most people who ride down here are into cutting horses or barrel racing and think riding to the hounds is something foreign and fancy. Sometimes when local people find out that I foxhunt, they look at me like I'm crazy, which I probably am—so that's OK!*

form our own pack and a hunt that would welcome children. The next generation is the future of foxhunting, so kids should be introduced to the sport and encouraged along the way. Albert Poe started coming down in the eighties to judge the hound show, and when I decided to start my own pack, he was instrumental in helping me do it. He's been like my brother, my best friend, for over thirty years. He introduced me to his brother Melvin and Jimmy Young, who were so supportive of my foxhound goals. Tommy Jackson of Mission Valley drafted me about twelve hounds to get started, and then I went to Virginia to speak to the head of the MFHA, John Glass, about starting a recognized hunt. He said, "You know you're going to upset a lot of people," and I said, "I've already done that because when I left Hickory Creek, a lot of their members came with me." He smiled and said, "At one time, there was only one hunt in the United States, and now look where we are. I suspect there's room for one more." I flew back to Texas with four more hounds from Albert Poe and Jim Atkins. Jimmy Young from Orange County drafted me a couple that I convinced a friend who worked at Southwest Airline to ship to me. In 1994, my motley pack of donated hounds became recognized as the Brazos Valley pack. The kennels are right behind my house. We've come a long way in our breeding program since those early days. One hound I'm especially proud of is Elliot, who has won the Warren Harrover Trophy at the Virginia Hound Show five years in a row.

I love the American foxhound because it's very dry and open here in Texas and you need a hound that can hunt without moisture. I love the English hounds, but they just do not hunt as well on our territory. It's also important to me that my hounds be biddable. I want to be able to take a baby into my kennel and not worry about them getting hurt. I wanted a tall, lanky, thoroughbred-looking hound that could cover big distances with great endurance. We need a lot of speed because our main quarry is coyote and there is wide-open space to run in Brazos Valley. The coyote is wily as a fox, often outsmarting the hounds. Like a fox, they don't dig dens, but if they are really being pressed by a pack of hounds, they can usually find a hole or a culvert to duck into. Young coyotes tend to stay with their mothers longer than fox do. They pack together to hunt and can do a lot of damage on domestic pets and farm animals as well as wildlife. When the cows are calving, the afterbirth draws in large packs of coyote, and they can do a lot of damage. The cattle ranchers want us to come in and hunt to keep their numbers down for the protection of their stock. Even though our quarry is coyote instead of fox, we're still carrying on the same traditions of foxhunting that were brought over here with the first European settlers.

Jake Carle and Larry Pitts have also been invaluable in their knowledge of hound breeding through the years. Larry gave me a bitch in 2004 that has been a great foundation for the type of hound I need to hunt coyote in this territory. A couple of years ago, I was traveling to the Bryn Mawr show, and one of my bitches came in heat on the drive out. I asked Larry if his dog Jefferson could pay her a visit while we were at the hound show, and he graciously agreed, only asking that any puppies that resulted have "J" names, which is a more than reasonable request. Every one of those puppies are great. Even though we're out here in Texas and our territory is nothing like the beautiful mowed paths through the trees back East, our hounds and horses are definitely like the Virginia and Maryland hunts. I'm so grateful to have Albert Poe's horse Mr. Williamson, who was passed on from Melvin when he stopped hunting at Bath County. I'd been fortunate to ride him when I'd come East to hunt, and last year at the Virginia Hound Show, I told Albert that I wanted that horse. Not that I expected him to give him to me, but sure enough, when we were packing up to leave, Albert said, "Come by the house on the way out," and when I did, he loaded Mr. Williamson on my trailer. I cried all the way through the state of Virginia on the way back to Texas.

We have a small pack, thirty-six hounds, but we don't usually hunt on the weekdays, so that's enough. If we're going to one of the larger fixtures, I'll take thirty to thirty-five hounds out on a Saturday. My number one priority is to give the members good sport, and my number two priority is safety. I know some huntsmen are a lot more concerned with their hounds than they are the field, but we're a small group down here, and the people riding behind me are the ones paying the bills. If I don't keep them in mind and leave them behind, they aren't going to be happy with me. In this part of the country, foxhunting isn't as established and popular. We have to take care of each other. Most people who ride down here are into cutting horses or barrel racing and think riding to the hounds is something foreign and fancy. Sometimes when local people find out that I foxhunt, they look at me like I'm crazy, which I probably am—so that's okay! When my husband Bobby first started hunting with Hickory Creek, he would

*Sandy hunting Brazos Valley hounds.*
CRAIG BUCZOWSKI

not get out of the truck to change a flat tire if he was in his riding pants for fear someone he knew would drive by and see him! The first thing he'd do when we'd get home from hunting was run into the house and put his jeans back on. Over the years, he's come to love the Brazos hounds as much as I do. He's the kennel man and first whip. We are definitely a team. Even though we only hunt one day a week, the hounds still need to be exercised, and they are so biddable—either one of us can walk them out by ourselves. They are our children. I don't think I could be huntsman and MFH if I didn't have Joint Masters, who deal with the field and fund-raising, leaving the hounds and landowner relations to me. You have to have an impeccable relationship with your landowners because one mistake, and you're out. That territory is lost to the hunt. I don't really blame them. In today's culture of liability and negligence, farmers feel like they have a lot more at risk than an open gate or hoofprints in a field.

A lot of our ranchers down here lease their land to deer hunters, so when you come talk to them about hunting through their property, they just assume that they should get paid for that privilege. Some charge by the head and some by a seasonal lease. That's just the culture down here, and not one member has objected to paying ten dollars each when we hunt certain ranches. The ranchers use that money to build new jumps or bring in gravel where it's needed to park our trailers, so it's worth every penny. There's no entrenched foxhunting tradition in this part of the country, like there is in the mid-Atlantic states. Down here, if I walk up to a rancher and say, "I want bring about thirty horses and riders and about forty dogs to your ranch and run all over your property. You don't mind, do you?" they'd probably think I was crazy to even ask such a thing. You have to have a rela-tionship with the farm manager or other property owners—a friend-of-a-friend situation at least, if you want to have a chance of getting permission to hunt on someone's land. We can hunt on the national grasslands, but it's public land, so I have to stay away from the deer hunters and the campers. I've had hunters shoot at me there, so it's not my favorite place to go, even though it is thirty thousand acres.

Despite getting shot at, enduring extreme weather, and the daily physical work, foxhunting is a passion, the joy of my life. When I walk into my kennel and thirty-six hounds look up at me with that look in their eye, waiting to see what I need them to do—I melt every time. I never take it for granted. Each time I whelp out a new litter of puppies, it's as exciting as when Bobby and I were first getting started. I can't imagine a life with-out horses and hounds. Sometimes I worry about what I'm going to do when I get really old, and then I laugh when I realize I'm already really old, and life is good! 🐾

# Tommy Lee Jones

HE'S BEEN HUNTSMAN OF CASANOVA HUNT SINCE 1970.
TOMMY LEE IS A RENOWNED HORSEMAN AS WELL AS A
HUNTSMAN. HE'S ALSO A PROLIFIC EQUINE SPORTSWRITER.

I started foxhunting when I was about nine years old. Even as a little kid, I preferred a horse. I thought ponies were rats with better tails. One summer, I counted that I fell off twenty-six times on those nasty little things, so I told my dad I wanted a horse. He found me this horse named Freckles when I was ten, and I won the high jump at six foot the first time I ever rode that horse in a horse show. She'd jump me off over a fence, then kind of move over and catch me on my way down. Talk about a confidence builder. Back then, most horses hunted—show horses and racehorses too. Now there's so much money involved, everyone's a specialist. Because my dad was a horse trainer, everything I rode was for sale, so when I foxhunted, I got to go up front, where I could watch the hounds. Mrs. Randolph at Piedmont really encouraged my enthusiasm, and it wasn't long before I was out there for the hounds as well as the horses. Hunting with Albert Poe in his prime and his brother Melvin at Old Dominion was a wonderful education for a boy. Growing up, my dad and grandfather always hunted rabbits with beagles, which I always enjoyed, but foxhunting was even better as far as I was concerned because you could add horses to the mix.

My family moved to Warrenton when I was in my late teens, and I started hunting with Casanova. Because we were selling horses, we hunted all over the place to get the most exposure. When Casanova hired Captain Benson from Ireland, they asked me to whip-in, and he taught me everything he knew about the handling and breeding of hounds as well as how to hunt them. When Ian Benson wanted to go back to Ireland a few years later, they asked me if I wanted to be huntsman. Our Master Mr. Gulick

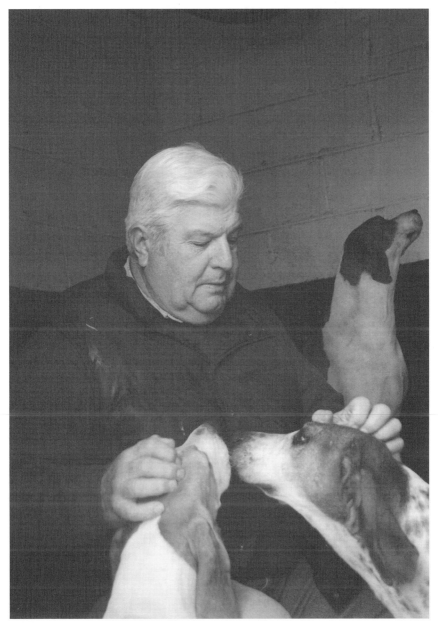

*That old dog of Hardaway's didn't look like it was worth a plug nickel to me, but he produced some great hounds. Breeding crossbreds isn't as unpredictable as Jack Russell terriers, but sometimes you get something that wasn't quite what you were looking for!*

promised to be out there with me my first season to guide me along, but he was on a toot that year and was only out once all season. I was just thrown in the deep end, which can be an excellent way to learn. I still sought Mr. Gulick out for advice from time to time, and he was always generous. That was 1970, and I'm still here. It's been fun too. When I took the job, I had no idea it would be a lifetime commitment. After a few years as huntsman, I stopped competing in horse shows and started managing them. In the summer, I worked in Kentucky at Fasig Tipton Sales and Spendthrift Farm, then Saratoga in August. Come September, it was back to the cubbing season and foxhunting.

When I first got to Casanova, we had a real deer problem. When they first showed up, their scent was a real distraction for the hounds. When I delivered a horse to Rolling Rock in Pennsylvania and went hunting the next day, I'd never seen so many deer. There were herds everywhere, and when their hounds were running, they'd run straight through the herd and stay on the fox line. I quickly realized I needed to breed to these hounds. A lot of them came from the Essex pack in New Jersey, so I spent a lot of time on the road getting our bitches bred. There was one Potomac bitch in the Casanova kennel when I first started as huntsman. If she was coming back to you when the rest of the pack was running, you knew you were in trouble and had to stop them. She would not run a deer, so she was bred to Rolling Rock Toby and later Essex's Triumph, and that was the beginning of our new foundation. Of course, now there are so many deer around here, they don't even run from the hounds. They move out of the way, but they don't take off. When Jimmy Atkins was at Old Dominion, he bred to Essex hounds a lot too, so that shortened my trip during breeding season. Now I'm breeding mostly to Potomac dogs because I trust Larry Pitts. He won't tell me anything about them until after I pick them out. I use my eye, and he fills me in on the details. You want to complement the bitch you're breeding at the time. I like my crossbreds to look like American foxhounds. I like strong loins and long legs.

When I saw Ben Hardaway's pack of white Cotswold hounds hunt, I loved how they were so free and fluid. I asked him to send me a dog that I could breed to one of ours, and he sent me one that looked like one of those old English hounds. He hunted great, but he'd end up running two fields behind the pack because he just couldn't keep up, so when the time came to breed him to one of our bitches, I decided I wasn't going

*Tommy Lee with Casanova Hunt.*
DOUGLAS LEES

to, but our Master Colonel Richards said, "You've got to breed him to something, otherwise it's just insulting!" Well, the last thing I wanted to do was insult Ben Hardaway, so I bred his dog to one of our older whiter bitches that I wasn't even going to breed anymore, and all of her puppies came out white, with a little more leg on them than their dad. I gave the three bitches to Jimmy Atkins at Old Dominion and kept the dogs because at that time, that was what we needed. Well those three bitches turned out to be the three best hounds they had at the kennel. That old dog of Hardaway's didn't look like it was worth a plug nickel to me, but he produced some great hounds. Breeding crossbreds isn't as unpredictable as Jack Russell terriers, but sometimes you get something that wasn't quite what you were looking for! I enjoy participating in the Virginia Hound Show in Leesburg, but otherwise, I'm not too interested in hound shows. I like to see young kids participating in showing the hounds because it makes them pay more attention when they are out foxhunting. Captain Benson told me that every now and then, you should dock a piece of tail off of one of your puppies so everyone in the field can recognize it and they'll be looking for him and more likely to watch him hunt and then more appreciate hound work. I did have a puppy born with a bent tail, and sure enough, hunt club members became so attached to that hound because they knew his name.

When winter closes in and the footing is too bad to hunt on horse-back, I still have to exercise the hounds every day, so I let them follow my pickup truck. I remember watching Melvin Poe do that when I was a boy, and I felt like a real huntsman once I could get my pack of hounds to follow my truck down the road like that. There's a wonderful description in Mackay-Smith's book on foxhunting about Mr. Bywaters having his hounds follow his buggy for miles down the road until they got to the meet and then he'd cast them into the covert. If you have a biddable pack of hounds, you don't even have to have a horse. Sometimes Melvin hunts his hounds from his tractor. I love to read about the history of hunting. Everybody who could write did write back in the day. Now everybody's a specialist, just like our horses. I've got several articles I'm working on right now. If you love the sport as much as I do, you want to read and write about the experiences. 🐾

# Bobby and Susie Ashcom

BOTH SUSIE AND BOBBY FOXHUNTED AS CHILDREN AND
HAVE WHIPPED-IN AND BEEN FIELD MASTER AT VARIOUS
HUNTS AROUND THE COUNTRY—EVEN FORMING THEIR
OWN FARM PACK. AS A FORTY-TWO-YEAR-OLD ENGLISH
PROFESSOR, BOBBY DECIDED TO BECOME A
PROFESSIONAL HUNTSMAN FOR TRYON HOUNDS.

**Susie:** After my father died when I was seven, all hell was breaking loose at home, so my sister Lois and I found refuge at Ellie Wood Keith's barn. We were barn rats, there seven days a week. We'd hack two hours or more to get to and from the Farmington Hunt meets. My mother whipped-in, and just about everyone I knew as a kid hunted. We hunted on Saturdays like some people go to church on Sundays—we never missed a day. Farmington Hunt Club was right in the middle of all our territory, and there were parties almost every weekend. The kids would gather in the basement, and our huntsman Grover Vandevender would play the piano for us. There was a crazy cast of characters in those days. Leaving a hunt breakfast at the club, Evernghim Blake jumped on his motorcycle and crashed it into a coop, thinking he was still on his horse.

**Bobby:** I got my first pony when I was eight, after wanting one for as long as I could want. My father told me I wasn't supposed to canter for the first six months. Well, as a result, I never learned how to post until I was about twelve because, of course, all that restriction did was make me want to canter every chance I could! Unlike Susie, I didn't have a barn experience and lessons. I just got on and rode. My brother David took lessons at Ellie Wood's, but I just flew around the farm. When I got a little older, I made my way over to Grover Vandevender's barn and rode out of there.

*Venery is either in your blood or it's not. Hunting with hounds really puts you in touch with the fact that the dog is the conduit between civilized man and nature at its most primal.*

But when I got my driver's license, I was no longer interested in horses. Hormones kicked in, and I wanted to stay out late and sleep late in the morning all through the rest of high school. But after my freshman year in college, I was helping my brother tack up at a horse show, and it was a singular experience. The smell of the horse and tack reawakened my love for horses, just like I had as a little kid. When I'd come home from college on holidays, I'd ride Ellie Wood's horse Toby out foxhunting, and my love of the sport returned stronger than ever.

**Susie:** Oh, we all rode Toby. He was a great horse, except he'd jig so bad hacking back to the barn that when I was about eleven years old, I burst into tears with exasperation, and Ellie Wood said, "Do you know what a balanced seat is?" And with that, she unhooked her girth and laid it over her lap, riding the rest of the way home with no girth. I was so impressed, I completely forgot my own misery.

**Bobby:** I remember the day when I lost my heart to foxhunting. I was home from college and riding a ugly horse of Ellie Wood's named Dixie that was a ton of fun to hunt. Grover had retired but was out hunting with us. Flying with him through the pines while the hounds were at full cry, I realized this is as good as it gets. I was hooked for life.

**Susie:** We started hunting together, and three months after we started dating, we got engaged. Bobby got a job teaching at boarding school, and we started foxhunting with Mission Valley. They treated us like celebrities because we had our Farmington colors. Back forty to fifty years ago, the Virginia hunts impressed the Midwest. They had Bobby whipping-in even though he didn't know the territory.

**Bobby:** After four years there, I went back to Brown for graduate school. Someone had left the college a marvelous foxhunting library. I spent hours poring over those books instead of doing what I was supposed to be doing. By the next year there, I had somehow pulled together forty foxhounds and registered with the MFHA.

**Susie:** We had a pony club down the street, so we had a ready-made field of enthusiasts.

**Bobby:** You start a pack of hounds, and the word gets out like lightning. People will show up. The territory was really tough going, rocky with few open fields, but that didn't deter our enthusiasm. We named our pack the Bradbury Foxhounds, and the country we hunted was around Rehoboth, Massachusetts. Susie and I were Joint Masters. Susie could hunt those hounds as well as I could. Mr. William Almy Jr., then currently president of the MFHA, had founded Quansett Hounds years ago and was a tough and bitter old man when I showed up. We became drinking buddies, and he taught me how to be a Master. Our shared enthusiasm for drinking got the best of me, and I was too sick to hunt the last year we were there, and Susie had to carry the horn. Every time I hunted my hounds, Almy would tick off a list of instructions—and he didn't talk, he yelled. He was tough, but I swallowed my pride and took all the wisdom he had to share.

**Susie:** You really were a gift to him because his daughters didn't give a damn about hunting, and here you were with all this enthusiasm and willingness.

**Bobby:** "Decorum" is a word today that is almost always denigrated, but there's nothing wrong with respect and good manners. Almy fought always to keep those traditions going in his beloved sport, though he was embittered by the prospect of a changing world.

**Susie:** Bobby knew he had to stop drinking, so he thought he'd try the geographic cure and move back to Charlottesville, Virginia. It wasn't exactly a smooth process, but eventually, he was able to stay sober starting in 1973.

**Bobby:** We started a horse breeding operation. I had a bloodstock agency and sold horse insurance. I was Field Master at Farmington, and Susie was whipping-in.

**Susie:** Jack Eicher was like no other huntsman I've whipped-in for. Like a football coach, he'd draw out on a chalkboard his strategy for the day. He'd draw little X's where he wanted us to be, and, of course, you'd get out there and the fox would have other plans! After each hunt, he'd meet again with his whips and talk over the day. You learned a lot with that system.

**Bobby:** Suddenly, when I was forty-two years old, I couldn't stand it any longer. It was now or never to be a professional huntsman. Neither my wife nor my mother thought this was a very good idea for someone who had a graduate degree from an Ivy League university, but I was determined to do this thing. We didn't have the money to go off somewhere and get me a Mastership, so the only way I could hunt hounds was to be a professional huntsman. When I told Jake Carle my plan, he laughed and said, "Once you start hunting the hounds, you'll be Master in two years." And that's exactly what happened. When I left to be huntsman for Tryon in North Carolina, there were no deer or groundhogs in that country, and when they started showing up, it was a nightmare. Thank God for Albert Poe and the telephone. He was a tremendous help to me during that difficult time.

**Susie:** Albert told me that once you weed out the incorrigible deer chasers, your core of trustworthy foxhounds can train the puppies by just not being interested in deer scent. It takes some strict discipline and heartbreaking culling of the pack to even get to that point, but it's what has to be done.

**Bobby:** The first person to figure this out was Buster Chadwell, so Albert Poe, then huntsman at Piedmont, drove up to New Jersey to get his counsel and taught me what Buster taught him. For years, deer were hunted down for food. The Great Depression in the 1930s almost wiped them out completely. Once the economy recovered after World War II, every foxhunting pack on the East Coast was having a deer problem. Susie was a saint when I gave up our business and took over eighty foxhounds at Tryon that weren't even pack broken. The first time I walked out with them, we made it about fifty feet away from the kennels, and they all ran away. By the end of that summer, I gave most of the pack to Belle Meade and kept the best young hounds. I called Melvin Poe for help, and he sent me six pack-broke hounds to train the puppies. That's how we got things started. No one at Tryon had ever seen pack-broke hounds. There was no way I was going to just drop the tailgate and let them run wherever they wanted to. Good God—William Almy would jump out of his grave and haunt me!

**Susie:** Our pack in New England were so tractable that when Bobby was teaching school, I would walk them out by myself with our two young children. My son was on his tricycle, and my daughter would have her hound whip and keep them all in line. That's the kind of pack broke we came to expect.

**Bobby:** We were so lucky to have all those wonderful Piedmont hounds at Bradbury. That first winter, the snow was so high on either side of the road that they couldn't do anything but pack up because they couldn't get over the snowbanks.

**Susie:** We brought Piedmont Rhonda to Tryon with us to breed, even though she was ancient and ugly. Man, could she hunt, so we were determined to have her puppies. Her pups were so important to us that we moved her into our house when she neared her due date.

**Bobby:** She whelped them in our bedroom closet, and the damn puppies were dying left and right even though Susie had 'em in our bed keeping them warm. We were able to save three of them—Rambler, Regent, and Robin. They were everything we hoped for and then some. By the second year at Tryon, we were on our way to having a biddable,

*Bobby jumping Fluter at 1975 Virginia Field Hunter Championship.*
Jim Carr

keen pack of hounds, with Melvin's hounds showing our wonderful puppies the ropes. I also called his brother Albert whenever I had a hound problem, and he likes to say, "I taught Bobby Ashcom how to hunt over the telephone!" Poe doctrine says you've got to ease your hounds into the covert and get the fox up and moving without scaring him so bad he flees and jumps in the first hole he can find. Poe doctrine says your hounds get faster every generation without you trying to make them faster, so there comes a point where you have to cull your lead hounds as well as the laggards. You either care about this stuff or you don't. There are people out hunting their whole lives, and they haven't a clue what happens when the hounds go into the covert and put their noses to the ground. Venery is either in your blood or it's not. Hunting with hounds really puts you in touch with the fact that the dog is the conduit between civilized man and nature at its most primal.

# Jordan Hicks

HE GREW UP HUNTING ALL KINDS OF DOGS ON ALL KINDS OF
QUARRY. HUNTSMAN FOR TRYON HOUNDS AT TWENTY-ONE,
EIGHT YEARS LATER, HE'S GOT A POSITION AS HUNTSMAN
FOR PIEDMONT IN UPPERVILLE, VIRGINIA.

I grew up on a farm in South Carolina, and my family has had hounds forever. I don't ever remember not following behind hounds—beagles, foxhounds, coonhounds, bulldogs, even some old mountain cur dogs. We ran fox, coon, bear, hog, deer, rabbit—you name it, we chased it. Wild hog is the tastiest critter in the South. Our night hounds for fox were usually Walkers, black and tans, even some Julys—whatever we could get. If it hunted, we hunted with it! I've always felt lucky to have grown up in this part of South Carolina because there are some real deal dog men in this neck of the woods. In those mountains, every truck has a dog box.

I grew up riding western, with a little hay string bridle. My horn was a cow horn, a PVC pipe, even a shotgun barrel. We made do and had fun. My Aunt Lydia whipped-in for the Greenville County Hounds, and she got me started on an English saddle. When I was seven years old, my daddy and I were following the Greenville hunt by car on the road, and I can still take you to the exact spot where I first saw and heard a mounted foxhunt. We saw the fox cross the road and heard the whole pack in full cry as they gained on him and crossed close behind. I'll never forget seeing the huntsman, Gerald Pack, thundering down the road blowing Gone Away full tilt, with his coat flapping in the breeze. At that moment, I knew what I wanted to be when I grew up. It's not even like there was a choice. I knew what path I had to take. After that, I shadowed Gerald everywhere, spending every free moment I had in the kennels, doing whatever needed to be done and learning along the way. By the time I was seventeen, Gerald would sometimes let me hunt the

*When it comes to genetics, it can get awfully tight right quick if you're not careful. The old night hunters used to say, "If it works, it's line breeding. If it doesn't work, it's inbreeding." Sometimes it's a fine science, and sometimes it's just luck. Like in anything else, don't over think it. After a while your intuition improves from experience.*

Greenville hounds myself. I got my first English hunt horn, and he taught me how to use it well. He helped me get together a pretty good pack of hounds that I'd hunt myself on foot after school. Back then, there were still a lot of fox about, but nowadays, the coyote have taken over, and it wouldn't work as well now to hunt foxhounds on foot. You'd just have to wave good-bye as your pack ran over the mountains. The foxes used to just stay in the bowls; and your foot pack could run the valley, but the coyote runs so fast and far, you need a horse to keep up with your hounds.

Between my Aunt Lydia and Gerald, as well as Tot Goodwin, who was nearby with Green Creek Hounds, I was really fortunate as a boy to have a lot of support. Tot's pack is old-school Deep South, with a lot of big old crossbred and July hounds. He thinks nothing about hunting out thirty, forty, couple at a time. He pushes them hard and is always with them. What a show—a wall of sound. I idolized him as a kid. I'd still like to know half of what he knows. Those three were tirelessly generous with their knowledge and really encouraged my enthusiasm. At eighteen, I moved out of my parent's house and to Moore County to whip-in for a season, then

I got a job as huntsman up in New York at Windy Hollow for two years. When I got the position at Tryon eight years ago, I was grateful to be back in the landscape I knew and loved. Even though I was barely twenty-one when I became Tryon huntsman, I knew everyone in the area and was able to help open up a ton of new countryside. The old Greenville Hunt territory was available, as that hunt had disbanded, so now it's part of Tryon's territory. I now hunt through that same road where I first saw Gerald Pack blowing the horn when I was seven years old.

Bobby Ashcom, with the help of Albert Poe, did a great job with the breeding program back in the eighties and nineties, so I had a pretty good pack of hounds when I first became huntsman here. When I first started hunting the Tryon pack, I felt like I had to slow 'em down to speed 'em up. I believe the hounds have to find the fox themselves. If you help 'em too much, you're doing more harm than good. Especially with American foxhounds—if it's their idea, they are a hundred and 10 percent on it. Once they settle on a line, you put your horn in your coat and let them have at it. I have no problem letting them cold trail for a while, getting as far ahead of me as they need to settle on the trail. It took a while for some of the members of the field to appreciate what I was doing, but after they started seeing the results, everyone came around. Now most of the field enjoys the anticipation as the hounds spread out and find. I love the slow buildup of one, then two, then three voices before the whole pack opens up and we're off and running. That's true foxhunting—not just running and jumping from covert to covert. A good pack always puts on a show no matter what. They are always so much fun to watch. As far as I'm concerned, American hounds have everything you need to hunt this country. People are always talking about breeding for voice, drive, speed, and biddability. Well, that pretty much describes the American foxhound! I know a lot of folks say they are too sensitive—shy and skittish. Well, they just don't know how to speak their language. I like it that they listen to me. It doesn't take much to get their attention, where a big ole crossbred hound will look up at you and wag his tail and keep on doing what you told him not to. I feel like they might flip you the bird if they could! I grew up with American hounds. They are bred to go out in the woods and find that quarry and stick with it. And that's what we want, isn't it? They don't get strung out because every single one of them is single-minded.

One of the good things about hunting coyote is that it has opened up so much more hunting territory for us because the farmers want them gone. Foxes were never the same menace to livestock as the coyote, who hunt in packs and can do some real damage. Our field would just as soon chase 'em without catching them, but if I know a landowner is really counting on us to get rid of some of the predators, I certainly won't discourage the hounds from getting the job done. I've never had any trouble getting along with the farmers. What gets me are people who move here to have a horse farm on Fox Hunting Ridge and they board up every coop. Tryon has been hunting hounds here since 1926, and our kennel is located between the humane society and the gun range. We're the quietest neighbors around. I have to watch out for the spay and neuter mobile when I'm walking out hounds on the road. Every time it snows, I go over to the SPCA and help clean their kennels, so they never cause us any trouble. I'm a southerner, so I know how to get along—kill 'em with kindness!

Even though being a huntsman is a dangerous occupation, the two things that mess us up more than riding accidents are whiskey and women. Huntsmen are rarely fired for hunting hounds poorly. It's their after-hours behavior that usually gets them in trouble.

At the end of this season, I'm moving to Virginia to be huntsman at Piedmont. I'm really excited to have the opportunity to hunt hounds three instead of two days a week. And Piedmont territory still has plenty of red foxes, which is becoming harder to find everywhere. By the time hunting season rolls around again, I should know the pack pretty well, just by walking out and staff cubbing. It's not going to be easy to make the transition to new Masters and countryside, but that's a challenge I'm looking forward to. When they interviewed me for the job, I told 'em I'm just like an American foxhound—turn me loose, and I'll make you look good! I can use a chainsaw and a bush hog as well as I can hunt hounds and ride a horse, and I'm really looking forward to getting up there and getting started on a new chapter in my life. I know it's not going to be easy to leave my Tryon hounds, but at least I have the satisfaction that I'm leaving behind a better pack than I started with. I know the new huntsman won't have any trouble with them.

Even though I don't know the landowners in the Piedmont territory yet, I will, as that's an important part of my job as huntsman. I mend fences by literally mending fences! You have to be able to talk to all

*Jordan hunting Tryon hounds.*
DON WEST

kinds of people—loggers and deer hunters, rich landowners from out of town, and backwoods local country people. You have to come into any situation with your hat in your hand and an open heart. At the same time, you have to be driven—you have to have a goal whenever you're dealing with any situation. When I breed a hound, I'm thinking about what I'm going to breed those puppies to five years down the road. I like to look ahead and have a plan. Like most huntsman, we want to look good and have fun while doin' it, and the best way to achieve that goal is to have a great pack of American foxhounds. When it comes to genetics, it can get awfully tight right quick if you're not careful. The old night hunters used to say, "If it works, it's line breeding. If it doesn't work, it's inbreeding." Sometimes it's a fine science, and sometimes it's just luck. Like in anything else, don't over think it. After a while your intuition improves from experience.

Even though tracking collars can be helpful, they can also do more harm than good by teaching a hound that they don't have to come to you because you're going to come get them sooner or later. I still follow the old trick of leaving my coat behind at the meet, so nine times out of ten, you'll find the lost puppy lying on it when you come back to the meet later in the day. Two things I cull for the most are running deer and wandering off. When I get a new person whipping-in for me, I don't want them to carry a radio for at least a year, so they learn to use their eyes and ears instead of becoming dependent on the radio. A huntsman is only as good as his whips, so it's important that a whipper-in really knows how to listen and make decisions on their own. If you just chase what people are saying on the radios instead of listening to hounds, that'll get you in trouble. You've got to trust your own judgment instead of what someone else is saying. You'll lose your instincts if you rely too heavily on technology. Heck, if you have really good hunting, the hounds will sometimes get away from you. It's the bad packs that'll never leave ya!

# Larry Pitts
# (with Peggy and Laura)

RETIRING THIS YEAR AS HUNTSMAN FOR POTOMAC HOUNDS
AFTER THIRTY-FIVE YEARS THERE. LARRY'S HOUNDS ARE
RECOGNIZED AS ONE OF THE BEST-BRED PACKS OF AMERICAN
FOXHOUNDS. HIS WIFE AND DAUGHTER HAVE BEEN AN
INTEGRAL PART OF THE HUNTING AND SHOWING OPERATION.

**Larry:** When I was in college, I worked on a friend's farm on the week-ends. I was told to go to the huntsman's house and clean up. I said, "Sure, but what in the hell is a huntsman?" At that time, I'd never even ridden a horse! I grew up hunting rabbits, so hounds were not a mystery to me. I always liked messin' with dogs. I saw the hounds in the kennels, and I'm thinking, "You get paid to do this? Sounds like a pretty good deal." I met Ian Milne at the Sedgefield Hunt that day and started hanging around the kennel every chance I got. He started asking me to help out, and by that fall, I left college to whip-in for him full-time. Two years later, I saw an ad in the *Chronicle* for a professional whipper-in at Old Dominion, and Ian encouraged me to take the job. He said Mr. Brainard was the type of Master who could really teach me a lot. When Brainard resigned, he got me a job as a huntsman with Eglinton & Caledon in Canada. After four years up there, I was ready to get back to a warmer climate. Seems like we did more snow shoveling than hunting. I applied for the job at Potomac Hunt in 1980, and there I stayed until I retired this year, thirty-five years later.

**Peggy:** I was working as a groom at the farm near Larry's hunt in Canada, and that's how we met. We got married right before we moved to

*Any good huntsman knows you want to give away some of your good hounds to another pack so they'll breed them to their good hounds and you can come back there in a few generations and improve your own line.*

Maryland, when Larry got the job at Potomac. I really hadn't foxhunted that much at that point, but I knew about horses. Soon after he started hunting the hounds, his professional whip left to be huntsman elsewhere, so after a while and initial hesitation, I found myself whipping-in to Larry. Now if you don't know much about hunting and you really want to learn something about it, you just have to talk to the huntsman after the hunt, and you'll learn everything everyone did wrong that day! After about ten years, I got a job as a vet tech, and I was really able to be helpful to Larry by taking care of the hounds.

**Larry:** Peggy's very involved in the kennel. She's the one that analyzes a wound or cares for a sick hound. She worked for our hunt vet, so our kennel got really good care between the two of them.

**Peggy:** I've always enjoyed walking out the hounds with Larry every day, and that helped me a lot both as a whipper-in and a vet tech because I had my eye on them daily. When you know each and every hound and they know you, it makes a tremendous difference when it's time to get them to do what you want.

**Larry:** When I arrived at Potomac, the pack was already the Virginia-style American hounds—the Bywaters. With my first whipper-in job in North Carolina and later up in Canada, both Ian Milne and Major Kindersley preferred English hounds, and I think that helped me getting started because they were so darn biddable. Handling American hounds is quite different. They want to hunt on their own and don't need to wait around for you to tell them what to do. Seems like with English hounds, they always had one eye looking at you, whereas with American hounds, they're too busy hunting to be watching what you're doing.

**Peggy:** That being said, a lot of those Potomac hounds will come looking for you if they haven't heard from you in a while.

**Larry:** When I arrived at Potomac thirty-five years ago, I thought I wanted to hunt English hounds, but after you hunt American hounds a while, you realize you've got a better beast. English hounds handle well, but they're just not as good at hunting. I don't think they have to worry a whole lot about good scent in England, but we have some dry spells here, and I want an American hound for those conditions. When I first started the breeding program at Potomac, Jim Atkins at Old Dominion drafted me some good steady hounds to help me settle the Maryland pack down a bit. He gave me Apollo and . . . what was that hound's name?

**Peggy:** Applause. They were brother and sister.

**Larry**: Apollo was a big, rangy dog, and I bred him to . . . what was her name?

**Peggy:** Tumble. She was by Rolling Rock Toby.

**Larry:** That's right. What a great litter she gave us, and that was the start of something mighty fine.

**Peggy:** Applejack was from that first litter, and he won the American Championship in 1984. Jim Atkins was at the hound show, and he said, "If I'd known that ugly old Apollo would have puppies as pretty as that, I never would have given him to you!"

**Larry:** Of course, Atkins was just joking because any good huntsman knows you want to give away some of your good hounds to another pack so they'll breed them to their good hounds and you can come back there in a few generations and improve your own line.

**Laura:** I came along the same year as Apollo and Applause. I guess that was a good year! My brother was born before me, and he never took to the kennels and stables like I did.

**Peggy:** When they were young, we really counted on the kids walking out the hounds on the weekends so we could clean the kennels.

**Laura:** Jim Atkins came through for me too and got me my first pony. I hunted him for years because he was a little big for me at first. He ran away with me more than once, but that didn't discourage me at all. I can recall my mom chasing me down trying to catch my pony as we tore away from the field.

**Peggy:** And all the while, she had this big smile on her face!

**Laura:** I always loved handling the puppies at home, but it wasn't until I was thirteen that my parents gave me two puppies to bring along and train for the hound shows. Tequila was hyper and superexcited all the time, and Foresight was shy and quiet. When you're a young teenager, you're embarrassed by just about anything, and when I had Tequila in the show ring, she kept licking me and wiggling. It was a mess but not so horrible that I didn't enjoy it and want to do it again. Through the years, I've come to realize that you're going to have some wild ones and you're going to have some shy ones in the ring and that's no reason not to go with the flow and enjoy it. I really enjoy the hound shows because I really enjoy the hounds.

**Peggy:** The hounds really like Laura. That's one reason she's so good handling them at the shows.

**Larry:** We took a lovely Potomac bitch to Essex and bred with Buster Chadwell's Joker. That's where the "J"s in our pack came from eight generations later. Our hound Jefferson was named the Centennial Fox Hound

at the Virginia Hound Show in 2006. He was like
a dressage horse—when he stopped, he squared
up. Back in 1990, we bred one of our dogs to one

*Larry and Peggy Pitts hunting
the Potomac hounds.* KAREN
KANDRA

of Melvin Poe's bitches, and he gave us a puppy out of that litter named
Breezy. That cross came out in another gear, and that was the beginning of
a much faster pack for Potomac. We picked up the pace considerably once
her puppies had puppies. After about ten years, I asked the Masters if we
should slow 'em down a bit, and they said, "No—leave 'em just like they
are." Of course, sometimes you've got to cull your lead hounds as well as
your stragglers so your pack doesn't get too strung out. We had a great
hound from that line named Brampton, and there was nothing wrong with
his nose or his voice, but he was so fast, the rest of the pack was always
at least fifty yards behind him, so we sent him out West, where they hunt
coyote in wide-open territory.

Now that I'm retiring this year, I'm going to get some rabbit dogs
and hunt on foot. Of course, I'm taking Jefferson with us. He's old as the
hills, and he's our pet—along with two of his puppies that are old as well.
I've had both knees and hips replaced, and it's time to take better care of
the new ones than I did the old ones. It's time to hang up my spurs, but I'm
not done following hounds.

**Peggy:** The hound shows were always like a vacation for us, to get away from the kennels and meet people. I'm sure we'll keep coming to them even though we won't be handling the hounds. It'll be fun to sit back and observe.

**Larry:** We're bringing our hunt horses to Virginia when we retire, and maybe we'll go out hunting from time to time. I've got a bass boat I never used enough while I was huntsman. We plan on enjoying ourselves and each other. 🐾

# Marion Thorne

WHEN SHE WAS A LITTLE GIRL, HER MOTHER MARRIED
AUSTIN WADSWORTH, GRANDSON OF MAJOR AUSTIN
WADSWORTH, WHO FOUNDED GENESEE VALLEY HUNT
IN 1876. SHE BECAME MFH AND HUNTSMAN WHEN
AUSTIN WAS READY TO RETIRE.

My grandparents hunted with Rose Tree, but I was born in Philadelphia, and there was no place to ride when I was really young. At six, I started taking riding lessons in Unionville, and that was it—I was hooked! Of course, I kept begging my mother for a pony of my own, but that wasn't very practical living where we did. In a wonderful stroke of good luck for me, my mother married Austin Wadsworth, the son of W. P. Wadsworth, Master of Genesee Valley and grandson of the hunt's founder. Talk about being in the right place at the right time! As a pony-obsessed little girl, it was like a dream come true. We moved to a farm in Geneseo, New York, and I got a pony and started foxhunting. Austin was whipping-in to his dad, and I got to ride with my stepfather. I can't imagine a better education in the sport. Austin didn't say much. I just learned in probably the same way he was taught, by observation. The Wadsworth family was one of the founding members of the MFHA and had been totally immersed in the sport for over a hundred years when I started hunting at seven. My mother had six kids, and Austin had three when they got married, and then they had a child together. With ten kids in the family, my mother had her hands full and left my hunting education in my stepfather's capable hands. Once Austin became Master, my mother became the hunt secretary and did start hunting again. I remember when she sent eight of us to a regional pony club rally. It was a four-day event. That's quite a packing job. I think her organizational skills were an inspiration to me when I grew

up. She showed me that you could do what needed to be done.

After a few years under Austin's wing, I was sent back to join my siblings and pony club friends back in the field. At twelve, I got a job riding one of the Genesee whip's horses, and I rode with him for a couple of seasons. After high school and college, I started my own horse business and was able to whip-in all the time. After I got married, we had three daughters, and I continued to whip-in through all of my pregnancies. I think I took a week off after I gave birth, then was right back at it. Having a mother like mine made me think I didn't have to stop one thing to do another. Running my own business gave me a lot of flexibility with my time that many mothers with young children don't have. My three girls all went through pony

*They both turn to me and tell me I'm hunting the hounds that day. By now, it's time to let the hounds out of the trailer, and the field is mounted up and ready to go. They gave me the horn and case because, of course, I didn't have one. It was sort of like learning to swim by being thrown in deep water. A lifetime of whipping-in and walking out paid off. At the end of the hunt, I came back to the kennels as happy as I'd ever been in my life.*

club like we did, and they hunted with Genesee every chance they could and still do when they come home to visit. Like my mother, I also got divorced and remarried and had another child. I evented and did amateur owner steeplechase racing as well as whipping-in. I had a full, gratifying life when I was younger and wasn't expecting to become the huntsman—and certainly not the Master—of Genesee Valley. Everyone knew my stepbrother Will Wadsworth was the next in line. He loved to hunt and had a lifetime of experience, but over time, his priorities changed, and he didn't want that kind of commitment to the sport. It dawned on me that I could probably step in.

My Aunt Martha Wadsworth used to carry the horn when Austin couldn't be there. She was also an excellent whipper-in. She had a wonderful ability to know what was needed and when to blend in when it was not. Even though she was a reluctant huntsman, she did a fantastic job. Though she preferred whipping-in, she certainly could hunt those hounds if she had to, and that was a great role model for me. Seeing a woman hunt the hounds made me realize that was a possibility for me. She was the real deal—one of the most influential people in my life. She taught me how to prepare the young entry for hunt season. She was a dedicated hound walker and carried on the traditions of training that her father W. P. had taught her. She never missed a day at the kennels, and I saw how that paid off—both for the hounds' performance and her enjoyment of the sport. Unlike my stepdad, Martha taught me by explaining things instead of just by example. Her behavior was an inspirational example, and she was the one I went to if I had a question. Because she was MFH before me, everyone involved in the hunt, including the landowners, were used to dealing with a lady Master, so being female was never an obstacle to the job. I couldn't ride with her while she was whipping-in because whips are always supposed to ride separately, but she was always my go-to person whenever I was trying to figure things out. As brother and sister, Martha and Austin had the greatest relationship. They never let their ego get in the way of hunting the hounds.

As Austin got older and started having problems with his knees, he was getting Martha to hunt the pack more and more often. One day as we're gathering at the meet, Austin tells Martha to hunt the hounds, and she says she wants him to do it. Well, this goes back and forth for a while until she says, "I'm not hunting hounds anymore. I like to whip-in." And he says, "Well, if you quit, I do too!" I'm just sitting there on my horse listening to all this when they both turn to me and tell me I'm hunting the hounds that day. By now, it's time to let the hounds out of the trailer, and the field is mounted up and ready to go. They gave me the horn and case because, of course, I didn't have one. I'd only carried one once before when we were exercising hounds in the winter years ago. I really didn't have time to get nervous because the hounds were pouring out and ready to go. It was sort of like learning to swim by being thrown in deep water. I did okay. A lifetime of whipping-in and walking out paid off. Of course, our pack gets a lot of credit because they were so keen and honest that they pretty much hunted themselves. At the end of the hunt, I came back to the kennels as happy as I'd ever been in my life.

*Marion hunting Genesee Valley hounds with whippers-in Annie Morss on her right and her mentor, Martha Wadsworth, on her left.*
BILL GAMBLE

Both Austin and Martha had gone down and hunted coyote in Georgia at Midland, so when coyote showed up in our upstate New York hunt country, we didn't hesitate to chase them. Our quarry is still about 80 percent red fox, so the coyote haven't driven them away like you often hear. Maybe that's because our country is so abundant with ample food sources for game that fox and coyote can coexist. I breed my hounds for a good fox nose and enough speed to pursue a coyote if one shows up. I've been involved with the breeding program even before I started carrying the horn. It's a key aspect of the whole deal. Our crossbred English/July line is heavily Midland, and our American blood goes way back through Brandywine lineage. I love their nose and cry. You'll find Potomac and Piedmont bloodlines in our pack as well. Most of my crossbreds are predominantly American.

The Genesee Valley kennels are modest, but I'd hunt our hounds next to anyone's. The club runs on a small budget, but we have lovely hunt country. As Master and huntsman, I work as a volunteer and still make a living with my horse business. Unlike a lot of Masters, I don't have a lot of money to put into the hunt, but I give them all my elbow grease! It's a subscription hunt, and we do a lot of fund-raising. My husband is our professional whipper-in and kennelman. He's on paid staff, while my positions are honorary. I wish we got along as well as Austin and Martha did out hunting, but they were brother and sister—not husband and wife! Sometimes it's hard for a husband to work for his wife, but a lot of times our teamwork is really good. One thing that I appreciate is how much I miss Travis when he's not out hunting with me. He's a really good whip, and I know it. He's got a great big scary man voice that comes in handy when discipline is in order. He's been professional hunt staff his entire working life and knows his stuff. My husband grew up whipping-in for Martha just like I did, so he's completely comfortable with a female Master and huntsman. 🐾

# Iona Pillion

SHE GREW UP HUNTING IN WALES AND AS A YOUNG WOMAN
IMMIGRATED TO THE UNITED STATES, WHERE SHE HAS BEEN
A MEMBER OF BLUE RIDGE HUNT IN VIRGINIA FOR FIFTY
YEARS. WITH DOUGLAS WISE-STUART, SHE ESTABLISHED THE
JUNIOR NORTH AMERICAN FIELD HUNTER CHAMPIONSHIP.

I grew up in North Wales, hunting with the Flint and Denbigh. I was also very involved with pony club. Anything having to do with horses, I was there! I used to have to ride miles on my little Welsh pony just to get to the meets. I didn't care how deep the mud or cold the rain, I was determined to show up. I used to ride my bike to my pony's field, with my tack on the handlebars. My mother was a farmer's daughter who never rode, and my father had no interest in horses, so I didn't get much support at home. I think they were rather mystified by my enthusiasm. I thought nothing of riding eight miles on my eleven-three pony to get to the hunt fixture. I was such a pathetically tiny child, at ten or eleven I looked much younger than my age. I spent every chance I could get in my bowler hat and rubber raincoat on my pony, Robin. Mother would say when I used to hack back from hunting, the only white she could see was the whites of my eyes. The rest of me was covered in mud!

When I got older and it was time for me to go off to boarding school, my parents tried to dissuade me from horses by sending me to horticultural school. Well, that didn't take. Instead, I started learning to ride sidesaddle with a woman named Betty Skelton in Hampshire. I was a working student who paid for lessons by doing barn chores. And let me tell you, she got her money's worth out of us. There wasn't an hour in the day when we weren't on the clock. I learned to break ponies during my time there and made friends with a girl who had gone to America in 1965. Mrs.

*If we encourage their love of the sport, perhaps when they grow up they'll be interested in preserving the countryside. I'll never forget being out hunting with this kid, and we were running through an area that had a huge McMansion. She said, "Why would anyone build their house right in the middle of such good covert? It really messes up the hunting!"*

Mackay-Smith was starting to export Welsh ponies to the US, and I found my way over to that farm to work as well. Back then, they happily issued out work visas. When I told the consulate in England that I had a job in America earning a hundred dollars a month, I'll never forget this fat American with stains on his tie telling me I could never live over there with so little money. My great uncle was a purser for the Cunard Line, so I took a ship to America. I got the royal treatment on the way across the ocean, even sitting at the captain's table. I felt quite grown up at twenty-two with my newly pierced ears and enormous steamer trunk. It was so large, Mrs. Mackay-Smith couldn't get it in her car when she came to pick me up. It didn't take me long to feel like Farnley Farm in White Post, Virginia, was home. I started hunting the Welsh ponies with Blue Ridge Hunt as soon as I arrived. Back then, the fancy show ponies went hunting. I used to love to hunt their champion stallion Downland Drummer Boy. He was only thirteen two, but he didn't know it! People said they couldn't see me coming until I took off over those big fences. When I left Farnley about ten years later, they gave me one of Drummer Boy's children, who had grown too big to show in the pony division, and he was so much fun to hunt. That's one of the best things about foxhunting—so many horses, whether off the track or out of the show rings, can find second careers there.

I met my husband Bobby in the hunt field soon after I came to work at Farnley, and we got married in 1970. We had a daughter who grew up hunting with us every weekend, but she never was as keen on it as we were. When she'd say, "Mommie, why can't I do ballet?," I'd say, "Because we foxhunt. That's what we do." As soon as she went off to college, she stopped riding, and that was over twenty years ago. Bobby was one of the most marvelous riders. Norman Fine said that watching Bobby ride across a field was like music. He could make any horse go well. He never took contact on them, and they just loped along. He was the ringmaster at the Upperville Horse Show for forty years. He died ten months ago, and they dedicated the horse show to him this year. I've still got his ashes right here beside me. We'll scatter them over our hunt territory as soon as the leaves come off the trees. He whipped-in for Blue Ridge Hunt for almost all of our time together. Next year, I'll have been a member of that hunt for fifty years.

One of my passions is bringing children out to hunt and helping them find good ponies. Foxhunting meant so much to me when I was a child, and I want to pass it on. About twelve years ago, Douglas (Wise-Stuart) and I were on a hill watching the field go over a jump during a children's meet at Old Dominion. All the kids were riding up front and flew over the coop perfectly. Then the adults arrived, and it was painful to watch. We decided then and there that the children needed to have their own division at the North American Field Hunter Championships and set about to make it happen. It's such a marvelous opportunity for kids to hunt with other hunts and experience different territories and hounds. If we encourage their love of the sport, perhaps when they grow up they'll be interested in preserving the countryside. I'll never forget being out hunting with this kid, and we were running through an area that had a huge McMansion. She said, "Why would anyone build their house right in the middle of such good covert? It really messes up the hunting!" She'll probably be interested in conservation when she grows up. The Junior North American has given over $35,000 to conservation over the years. It's my hope that the kids will be able to ride behind hounds for generations to come.

Riding in a show ring is like being in a playpen. I say let them out to explore! Let ponies be ponies and kids be kids. I've so enjoyed watching

*Iona on her pony in Wales.*

them enjoy each other. It all started when I had my daughter, and the mothers of her friends wanted me to teach their kids to ride. I leased a barn at Clay Hill, and the kids started showing up to hunt. There was pony club and horse shows too, but the most fun was always foxhunting. Mrs. DuPont always said, "Good ponies make good children," and I think there's a lot of truth to that. I always had wonderful ponies to hunt in the barn because the horse show folks would send me the ones that wouldn't do their lead changes. Who cares, out hunting! I can't tell you how many thrown-away show ponies I had go on to have wonderful careers in the hunt field.

I've been involved with pony club for fifty-five years. I've taken two groups of kids to my old pony club in Wales, and it was like being in a time warp. It was great fun to take these little American girls to a place where there were no modern conveniences. They absolutely loved it. Life over there is like camping out—a great adventure. Every kid who rides out of my barn here has to be in pony club. It's just such a good education. The teamwork involved doesn't let the girls be a princess. Everyone gets their hands dirty and gets involved in every aspect of horsemanship. I think foxhunting is such an important legacy to pass on to the next generation because if the kids grow up loving the landscape and wildlife, they'll work to preserve it when they grow up. It breaks my heart to see what's happened to the countryside in Northern Virginia. Loudon County has transformed from a farming community to a bedroom community for Washington. Blue Ridge Hunt is fortunate that our hunt territory is located west of the Blue Ridge Mountains. It's a great protective barrier from development. But we can't assume it won't happen here. Our landscape is so open and undeveloped, we don't need tracking collars on our hounds.

The little bowler hat I used to proudly wear out hunting in Wales is in this country today, still used every May at the Virginia Hound Show. The children who show in the English hound ring have to wear a bowler, and apparently it's almost impossible nowadays to get a child-sized bowler, so they use mine. That hat is still hard at work after all these years. Foxhunting has always been a sport that honors continuity and traditions. I love to see a child out hunting in a coat that was made for me when I was fifteen. I love that we pass down these things from one generation to the next. 🐾

# M. Douglas Wise-Stuart

GRANDDAUGHTER OF THE WELL-RESPECTED MFH OF OLD
DOMINION HOUNDS, ALBERT HINCKLEY, SHE HAS NOW BEEN
JOINT MASTER OF ODH FOR TWENTY YEARS. HER LEGACY
IS ENCOURAGING CHILDREN TO FOXHUNT THROUGH JUNIOR
MEETS AND PONY CLUBS.

I raised my four children in the hunt field. Old Dominion used to not have a second field, but when my kids were too little to jump, we instituted a separate group, and that's when the young children really started showing up. Of course, most kids want to run and jump, so they moved up to first flight in no time. Before I knew it, there were more people following me in second flight than there were behind my Joint Master, Gus Forbush, in the field. What better way to spend a Saturday than out foxhunting with your children. Once we had the second field, other folks started bringing their kids along. I always showed up with a trailer full of children on weekends and holidays, and it was a blast. When we'd get back to the barn when the weather was warm, we'd ride the ponies bareback in the pond to clean them off. I had a wonderful Irish sport horse that three kids could get on top of at the same time, and he'd just stand in the water like a hippopotamus while the kids did cannonballs off his back.

I was brought up foxhunting every chance I got. I don't remember many kids out with me at the time. I always thought that when I had the opportunity, I'd encourage kids to go foxhunting. They are the future of our sport. One of the first things I did twenty years ago when I first became Master was start having regular junior meets. Now we have at least ten to twelve juniors hunting every Saturday. The Old Dominion Hounds pony club has been instrumental in making sure that any kid who wants to hunt with us can show up. At the last junior meet, we had

*I was brought up foxhunting every chance I got. I don't remember many kids out with me at the time. I always thought that when I had the opportunity, I'd encourage kids to go foxhunting. They are the future of our sport. One of the first things I did twenty years ago when I first became Master was start having regular junior meets. At the last junior meet we had fifty-one kids out hunting.*

fifty-one kids out hunting. Sadly, I did not do pony club growing up. I grew up in Boston and got down to hunt with my grandfather, Albert Hinckley, who was Master of Old Dominion, every chance I could. I lived and breathed the kennels from the time I was old enough to walk across the field by myself. From the time I was practically a baby, you couldn't get me off a horse. The kennels were right next to the barn, so anytime I was down at my grandfather's, I was in heaven. When the weather was mild, I practically lived in the barnyard, except when Leroy Ryan would take me down to the Orlean market for my sticky bun and Mountain Dew. My grandfather gave Melvin Poe his first job as huntsman after the war, but by the time I showed up, he'd moved on to Orange County, and my first huntsman was Ray Pierson. Later on, Bill Brainard was Joint Master with my grandfather, and he would hunt a pack of English hounds one day and Pierson would hunt the American hounds the next. Of course, we eventually ended up with some wonderful crossbred hounds! As a little girl, I'd love to hang out in the tack room with the hunt staff, listening to their stories—unbelievable stories that kept me wide-eyed and silent. I loved the stories of the night hunting, which doesn't happen too much anymore because there's too much traffic on the road. Melvin Poe used to hunt his own pack at night after a day of hunting Orange County hounds. I used to love going up to Bath County when Melvin hunted up there after he retired. There's so much shared history between the Hinckleys and the Poes.

I'll never forget my first pony and my first time out foxhunting. I was probably five. Jimmy was a really well behaved little paint, and I never had to go on a lead line. My grandmother always hunted sidesaddle with a groom in tow, so he was always there to keep an eye on me. I probably wasn't jumping yet, but somehow, we'd hunt and peck our way through to where we needed to be. My next pony was a medium that could jump the moon. I was able to ride in high school at Ethel Walker's, but there was nothing like hunting with my grandfather at Old Dominion and staying at Henchman's Lea—which the family always referred to as "the big house." I'll always remember my sister and me coming down to my grandparent's place after a debutante ball. We left the party at one o'clock in the morning and changed from our gowns into our riding gear in the car from Boston to Henchman's Lea and made it in time for the eleven o'clock meet.

*Douglas with her Joint Master of Old Dominion, Gus Forbush.*

My grandfather got some wonderful stallions from the remount station in Front Royal and bred them to all the farmer's workhorses as a thank-you for letting us hunt through their farms. He had a big Imperator horse van, and I painted a hunt cap and horn on both sides. We still have that old thing on the back forty, rusting out and long inoperable. Too many good memories to let it go.

In 1981, I didn't have a job or a place to live, but I bought a horse and moved to Virginia. I lived in the "big house" for a while until I got a job and apartment. As soon as I arrived, I started hunting every day I possibly could get out. Even though I had four kids, I hunted up until the last month or two of pregnancy and was back in the saddle again within a few weeks after they were born. There were years when they were young that the older kids would be out hunting, and I'd follow the hunt in the car with the babies in the car seats.

When Gus Forbush and I were asked to be Joint Masters of Old Dominion twenty years ago, Gerald Keal was huntsman, and he stayed with us for nineteen years. Now we have a young man from Wales, Ross Salter, and he's doing a great job. He's a lovely rider and has a nice touch with the hounds.

Twelve years ago, Iona Pillion and I had the inspiration to have a junior North American Field Hunter Championship. We were at a junior meet at Old Dominion, and we couldn't get over how spot-on those young riders were. They made the adults look bad! Today we have competitors from all over. We're going to renew the old hunter trial course at Old Dominion so the pony club can hold events there. We're always thinking of ways to encourage kids to ride cross country. At our junior meets, we let the kids ride with the staff. There's always a junior huntsman as well. They actually get to participate in hunting the hounds. It's a lottery system because so many kids want to do it. There's junior Field Masters as well as whips. Every Saturday and holiday, our huntsman Ross always invites all the kids to ride with him and the hounds on the hack home. When our kennel man was injured, the kids started coming to the kennels and doing his chores. These tiny little things were moving mountains of muck. If you're a member of a pony club, you can hunt with Old Dominion for free. We also have a reduced subscription for pony club parents because if they're going to be hauling kids to the meets, we'd love to have them join us too. At every junior meet, a parent can ride with their child for free. We end up getting great members that way. They see what fun we have and what a great family sport we offer.

# Gus Forbush

My house was right next to Casanova hunt territory, so I called their Master at the time, Colonel Sam Richards, and asked if I could come out foxhunting with them. Well, my horse acted like a lunatic, and I spent most of my first time out apologizing to people around me. Somehow I hunted that crazy thoroughbred for about a year until I came to my senses and got a good field hunter who knew how to behave on the hunt field. I went out every chance I could and got my colors in 1974. At the end of every season, my horse was fit, and I was still ready to keep going, so I got into point-to-point racing. I started racing my good field hunter, Chandler, and we had a ball. I was so scrawny back then, I had to carry thirty pounds of lead in my saddle to race. In those days, horses carried a hundred and eighty pounds. In 1982, I met my wife Sandra and moved up to Old Dominion territory. I hunted Rappahannock a lot back then because they hunted on Sundays and that was easier for my work schedule. Foxhunting was always something my wife and her daughter Nancy really enjoyed doing together, and we still do. Today, Sandra and I hunted with Nancy's daughter Gigi.

About twenty years ago, Old Dominion asked me to be Master, and at first that was the last thing I wanted to do. But they kept a slow and steady pressure on, and I realized that because I knew everyone around for miles, I could probably do some good for the club as far as landowner relations were concerned. I grew up in Warrenton, so people knew and trusted me. I knew all the landowners and farm managers because my dad had a welding shop when I was growing up and everyone brought their equipment there. I wouldn't have taken the position without Doug-

*As Field Master, when we're on a run, it's everyone for themselves. My eyes and ears are on those hounds. If anyone behind me can't keep up, it's not my job to slow down. My job is to keep the field as close as possible to the action without getting in the way.*

las (Wise-Stuart) as Joint Master. She takes care of all the events, which are so important for keeping the club profitable, and is as knowledgeable about the sport as anyone I know. Also, Sandra encouraged me to take the Mastership. I value her opinion. She finds my horses for me and ties my stock. I couldn't do it without her. I'd been hunting for about ten years when we met, and I thought I really knew how to ride. But Sandra was not impressed. She got me a flat saddle, and I flew right out of it at the first coop. She said once I could stay balanced in that, my riding would improve tremendously. And, as usual, she was right!

I still try to make sure I know who lives where as much as possible. I read the paper every day to follow the real estate transactions so I can introduce myself to new landowners. When I started as Master twenty years ago, we had about two hundred landowners, and today there are over five hundred that I have to keep track of. It's still the same amount of acreage, just smaller parcels. Newcomers to the area are often unfamiliar with our sport, and it takes some explaining to get them to let us hunt through their property. My job is to keep landowners happy so our members can have the hunting territory that makes them happy. Sometimes a little house dog or barn cat crosses the hounds' path when they're on a run, and we have to patch things up with their owners. I've had guns drawn on me and have even been shot at, but somehow I've been able to talk my way out of it. When landowners do get upset, I feel like I've made a mistake. These people should have known we were coming, but sometimes the fox takes you places you don't expect to go. Because I grew up around here, I'll sometimes find myself on the property of someone I went to high school with forty years ago, and that helps when you show up unexpected with forty hounds and horses.

Old Dominion is probably one of the few hunts in the country that always has its books in the black. We do all the work of paneling and clearing ourselves with volunteers, and we put on a lot of profitable events. Most of our members roll up their sleeves and pitch in. A lot of our landowners who hunt with us clear their own trails and build the jumps on their property. Because I'm in the steel erection business, I can do the repairs on all the hunt club's equipment, and that helps hold down our expenses. I haven't been able to contribute as generously financially as Douglas has over the years, but I'm more than willing to put in the sweat equity. She's thinking about retiring after this season. After so many years of working together, I hate to see her go, but she's certainly done more than her fair share. We've always talked on the phone every day during hunting season and really communicate well together. That—and a pretty clear division of labor—has kept our partnership smooth for twenty years. A few years ago, we got a third MFH, Dr. Scott Dove, and as a veterinarian, we rely on him to make most of the decisions in the kennel. It's my belief that one reason Old Dominion operates so smoothly is because we are not a democratic hunt. Only our thirteen-member board has voting rights. The general membership doesn't. The board votes on the Masters every year, then the Masters run the hunt. Our Masters are also our Field Masters, and I think that's as it should be. Ideally, the Master should be a bold rider on a brave horse and an example for the rest of the field. I don't get involved with the MFHA stuff. My focus is on all things Old Dominion.

We hunt every chance we get—not just Tuesday, Thursday, and Saturday but also any holiday that is on the calendar. We go out on both Lee Jackson Day and MLK Day. If school's out, the hounds go out. The Old Dominion Pony Club members can hunt for free with us, so we always have a lot of juniors in our field. Douglas gets most of the credit for that happy arrangement. For any hunt club, young people loving the sport is better than money in the bank. We love our junior days, when the kids get to ride with the staff. Some of the older members will sometimes complain, but I think that's just because they are jealous that the kids can ride better than they can! When the kids are leading the way on junior days, I have to ride behind the junior Master, and I swear they'll jump my tail off! I'll say, "You don't have to jump every jump out here." And they'll just smile and kick on. Cap fees also really keep us going. Because there are so many hunts in this area, we usually get between fifteen and twenty thousand dollars a year in additional revenue over membership dues.

When I started hunting in the early seventies, almost everyone in the field was on a thoroughbred horse, and most packs in this part of Virginia were American hounds. Now most people are on some Irish potato plow horses, and the Bywaters hounds are mixed with the slower Penn Marydels. A thoroughbred just floats. You can sit on them all day, and neither one of you gets tired. Another thing that's really changed since I started hunting forty years ago is that we have more hilltoppers than we do jumpers now. There used to be no second flight, where folks can follow the hounds by going through the gates instead of going over the jumps. Our hilltoppers go from hill to hill and watch the hunt from a distance, and the field goes as fast as they can go over obstacles to keep up with the huntsman and hounds.

The thing I love most about foxhunting is every day is a new day. You never know what's going to happen. I know a lot of people like a drag hunt because you're always guaranteed to run and jump, but here in this part of Virginia, we are fortunate to have enough land and foxes that we can just let the hounds do what they can do. We make a constant effort to keep our fox population strong and healthy.

Like a lot of us, I started off hunting to ride, but now I find myself riding to hunt. I love to watch and listen to the hounds. As Field Master, when we're on a run, it's everyone for themselves. My eyes and ears are on those hounds. If anyone behind me can't keep up, it's not my job to slow down. My job is to keep the field as close as possible to the action without getting in the way. I take a lot of pride in the fact that Old Dominion doesn't use any electronic devices. I don't want to hear anyone's cell phone ringing. You can carry one for emergencies but keep it turned off. When the fox can carry a radio or cell phone, I'll use one too. But until then, I'll do it the old-fashioned way—with a good pack of hounds and years of fox-

*Gus on Chandler (#2) ahead of Randy Waterman on Mermydon (#6) at the 1978 Old Dominion Hunt Cup.*
PAINTING BY SANDRA FORBUSH

hunting experience among our club's members. Sure, I get lost sometimes, and it'd be so convenient to call the huntsman or a whip and ask where they are, but that's not foxhunting to my mind. The fun of it is figuring things out. Yes, it might take more time to get yourself on a high ground and listen, but that's what we do. We use our wits to get it done. If you always knew what was going to happen, it wouldn't be nearly as much fun. I don't just rely on my own ears. There's younger people in the field that often can hear something before I do, and I'll go with that. I've got them trained to just quietly point in the direction of the hounds, and off we go. It makes me look good! Figuring things out is what it's all about. It's so gratifying (and sometimes humbling!) to use your instincts. The main thing that can trip you up is to second-guess yourself. You can't hesitate. You have to go with your first instinct. Of course, you try to minimize the danger of riding at top speed cross country, but it's that adrenaline rush that heightens the senses and makes both you and your horse much braver than you'd be if the hounds weren't running. Since no two days out foxhunting are ever quite the same, it's something that you can do your whole life and never tire of. 🐾

# Billy Dodson

HE BEGAN WHIPPING-IN FOR HIS FATHER OLLIE SIXTY
YEARS AGO AND WHIPPED FOR HIS BROTHER OLIVER
BEFORE HE BECAME THE HUNTSMAN OF THORTON HILL
SEVENTEEN YEARS AGO.

I always wanted to go foxhunting with my daddy from the time I was just a little boy. We had two workhorses named Maggie and Nell, and when he said he didn't have anything for me to ride, I just showed up at the hunt bareback on old Maggie. One of the few times I can remember my dad getting really mad at me was when I was on a damn pony that could jump anything. When the Warrington hunt passed near our place, I just tied a bridle together and went off bareback riding with the whip for about four hours. Daddy was looking everywhere for me, worried to death. Luckily for me, the Master of the hunt came by the house and told him how much everyone at Warrington enjoyed having me along. When I heard what Mr. Bill Rochester had to say, I was the happiest little fella there ever was because he saved my hind end, I can tell you that. I started whipping for my daddy at Rappahannock Hunt when I was nine years old. Jim Atkins always said my father, Ollie Dodson, was the best huntsman he ever followed. I got my first pink coat when I was ten years old. I just stuck with it and watched my dad over the years, and what I know about horses and hounds I learned from him.

I've been professional hunt staff for all my life, first as a paid whip until I became huntsman for the Thorton Hill Hunt seventeen years ago. Back when I was a boy, there were very few groundhog holes, and foxes would run for three or four hours at a time. Mr. Fletcher, Master at Rappahannock, would pay me fifty cents apiece to kill every ground-hog I could find. I went after 'em every day and could usually count on

*You've got to breed your pack of hounds for your territory. In these mountains, you need something with a deep good voice so you can hear 'em when you can't see 'em. I don't want dogs that run so fast that I can't follow them on horseback in this steep terrain and thick covert.*

putting a couple of dollars in my pocket every evening. In 1967, my dad retired, and my brother Jimmy hunted the Rappahannock hounds for a while. Then I hunted them for a year or so, but in my early twenties, I was too damn wild for that much responsibility. Jim Bill Fletcher got me to come back to Rappahannock as a whip, which I did for about seven years, whipping for my brother when he got out of the army. After Oliver Brown started carrying the horn, Jim Atkins had me whip for Old Dominion and Warrington when I wasn't working for Rappahannock, so I was hunting almost every day in the seventies. Except for when I had a back operation in eighty-one, I've been foxhunting this part of Rappahannock County nonstop for sixty years.

In the mid-nineties, there was a split at Rappahannock, and Mr. Larry Lehew wanted me to hunt the hounds, and we formed Thorton Hill in 1998. We didn't take any of the Rappahannock hounds for our kennel, but we didn't have any trouble establishing a new pack. We got hounds from all over the United States. In three days' time, I had thirty-two hounds. Old Dominion, Warrington, Fairfax, and Mission Valley gave me some nice hounds to get established. What I like is a three-quarter Penn Marydel, one-quarter American foxhound. Now a Penn Marydel is very timid. You can get after one and scare the whole pack in the process. You put that American hound blood in there, and they are so much easier to handle. I love the Penn Marydels for their nose and voice and the American for their good sense. You've got to breed your pack of hounds for your territory. In these mountains, you need something with a deep, good voice so you can hear 'em when you can't see 'em. I don't want dogs that run so fast that I can't follow them on horseback in this steep terrain and thick covert. One thing about a Penn Marydel is when they get a little age on them, they'll dwell so bad that I just pass 'em on to a slower hunt. By six or seven, they're wore out for the job I want them to do here. We hunt over a hundred times a year, and they get tired over the years. We've got about the roughest territory you'd ever want to hunt, but I wouldn't trade this territory for Piedmont's or Keswick's because I just love the hills. This is where I grew up. It's in my blood and my hounds' blood too. They've been bred for these hills and valleys. Hounds have more roar to 'em in the mountains. Their cry starts bouncin' off these hills, and it's the best music in the world.

Some folks are terrified when we start running up and down these mountains. Well, I'm terrified when I'm running across an open field full of groundhog holes at Piedmont. It's whatever you're used to. The horse for this territory is an Appendix, but it's damn near impossible to find a good thoroughbred/quarter horse anymore. They've bred 'em so small, they are almost like ponies. Another horse trend I don't like is these big draft horses. They're made for pulling a plow, not running and jumping up and down these mountains. They can't keep up with a basset hound, much less a foxhound! Look at a field nowadays, and it looks like there's as many workhorses as there are hunting horses. A thoroughbred horse has the stamina you need to run up and down these hills. I usually have steeple-chase trainer Dougie Fout to thank for most of my horses at Thorton Hill.

Now my dad hunted mostly Bywaters hounds back in the fifties and sixties, but I was so young back then that I just knew their names instead of their pedigrees. Man, those dogs could run. With very few groundhog holes and no deer, it was great huntin'. Back then, the farms were much larger, and there was so little traffic, so we could let the pack roll with very few worries. Now the land is so split up and the traffic is so heavy, you gotta keep a lot closer eye on your pack. That's where a fast thoroughbred horse comes in handy, so you can get in front and turn 'em if ya have to.

Even though I've been a whip for a lot longer than I've been a huntsman, either way, it's all about teamwork. You've got to hunt with someone that wants to get the hounds in at the end of the day as much as you do. A huntsman's no good without good whips, and a whip's no good without a good huntsman. When I think about the huntsmen in my life that were an inspiration to me, they would be my dad Ollie Dodson, Jim Atkins, and Albert Poe. I think when Jim Atkins hunted the hounds at Old Dominion, that was one of the best-recognized packs ever. Back in the sixties, Rappahannock had one of the best packs in the world. If you hunted with them back then, you'd better bring a spare horse! But the best pack of hounds I've *ever* hunted with are Roger Gibson's. That man is one of the most outstanding foxhunters there ever was, even if he doesn't ride a horse, right up there with the greats. He's got that Bywaters breeding, which is almost gone from most recognized hunts today.

Coyotes haven't been in our part of Virginia long enough for anyone to be exactly sure what their appearance means in the long run. I do know

Billy on Cosmo, hunting
Thorton Hill hounds.
JAKE CARLE

that when they first showed up, our fox got mighty
scarce, but they've been coming back strong the last
couple of years. So that makes me believe eventually
they'll be able to live together. At the same time, the coyotes are packing up in larger groups instead of being more solitary, and to my way of
thinking, that's not going to do anyone any good. Six or seven of those big
muscular things hunting together could take down just about anything. As
smart as a fox is, I think a coyote is smarter. You ain't goin' to run a coyote
straight across the road. He'll turn one way or the other instead of rush-
ing into traffic. You won't see one dead on the side of the road hit by a car.
They're too smart for that. I break my hounds off coyote scent as soon as I
can because as long as there's fox around, that's what I want my foxhounds
to go after. Our territory is so steep and our covert so thick, there's no
horse alive that could follow a coyote like he can a fox. Now we might have
to run them one day, but for now, my hounds stick with fox.

Just this year, I started thinking about retiring. I just hope whoever replaces me understands the importance of landowner relations. Nothing's more important than having farmers welcome you on their land. Michael Jordan might be one of the greatest basketball players, but where would he be if he didn't have a basketball court? I always said I'd keep on going until I couldn't ride or keep up with all the work that a huntsman has to do. With all the rain we had this summer, clearing those trails and putting up all that hay was just too much damn work. I still love foxhunting as much as I did as a boy, but all the other stuff is starting to wear me out. We've got the roughest territory around to keep clean. It's nothing but solid hills and thick undergrowth. When I retire, I'll make sure to get rid of all my horses, or the Masters will worry me to death to take the hilltoppers or lead the field. But I'm not going to do nothing like that. My whip Charlie Brown and I will get in the truck and follow the hunt on the road. I tell you right now, I admire anyone who can lead the hilltoppers and not get in the hounds' way. I just don't want to do it because when the hounds are running, I want to pay attention to them instead of a field of people on horseback. Now Jake Carle has been following our hounds in the truck for years, but if I ride with him when I retire as huntsman, I'm gonna drive! To me it's all about the music of the hounds. That's why I do what I do for my entire life and will continue to do so, even when I'm no longer riding. One morning really early, our pack ran at full cry through a man's yard, and he came out all upset hollerin', "How'd you like it if a bunch of hounds came runnin' through your yard?" and I said I'd like it a lot! 🐾

# Charlie Brown

SON OF THE FAMOUS HORSEMAN ELZY BROWN, CHARLIE
HAS ALWAYS BEEN A HOUND MAN. HE STARTED WHIPPING-IN
AS A PROFESSIONAL WHIP AS A YOUNG TEENAGER AT
RAPPAHANNOCK AND HAS SPENT AT LEAST FIFTY YEARS
IN HUNT SERVICE.

I always liked huntin'. Even before I could ride, I always wanted to ride around in the hound truck. I learned about horses and hunting from my father, Elzy Brown. By the time I was nine or ten, I started going out hunting from time to time, and I really got goin' when I was in my early teens. We hunted with farm packs as well as recognized hunts like Rappahannock, and I remember the first time Billy (Dodson) asked me to help out with the hounds. I just loved it, and after a few more times helping Billy whip-in, I remember Mr. Fletcher sayin', "Young Brown, you goin' to help today?" I never said "yes sir" so fast in my life! I whipped at Rappahannock for years. I got my pink coat when I was sixteen and started getting paid as a professional whip. I was just paid by the day back then, not salaried. I'm probably the only one who was invited to hunt at Piedmont and was allowed to wear a pink coat in the field. When we were invited to a joint meet there, my father called Mrs. Randolph and told her all I had was a pink coat. I didn't own a black coat. She said to come on anyway. Albert Poe was huntsman back then, and my brother Oliver and I had the time of our lives, chasing a red fox from the Piedmont kennels to the base of the mountain. I remember seeing that sucker running atop of the stone walls. The thing about Mrs. Randolph is, if she liked you, she liked you. If she didn't, forget it! Now she used to like to come hunt with Rappahannock every Sunday, so she knew me since I was a little kid. Growing up, I used to always think I wished I'd come along in my father's time. Our

*I've had some hounds that were so good, they'd chase a fox just like they was tied to it—squalling every step of the way. Some things money can't buy and some hounds aren't for sale.*

joint meets with Potomac were some fun times. Larry Pitts hunts a hell of a pack of hounds. Coming along as a young man, I had this idea that it was better back in the day, when my father, Ennis Jenkins, and Delmar Twyman were hunting. They had such great horses and hounds, and those men were an inspiration to the next generation, but now I realize that my generation is just making more history. The story continues.

In 1974, I left Rappahannock to go work with the Master and huntsman of Keswick, Jake Carle. I was on his payroll, whipping-in for Keswick three days a week. Those were some good times. When I wasn't whipping for Keswick hounds, I was hunting with Roger Gibson. His foxhounds were the best pack I've ever hunted. Those hounds were completely broke off deer. You could really trust 'em. We'd go out in the evening and stay out all night long. I'd be lucky if I could grab a few hours' sleep before I had to work on Carle's farm or hunt with the Keswick hounds. Even though we hunted Roger's pack on foot, Jake invited them to have a joint meet with the Keswick hounds. Those two packs honored each other like they'd been hunting together all their lives.

As a boy, when I was hunting with a farm pack, I got blooded at my first kill, and I thought that was the best thing in the world. Nowadays, most hunts try their best not to kill foxes, so the bloodin' tradition has kind of fallen by the wayside. Now last year, my granddaughter was blooded when the hounds killed a coyote, but in Virginia, I don't think we should blood our juniors with coyote blood as long as there's a fox around to hunt.

After thirteen years of whipping for Keswick, I went to Old Dominion to be their huntsman. My brother Oliver was huntsman for Rappahannock. My brother Mike whipped for Oliver back then. My brothers and I were never really competitive about foxhunting, but back when it came to horse shows, Oliver and I were each other's competition. We went around to the shows every weekend in the summer.

Now I don't like to put up with a lot of bullshit. So I up and quit after seven years with Old Dominion because as huntsman, it's hard not to get messed up in hunt club politics, and that's something I have no interest in. I just want to follow the hounds. One thing I did enjoy as huntsman was my relationship with the landowners. When I first became huntsman, the Masters told me my first concern was the subscribers, and I said, "Whoa—the first thing is landowners because without their cooperation, there is no

*Charlie in the foreground with his brother Oliver and his father Elzy Brown.*

hunt club." I enjoyed helping 'em out whenever I could because that was a win-win situation—good for them and good for us. After I left Old Dominion, I went to take care of Cappy Smith's horses, but I'm one of those fellas who rides to hunt. If I'm not following hounds, I don't have much use for it. Randy Waterman had me transporting his racehorses in the nineties, but I wasn't interested in riding them if I couldn't hunt them. Heck, I wouldn't go on a trail ride! I'd rather follow hounds in a truck than ride a horse without following hounds. It's actually pretty amazing how much hound work you can see following with a truck. If you've hunted as many years as I have, you have a pretty good sense of things and know where to go to see the most action. Hell, you don't have to get that horse ready to go out or take care of him and your tack when you get back to the barn. I've ridden all my life because I've hunted all my life. It *is* my life. To hear those hounds squalling is as good as it gets. There have been so many great days when it all comes together and hounds are hot on the track and the fox is in a running mood. Too many to count. One thing I can never stop appreciating is when hounds run in the cornfields during cubbing season. There's something about the way they sound in there that I can't get over. I just love the way Thorton Hill hounds sound in full cry. Even though it's familiar, I could never get tired of it.

Back when I was huntsman at Old Dominion, Bill Brainard gave me three Bywaters hounds—Eskimo, Essex, and Echo. Eskimo was one of those hounds that when she started running a fox, she'd call out every time her feet hit the ground. Good God, I like that. Of course, I wanted to breed her for more of the same, but she died before she whelped out. Not many things tear me up, but that did. The worst thing that ever happened to me was when I lost five hounds at one time when I was huntsman at Old Dominion. I'm pretty sure a landowner shot them, but I could never prove it. I've had some hounds that were so good, they'd chase a fox just like they was tied to it—squalling every step of the way. Some things money can't buy, and some hounds aren't for sale.

One of the best days I ever had traveling was with Tony Gammell at Keswick. We got on a flat-out run for an hour and ten minutes. That man is a foxhunter all right. Those hounds took everything my horse and I got! I just love to hear hounds run. As long as they're chasing a fox, I'm happy. It's gettin' to the point where the coyote have driven out most of our fox, and I'm afraid one day that's going to be our prey because they pushed the red fox out. A hound is born to put his nose to the ground and chase quarry. They've got to do what they've got to do. And so do I! One time a while back, someone asked Ben Hardaway where was his favorite place to hunt, and he said, "Well you can't beat Rappahannock County. Those red foxes up there in that county will run your balls off!"

# Roger Gibson

AT SEVENTY-FIVE, HE STILL HUNTS HIS PACK OF WALKER
FOXHOUNDS ON FOOT AT LEAST THREE DAYS A WEEK. HE
STARTED NIGHT HUNTING WITH HIS DADDY WHEN HE WAS SIX.

When I drop the tailgate, my hounds are ready to hunt. I like to let my older deer-proof dogs out of the truck first so they can get started on the right quarry. They usually find their way back to the truck after the hunt, but I hunt all my hounds with tracking collars so I can always find them. The trouble with the collars is that your foxhounds can get used to you coming to them instead of them coming to you, but when you're not on horseback, it's not possible to keep up with them as closely, and it's the best way to get your pack back at the end of the hunt.

I started hunting with my father when I was about six years old. I've lived in the same house for seventy years. My daddy foxhunted all his life before I was born and did until he died. He was a hard hunter. He didn't want to see anything get away from him. Chasing 'em wasn't enough—he wanted to get it! He had an old mixed dog named Butch, and when he'd run a fox to ground, he'd go back to Daddy's truck, and Daddy would say, "Go back to him, Butch! Go back to him!" and that ole dog would lead us back to the earth, even if it was miles away. That was one smart dog. I guess foxhuntin' is in our blood. Once you get to huntin' hounds, it seems like you can never get it out of your mind. A little while back, I ran into an old fella who used to hunt with my daddy when I was a young man. The first thing he says to me is, "Mr. Gibson still got that old dog that run high?" That dog would be over fifty years old if he was still with us! Gone but not forgotten.

My daddy would take the hounds out every Saturday and Sunday and anytime I could convince him to let me skip school. Every Saturday

*It's nothing fancy, but when those hounds start running a fox, the mountains ring with their music. When you hunt on foot or in your truck, you learn to really use your ears. Men who night hunt have to use their ears, because it's dark!*

evening, we'd go down here to Turkey Sag Road and meet a bunch of other fellas with their hounds and have a big go all night long. About the edge of dark, we'd see an old black guy named Will Douglas coming down the road leading his two hounds on a piece of twine, a fox horn hanging off his side. It's nothing fancy, but when those hounds start running a fox, the mountains ring with their music. When you hunt on foot or in your truck, you learn to really use your ears. Men who night hunt have to use their ears because it's dark! Bobby Coles over at Cloverfields used to go out with us at night and run his hounds with Daddy's pack. I can still see his old raggedy truck, the bumper tied on with bailing wire, flying down the gravel road with him leaning out the window hollering, "Get out of the road! Get out of the road! I don't have any brakes!" Ennis Jenkins was a fine ole fella who used to bring his hounds out with us when I was younger. He was a real gentleman who thought nothing about spending days helping you find a lost hound after a hunt. That was back before tracking collars, and we spent a lot of time picking up hounds.

I usually like to meet up with one or two other fellas and their packs of foxhounds when I hunt at sunrise. Around here, I usually meet up with Brad and Ronnie Rhodes. The more hounds, the better the cry. I've always like to run a large pack. And I can recognize each and every one of them by their voice alone. One old boy told me he didn't like to hunt more than four or five dogs at a time, and I said, "Heck, I carry more dogs than that with me when I go fishing!" I like to hunt about twenty, and since I usually join up with a couple of other men who run about that many each, we'll have about sixty dogs howling through the woods. Some folks just want their hounds to open up and hunt just about anything, but I like to stick with fox. I like to just let 'em alone and not bother 'em as long as they are runnin' a fox. Then most of 'em will just head back to the truck after the run is through. I'll just use my voice to pick up the stragglers after the hunt's over. Most foot hunters don't carry a horn like we did in the old days. We used to use the horn to let a hound know where we were when picking up. With tracking collars, that's not as necessary. If I view a fox, I just have to holla, "Hark here! Hark here!" and they'll come running to me and pick up the line. You don't really need a horn like you do when a mounted huntsman needs to communicate with the field who's on horseback. I can get only so far away from anyone else who is out with me if I'm on foot.

We used to hunt mostly at night when I was young, but now we mostly run the hounds in the daylight. My daddy pretty much always hunted at night because he had to go to work in the daytime. He had an old thirty-nine Mercury car, and he'd pull the backseat out and carry the dogs back there. The thing that's great about night hunting is you have longer runs because the hounds can't see in the dark as well as the fox. We've run a gray fox for eight hours hard and straight at night. Come daybreak, the fox will go to ground if they don't get him first. I prefer running a gray fox when you're on foot because they run a tighter circle than a red. It's sort of like running a rabbit. You don't have to travel too far to keep up. When my daddy was night hunting, we'd often run two or three grays up a tree, but it seems like now, if you do find a gray, it just runs for a bit then goes in a hole. They don't run and climb like they used to. The problem is nowadays there are very few gray foxes around, so you pretty much have to jump a red if you want your hounds to hunt. I think we tend to hunt mostly red these days because the coyote have pretty much run off the grays. Coyotes didn't really show up around here until about ten years ago, and the gray fox has become scarce since they did. There's also bobcat in our area now, and they are really rough on a gray fox. They can climb like a gray, so it's hard for grays to escape. What I really like about the gray fox is because they run so tight, you're pack doesn't get too strung out. Running in a smaller circle, the slower hounds can eventually catch up with the lead hounds, and you get the best music then. I like a hound with a real good squallin' mouth. The females have a nice tenor that sounds great with the dogs. A hound with a real distinct voice better be a good hound because if he's up to no good, he'll always get caught. Of course, if he's doin' right, he'll always get the credit!

Now I like to hunt American hounds. Most of mine are Walkers. I've had some good Julys, but most of them are so daggone mean that I tend to stay away from them. They can really hunt a fox, but they love a dog-fight too—which is a problem. I hardly ever breed my bitches. I usually just buy what I need when I need it. I love the Walker hounds because they love to hunt and they handle so nicely. I can just look at them and say, "Get in the truck," and up they go. You don't even have to put your hands on them. I'm by myself, so I really need a pack that can listen to me. I'm seventy-five years old, but even though I've slowed down a bit, I like to hunt fox as much as I ever did. I try to get my hounds out huntin' at least three times a week. Now the hounds I hunt are different from the ones the mounted hunt clubs use because a lot of times at those hunt clubs, the horses scare the fox up, and most times when those hounds start running a fox, it's a hot track because the fox is already up and running when they find. Now hunting on foot is different because our hounds might hunt and peck for an hour or so before they jump the fox and he gets to runnin'. My pack will have their noses on the ground, and they'll speak from time to time on the cold line, smellin' where the fox has been. We call it trailin', and they'll keep beatin' and bangin' until they find where the fox is laying. Then he'll jump up and start runnin', and my pack will open up in full cry. I just love to watch a pack trailin' a fox, working that old line 'til they come to their quarry. If I ever see a fox when we're out huntin' I just have to holla, "Hark here!" and those hounds will come right to me and get right on that hot line.

By the time I was ten years old, I could tell you the voice of every single hound in my daddy's pack. It's important to recognize their voices because you can't see them as much as you can on horseback, and a huntsman needs to know what hound is saying what. Now, of course,

*Roger's father Lawrence with the Gibson family hounds in 1960.*

when I was a boy, there wasn't any deer around, and that was one thing you didn't have to worry about. Now we have to use training collars to get the young hounds to not run deer. There's nowhere you can find that doesn't have deer everywhere. When we turn 'em out of the truck and they start speaking, you can tell pretty quick by their voice if they're runnin' a deer, and you zap 'em with that trainin' collar and they'll back off. It doesn't take long for them to get with the program. Now that we have coyote coming in, we have some figuring out to do. If they jump a coyote, you'd better get over to the second road because by the time you drive over to the nearest road, they'll have crossed over and gone. Some of these new inventions like tracking collars can be pretty helpful. If a hound runs until she's really tired, she might lie down fifty yards off the road, and you might drive by there for days and not even know she's there. You can get 'em up so much quicker with the collars, and I really like that.

A foxhound was put on this earth to chase a fox, and that's what they gotta do. I'm just so glad that I've gotten to be part of it. Heck, it seems to me the red fox enjoys the chase himself. I've seen 'em so many times stop and sit while the hounds get organized and refind the line. Even though it's life or death for the fox, I swear sometimes it seems like he's playing with us! Now I know a lot of people don't like it, but if the hounds catch a fox every now and then, that really helps 'em to be interested to hunt that scent the next time they're out huntin'. They can get real discouraged if they never get their quarry. That'd be like if a man worked real hard all day and his boss said, "I'm not going to pay you." Well you'd lose interest in that job after a while, for sure! If you don't get paid every once in a while, sooner or later, you're goin' to stop showing up for work. The old-timers use the expression "they need to get some fur in their mouth." I often wonder what it would be like if I could get all the good hounds I've ever hunted up in one pack together—a fox wouldn't stand a chance! 🐾

# R. E. Lee Gildea

LEE GREW UP NIGHT HUNTING ON FOOT BEFORE HE
STARTED RIDING BOBBY COLES'S HORSES WITH KHC. HE'S
AN ACCOMPLISHED ARTIST IN BOTH CARVING AND DRAWING,
SPECIALIZING IN FOX, HORSE, AND HOUND.

Uncle Will Douglas, the old colored man who worked for grandfather, always had some hounds—as did most folks in these parts when I was a boy. Country people used to have hounds like they'd have a television set today. Either by previous arrangement or somebody just taking a notion to go huntin', someone would let their hounds out, then others would hear them runnin' and do the same thing until, before you know, the mountain were ringing with their cry. Frank Carter and Montgomery Dickerson always had a good pack of hounds. They were black fellas too, but no one seemed to care about anyone's race when the hounds were speaking. I've been reading a book about cockfighting in England, and it says that the great levelers of society have always been horse racing, cockfighting, and foxhunting. Now Uncle Will was as close as you can get to a relative without being related by blood. He and my grandfather were born the same year and died the same year. And they probably didn't have a year apart in their entire lives. Growing up together they were so close, they had their own secret language that no one else could understand. Even though I was around them constantly growing up, I never could pick up a word of what they were saying when they were speaking together. When I was too young to stay up late, if the night was warm enough and the whip-poor-wills weren't too loud, I could keep my windows open and listen to the night packs running through the dark after they were let out at Bruce's gate. Next morning, I'd have Uncle Will tell me every dodge and double back of the hunt, every step of both the

Country people used to have hounds like they'd have a television set today. Either by previous arrangement or somebody just taking a notion to go huntin', someone would let their hounds out, then others would hear them runnin' and do the same thing until, before you know, the mountains are ringing with their cry.

fox and hounds. He had a name for every hollow and spring branch, so he could describe everywhere they went, every step of the way.

Hunting hounds was always the great equalizer in these parts. Whether you were a backwoods moonshiner or a rich landowner, chances were you foxhunted. I've hunted with both and moonshiners were usually the most fun! Back then, we never had to worry about where the fox ran because no matter where the hounds ended up, you'd know the folks who had the land because, at one time or another, you'd run your hounds together.

My family home, Millwood, has been in the family since we stole it from the Indians in 1732. Like most people where I grew up, we always had ponies on the place. When I was about sixteen, the Rafferty sisters at Cloverfields got me going out foxhunting with Keswick Hunt on horseback instead of on foot. I rode our huntsman Roberts Coles's horses for years. I don't know if I taught them anything, but I put some mileage on them. I was always foolin' with horses—did a lot of trades, rode a lot of other people's as well as my own. Even though I loved following hounds on horseback, I never lost my love of night hunting and continued to do so all my life. Back then, we'd blow our horn, and the hounds would come to us. Now everybody uses those tracking collars, and it seems like we've trained ourselves to come to the hounds. With all the traffic on the roads today, you have to get to 'em as fast as you can.

When I was in my twenties, my friend Ronnie Rhodes and I got our first foot pack hounds. They were the old-time red Virginia hounds, descendants of the Irish hounds, Mountain and Muse, the ancestors of today's American foxhounds. The old-time reds were good all-around hounds, with good noses and voices, but they could be pretty crotchety. It's been said that Mountain and Muse were sent to this country because they were a little too rough for the Irish! Ronnie and I used to go through so many flashlight batteries running through the mountains in the dark that we figured out it was better to use the old coal oil lamps. They lasted all night and would keep us warm.

The best thing about night hunting is the air's cooling, and the scent doesn't rise like it does when the sun is warming up the ground. It's hard not to jump a fox out of his bed if you show up on horseback, but if you let the hounds hunt at night and you're on foot, they trail him up—follow the fox for quite a while before they open up and start chasing. I love the way they peck along until they get the fox on a hot run, then they open up and let loose. Back fifty years ago, when I was hunting with Bobby Coles on horseback, he'd leave the hounds alone and let them trail up a fox on their own. It oftentimes made for longer runs because the fox would have more of a head start and wouldn't have to jump in a hole to protect himself. Even though a good hound relies on his nose instead of his eyes to track a fox, at night the fox has more advantage because the hounds can't see him, even if they look up when he's right in front of them in an open field. Every advantage the fox has guarantees you'll have a longer run. In the daytime, you'll often see the lead hounds right on the line trailing the fox, and when the back hounds break covert and run out into an open field to catch up, they'll often have their head in the air and see the fox, and then the music changes to something even more exciting. Sometimes the hounds get so stirred up when they actually see the fox, it'll take 'em a while to settle down and get back on the line.

Back in the sixties, Coles used to run the hounds at night, and everyone would arrive in the field with their families and a picnic to enjoy the music. We still have the hilltopping tradition every full moon during the summer, but now it's just a field party because there's too many different landowners and too much traffic on the roads to let the hounds run free at night.

Back when I was first coming along, all those old boys, like Ennis Jenkins, Link Brookings, and Peck Watson, had the old-time red hounds. When Link started hunting hounds for Mrs. Scott at Montpelier, he rode over Chicken Mountain to show Dally Watson his fine red coat and white pants that Mrs. Scott had made up for him, and Watson replied, "What's the matter, Link? Did Mrs. Scott run out of that pretty red cloth before she got to the britches?" Peck's father, Dallas Watson, was a great foxhunter. He had two little mare mules that he worked on the farm and rode out foxhunting. If those mules were in the barn when the hunt ran by, that barn better be closed up tight, and those mules better be tied hard, or they were going to go with the hunt whether Dallas was there or not. The people that hunted with the Montpelier pack were mounted on the fanciest horses money could buy, but when it came to jumping a barbed-wire fence or crossing a railroad trestle, no one could keep up with Dallas Watson's mules! I think part of the fun for Dallas riding with the Montpelier pack was leaving those high-dollar horses behind.

*Lee as a baby with his father, Robert E. Lee, and their red hounds.*

Back when Coles was Master at Keswick, he'd run the hunt club's hounds with the foot packs in the area. The Gibsons were the first to break their hounds off deer, and so lots of huntsmen wanted to hunt their hounds with that pack so they could get a good education. They had two old black and tan coonhounds that would run a fox but not a deer. They'd turn out those two coonhounds, and when they were running good and steady, they'd turn out another hound. It took almost all night to get the hounds out of the truck that way, but they learned to stay on fox scent instead of being distracted by deer. If they put a fox to ground, they'd move a mountain to get him out because they have to bite one from time to time to get the idea of what they should be doing. In the summertime, we hunted with the Gibsons all the time. We'd start out Friday evening and hunt right on through 'til Sunday. There would be four or five kids sleeping on the top of the hound truck while we rolled back and forth on those back roads. Sunday morning, the mothers and wives and daughters would show up with their grills and cook a great big breakfast for everyone. In the wintertime, we'd go back to Roger's place, and his mother would cook for everyone. That big old round table only seated about eight, but as soon as someone had enough to eat, they'd get up and another fella would take his place.

Doris Coles's kitchen at Cloverfields was the center of our lives when I was hunting on horseback with Keswick. We'd all be there together cleaning tack Friday evening, and she fed everyone that showed up. Kids would often hack over the night before the hunt and spend the night because a lot of folks didn't have horse trailers back then. I was the kid following the Cloverfields' Rafferty sisters for years. Eventually, I became the one leading the kids along myself. They were a great bunch who could ride and knew the countryside. I loved it when I could get first-timers out where they could get a good view of the fox and hounds as well as getting a good run cross country. You can't underestimate how important it is to be on a horse that enjoys foxhunting as much as you do. My mare Sweet Marie would always know which direction the fox was running. That skill made me look good! My gelding Crackerjack loved to hear the hounds in full cry. That music would make him as happy as it did me. I swear, he'd hum on the hack home after a good run.

Seems like the foot packs and the mounted packs are more separate nowadays, and there's more separation of rich and not so rich. Some mounted hunt clubs are against the fox pens, but if you want to run hounds on foot, that's about the only way to do it. It's almost impossible to let your hounds run fox nowadays unless you're a member of some organization that has permission to go through private property. Gone are the days when almost everyone kept hounds and were glad to hear their music ringing from the hillside. That's why we have the pens—so people who aren't big property owners or don't have hunting rights from big landowners can run their foxhounds. Of course, you don't want the territory where you meet to ride behind the hounds to have all the foxes trapped out for the pens, but there's plenty of places along the roads and subdivisions where foxes live, and the trappers wouldn't be taking foxes off the hunt club fixtures. To my mind, both sides would be much better off if they'd work together. Foxhunters have enough trouble keeping their sport going without bickering amongst themselves. 🐾

# Larry Jenkins

SON OF THE LEGENDARY HUNTSMAN ENNIS JENKINS AND
BROTHER OF THE FAMOUS SHOW RIDER RODNEY JENKINS,
LARRY QUIT HUNTING AFTER HIS FATHER DIED, UNTIL TONY
GAMMELL STARTED HUNTING KESWICK HOUNDS IN 2000
AND LARRY BECAME FIELD MASTER.

My father Ennis was the huntsman for Manley Carter in Orange, and I was born on the Carter farm, right next to Montpelier. By the time I was old enough to know what was going on, my daddy was huntsman for the Rapidan Hunt. My dad had a small gray mare that taught all of us how to ride, and I started hunting regularly at about nine or ten. My dad had a mare that could jump anything you pointed her at, and my brother Rodney was always trying to find a horse that could outjump her. He was always very competitive, even out hunting. He and my brother Dale love to jump; the higher the better. I jumped a horse to keep up with the hounds but didn't need to jump to have fun. My brothers Rodney and Dale and our friend Noel Twyman and me always hunted together as kids. As children, we'd take a long time shutting the gates so we could race each other catching up with the rest of the field. Noel was like a brother to us. He stayed with our family all the time on the nights before we went out hunting. We used to love it when the field would go in and dad would keep the four of us out on our own private hunt. Of course, my mother wasn't too crazy about those extra-long hours of foxhunting because by the time we hacked back to the barn, it was getting dark. By the time the horses and tack were cleaned, we might not get home for dinner until eight o'clock, and my mother would have a fit. But my father had all the time in the world to pick up a good scent, no matter the consequences at home. If that meant you didn't start picking up a line until two

*If you've hunted the same country for enough years, you kind of know your foxes as well as your location, and you have a pretty good sense of how a particular fox is going to run. But sometimes, you're going to get thrown out, I don't care how much experience you have. The thing that makes foxhunting great is it's never the same. There's always surprises. No two days are alike.*

or three in the afternoon, then you'd keep on hunting as long as it lasted, even if you started at ten o'clock in the morning. My father didn't need any whipper-ins back then because there wasn't much traffic on the roads and there weren't any deer to pull them off of. He carried a cow horn but most of the time hunted with voice command. He could holler if his hounds were splitting on two foxes, and his voice was so strong, he'd pull their heads up and all fall in behind the same fox. His voice would give you cold chills when you heard him holler. You knew you were in for a chase that would be a thrill.

My father was an unusual huntsman in that he owned his pack of hounds, so he took them with him when he left Manley Carter's and went to Rapidan. He'd hunt red fox with his pack three times a week for the hunt club, and then a couple of days a week, he take them out with his friends to hunt gray foxes. He liked to hunt grays to slow his pack down so they'd hold the line better when they were running a red, which are much faster and easier to overrun as a result. In the early sixties, he bought his own place, and he took his hounds with him to our farm, Hilltop. At that time, Dad was hunting a lot with Link Brooking, who was Mrs. DuPont Scott's huntsman at Montpelier for about fifty years. He and my father were best of friends, and they foxhunted together every chance they could get, day and night. During moonlit nights, there's probably more fox activity after dark than in the daytime. When he hunted on horseback, he mainly hunted the Bywaters hounds. But in later years, when he hunted more on foot or from his truck, he crossed 'em with Penn-Marydel to slow them down. Now my father could walk any man into the ground when we hunted on foot at night. When the hounds would put the fox to ground, he'd be there with the hounds long before the rest of us could get there. He'd laugh and say, "Where have you been? The fox has been in the ground thirty minutes!" Those who hunted with him suspected he was part hound, part fox. My dad and Rodney traveled around the world to horse shows, and when he called home, he never asked about the horses, he just wanted to know how his hounds were doing.

My dad had all three of us boys working with the horses, but my sister never cared for them. I think Rodney scared the interest out of her when he'd try to make her jump before she found her seat. Rodney didn't particularly like to hunt. He'd go to gallop and jump but wasn't that interested in the hounds. I'd ride to hunt, whereas he'd hunt to ride. Viewing the fox and watching the hounds work is what I'm out there for. As soon as I was able, I got my own pack of hounds. My father had twenty-five, and I had twenty-five, and we hunted with a guy from Keswick named Roger Gibson, and he had about forty couple. The three of us would turn out about a hundred and forty hounds at a time, and man what music you'd have for night hunting. Sometimes we'd hunt the hounds all night Friday, I'd go to work Saturday, and then we'd hunt 'em again Saturday night. When it gets in your blood, you feel like you don't even need sleep. It was great times, some of the most fun I ever had. My father and Mr. Gibson could recognize each individual hound's voice, even mixed in with all those other hounds—not only their own hounds but the other packs as well. That's a gift. Not everyone can do that. Not me! I'm very good at recognizing any outstanding voice, but there's always some that have such similar voices that I can't tell them apart. It's important to recognize your hound's voices so you can be sure you're on the right quarry. Some hounds never run deer, so if they're speaking, you can trust the line and encourage them on. You've got to breed your bitches that don't run deer to your dogs that don't, and you'll have a good shot at getting a dependable pack. If you get an incorrigible deer chaser, you give them to a deer hunter and move on. You've got to get them out of the pack. In fact, I sometimes deer hunt with some of the boys who are hunting the hounds that I gave them.

After Dad had his first stroke, I kept his hounds with my pack and I'd take him out in the truck night hunting. He'd lost his speech and the use of his arm, but his hearing was unimpaired, and when he heard his hounds, he'd shake a finger on his good hand and say "Yeah!" when one of his pack spoke. It'd bring tears to my eyes every time he'd raise a finger. It was a blessing that he didn't lose his hearing because he could still listen to them run.

My dad was a heavy smoker and always had a cigar or pipe in his mouth. One time, the hounds were running, and his horse tripped on a wire and flipped him on his face. He still had his cigar clenched in his teeth, looking like it had exploded in his face, and he grabbed my brother's horse and kept on after his hounds. Another time, he was breaking a horse and rode back to the barn with a bad concussion. He wasn't making any sense, and the mouthpiece of his two-piece pipe was gone, and he had the front piece with the bowl in his mouth. We insisted on X-raying his stomach as well as his head because we were sure he had swallowed his pipe stem. Apparently, it broke in two when he fell, and he just popped the front piece back between his teeth without even noticing it was broken. After he died at sixty-three, I just hunted on foot or in my truck for about twenty years because I didn't think there would be anybody else that I would want to ride behind.

Now I know it sounds kind of strange, but even though I've always been surrounded by wonderful hunt and show horses, I've always loved a mule. I heard about this mule named Arthur that was supposed to be some kind of mule, and sure enough, it was love at first sight. He came right over to me and put his head on my shoulder, and that was it. I had to have him even though he wasn't for sale. My brother Rodney thought I was crazy, but my mind was made up. It took me quite a while to convince his owner to sell him to me, and she made me promise to never change his name. I swear, that mule could do everything but talk! My wife would get jealous when we'd go out riding together because everyone would make a fuss over Arthur instead of her pretty little gray mare. He was like a celebrity. He snapped his knees like you wouldn't believe going over

*Larry's father, renowned horseman and huntsman Ennis Jenkins.*

a jump, and there was no type of footing that would stop him. He was too slow to hunt, but I wasn't doing mounted hunting anyway after Daddy died. I broke my promise a bit when I changed his name to King Author, but his previous owner agreed that that title was well deserved.

When Tony Gammell started hunting Keswick hounds in 2000, my old friend Noel Twyman encouraged me to get back out there because he said Tony hunted a lot like my dad, and I rediscovered the type of hunting that I really loved and hadn't done in way too long. King Author was too slow for first flight, so I went back to thoroughbred horses with Keswick, but I still loved riding that mule whenever I went trail riding.

After I started hunting regularly again, I became Field Master and really enjoyed teaching people who were interested about what was going on when we were out there. It's a great joy to share your interest with someone who is really interested. If you've hunted the same country for enough years, you kind of know your foxes as well as your location, and you have a pretty good sense of how a particular fox is going to run. But sometimes, you're going to get thrown out, I don't care how much experience you have. The thing that makes foxhunting great is it's never the same. There's always surprises. No two days are alike. I finally had to hang up my spurs in 2008 because of health problems that disturbed my balance. I didn't think it was safe to take off at a full gallop, and that's the only way I want to go. If I can't keep up with the hounds on horseback, I don't have any reason to hunt. I still miss it, but I know I wouldn't be satisfied hilltopping. 🐾

# Barclay Rives

HONORARY WHIPPER-IN AT KESWICK FOR FORTY YEARS,
HE'S ALWAYS HUNTED ON A SHOESTRING BUDGET—
BREEDING, TRAINING, AND SHOEING HIS OWN HORSES.
EXCEPT FOR A BESPOKE SCARLET COAT THAT HIS MOTHER
HAD MADE FOR HIM MANY YEARS AGO, HE'S ALWAYS RIDDEN
IN HAND-ME-DOWN CLOTHES.

I always saw my parents and older brothers on horses as a child, but I didn't go on my first foxhunt until I was twelve years old. My brothers were five, six, and seven years older than me and did everything together while I was a bit too young to keep up with the pack until I was in fifth grade. My family had this wonderful pony named Glory Be, who was a school pony there at Ellie Wood Baxter's riding camp, and that's when I really started to love riding, with Ellie Wood and that great pony building up my confidence. Glory Be returned with me to the farm, and that year, I started hunting with my family. Our neighbor John Coles was my age and already had his colors and was whipping-in for his father at Keswick. Before we were old enough to ride, our job was to drop the tailgate and let the hounds take off. John's father would wait until everyone was ready to go, then he'd give us the nod, and we'd let the hounds go, and away they went! As a child growing up down the road from the Coles farm, Cloverfields, it was such fun to ride with the Rafferty sisters—Doris Coles, Caroline Hall, and Francis Rafferty. Running gray foxes in these mountains is a lot like beagling for rabbits. If you found a high spot and held still, you'd almost be guaranteed to see the chase. The ladies always had a knack for putting the kids in the best spot to see the most action. There were many

*I did without for a long time so I could hunt—including indoor plumbing. I remember our Master Jake Carle saying he wanted to get a picture of my scarlet coat hanging on the door of my outhouse as an emblem of my priorities.*

more children out hunting back then than there are today. It was a neighborhood thing, and most of the landowners were foxhunters.

We'd often ride our horses over to Cloverfields and bed them down there the night before a hunt. It was such a great scene in the front yard of that wonderful old place, where Keswick still gathers for our opening meet every year. Glory Be was such a good teacher that it didn't take much time for me to learn to jump and join the first flight, but the Rafferty sisters taught me a lot about hound work by setting the hilltoppers up where we could see both hounds and fox. I'll never forget one day when I was on Glory Be riding behind Doris, Caroline, and Francis when they lined us up along a fence line so we could hear the hounds coming down from the mountain. We saw a red fox run out into the pasture and zigzag across the field, and then we saw the hounds with their noses on the line, overrunning the crazy line and getting back on it again. Then the huntsman arrives with the back hounds and puts them on the line with the rest of the pack. It was my first comprehension of what we were doing out there. It was a magical moment—the first of many. I understood for the first time that I was clinging to my pony to keep up with the hounds and watch them use their hunting skills.

My father promoted me from the pony Glory Be to a white horse named Tim. Daddy was Field Master, and it was such a joy to ride behind him in the field. Unfortunately, I only had one year of doing that before he lost his hearing and balance as a side effect of antibiotics. He tried to keep going despite his physical limitations, but even if he was willing to get killed in a fall, his friends and family didn't want to see that happen. He would ride with me in the field after he became deaf and dizzy, and suddenly I was taking care of him instead of him taking care of me. He was such an inspiration to us all. He never let us forget that foxhunting was supposed to be fun. That was a lesson I appreciate to this day. As a child, I used to look up at Daddy on some nice horse, handsome in his pink coat. I thought that all I needed was one of those coats and I'd be a man too. I learned that it wasn't that simple. My father's beauty came from within; it was his courage, his honesty, his character that shone through that coat. The actual coat was faded and tattered. Scarlet doesn't bestow any virtue on its wearer. Clothes cannot correct a scoundrel.

The summer before my senior year in high school, I started walking out the hounds and learning their names and dispositions. Jake Carle was Master and started being huntsman a year later. He asked me to whip-in from time to time, and it is a responsibility that takes some gumption. Like anything else in life, sometimes you're gonna get it right, and sometimes you're gonna be wrong. One of my favorite things about whipping-in is that each day there are new challenges and what you did last week doesn't matter. You've got to step up and be alert. You've got to shake off your mistakes and try to do better. It's always interesting working as a team with the huntsman and other whippers-in. We usually have a discussion before the first draw about who should be where, but we have to always be open to the possibility that the best-intended plans can change in an instant! I've been whipping-in since the seventies, and no two days are ever alike. So many variables come into play that it never gets predictable, though experience can certainly help your luck from time to time.

I did without for a long time so I could hunt—including indoor plumbing. I remember our Master Jake Carle saying he wanted to get a picture of my scarlet coat hanging on the door of my outhouse as an emblem of my priorities. There were years when I was hunting with Bull Run as well as Keswick, going out four or five times a week. I kept a hunting journal, and it was not unusual for me to get out over a hundred times in a season. There were some days when I'd hunt with Keswick in the morning and with Bull Run in the afternoon. I think it was Hayden Trigg who said that foxhunting is either for the extremely wealthy or for those who have nothing and want nothing. I definitely fall into the latter category!

While home from college, I was riding my white horse Tim through our family's property and saw an old falling-down farmhouse. I had an *aha* moment where I imagined living there and hunting every chance I could get. There was a little screech owl in the gable of the house, and it winked at me, as if in approval of my idea. I've never seen a screech owl before or since, but I took his appearance as a wise omen. I thought I'd spend a couple of years fixing it up and foxhunting before I went on to the rest of my life. Well, it's been thirty-eight years and a wonderful life here with my wife and two daughters. My wife Aggie and I share the same understanding that the most important things in life don't involve money, and we don't mind deferred gratification. It makes us happy to see each other happy. I'm living proof that you can hunt on a budget if you're willing to put in the time. My horses are home bred and raised. That's a tremendous investment of time, but it keeps my expenses low. I do my own horseshoeing as well, so from the first day they are foaled, I start picking up their feet and getting them used to being handled because I do everything by myself.

My preference for hand-me-downs probably comes from my being the youngest of four brothers. New clothes never came my way when I was a kid. My mother hunted for twenty years and claimed she never bought any riding apparel. Older women in the neighborhood passed boots, britches, and coats on to her, grateful that someone would keep the old fabric sailing over fences and fields. I still use my father's eighty-year-old Whippy saddle and a whip with the initials of an uncle that died twenty years before I was born. My favorite vest was my grandfather's a hundred and fifteen years ago and was used by my father and then a close family friend before it was passed on to me. My mother ordered scarlet coats from Dege for my brother and me the year before she died. No one else has ever worn my coat, and when I put it on, I think of the passage from Proverbs 31, which was read at her funeral: "When it snows, she

*Barclay on Tim, with his father Alexander Rives on Jill, in front of Cloverfields in 1970.*
GEORGE BARKLEY

has no fear for her household; for all of them are clothed in scarlet."

I know some people ride to hunt and some hunt to ride, but I really don't think I could say whether I'm in it more for the horses or hounds. For me, a good day of hunting is if there is at least one transcendent moment. That moment might come from the hound work, the horses, or even the fox. There was a day when Jake Carle was Master and huntsman. The hounds were right on this fox for a long run, then they had missed it, and Jake had just about given up ever picking up the line again because most of the hounds had given up. Before he blew his horn to draw another covert, this hound named Chickadee just flung herself back around and put her nose on the ground, feathering excitedly. The rest of the pack noticed her excitement and came to follow, and we were up and running that same fox again. If your horse gives you a great ride, doing everything you ask and more—that can be a day to remember. Many books have been written on the fascinating character of the fox. What the anti-foxhunters can never understand is our profound admiration for our quarry. When we tip our caps in the direction of the fox, I've always felt that it wasn't just to let the huntsman know which way he went. You're also saluting the animal. Foxhunting puts you right in the middle of the wonderment of nature. Mason Houghland said it much better than I could. He said foxhunting goes on because "after all the adventures and misadventures of the sport, a few become attuned to nature's wondrous harmony, of which they themselves are a part." You get to feel yourself as a part of the big picture.

I've been so fortunate to get to spend a lifetime sharing this sport I love with my brother Sandy, who also whips in for Keswick. We have always used the time either hacking or trailering to a meet to catch up and stay close. Now his daughter Lizzie is hunting with us every time she's not in school, and it's been so wonderful to watch her grow to love the sport and teach her everything I know.

Foxhunting has been such a big part of my life for so long. Even when I wasn't actually doing it, I was thinking about it. I remember looking out of plane windows and wondering what the territory below me would be like to hunt. I've never been the most accomplished rider or the best-caliber whipper-in, but my skills are such that I can contribute to the hunt and have a heck of a good time doing it. I agree with people who say it's the most fun you can have with your clothes on! 🐎

# Lizzie Rives

SHE GREW UP RIDING WITH HER FATHER AND UNCLE—
BOTH WHIPPER-INS AT KHC. SHE WANTS TO BE AN EQUINE
VETERINARIAN AND BE A WHIP ONE DAY HERSELF.

My parents tell a story about when I got out of my crib in the middle of the night and went outside into the pasture. They found me the next morning in the middle of the field, with all the horses standing around me just staring at me. Mom and Dad were terrified, but apparently I was as happy as could be! I was such a tiny little kid that it was hard for me to stay on a horse. I broke my arm twice while still in grade school. My parents were waiting for me to grow before they got me my own pony, so I just went to friends' barns and rode their ponies. Riding all sorts of different ponies helped build up my confidence in the saddle. By sixth grade, I was riding every day and, in the summer, sometimes four or five ponies a day. My dad and my uncle foxhunted all their lives, but neither of Barclay's daughters or my big sister were interested in foxhunting. To this day, my sister and cousins really don't understand why I want to get up when it's still dark and cold and ride with the hounds. You either get it or you don't. To me, there's so much to like about the sport, it's hard to know where to begin to explain it.

I always liked talking to my dad about his foxhunting when he drove me to the school bus stop. I never felt any pressure to do it; it was just something that interested me. As a little kid, I loved to read the *Pony Pal* books, and after I started hunting, I researched everything I could find about the sport. The fact that my parents never expected me to foxhunt is probably the reason that I'm still hunting at eighteen, which is an age when so many kids back off for other things. I always had the opportunity to go out with my dad or my uncle without the pressure that I had to do

*To this day, my sister and cousins really don't understand why I want to get up when it's still dark and cold and ride with the hounds. You either get it or you don't. To me, there's so much to like about the sport, it's hard to know where to begin to explain it.*

it. Positive reinforcement is a powerful thing. I always felt so welcome when I did show up in the hunt field. When hunting season is over, I have fun in the show ring over the summer. But by September, I'm ready to get out of the ring and start hunting again. My biggest thrill in the show ring was winning the hunt night pairs class with my dad at Warrenton. In ninth grade, I won the Corinthian Class at hunt night. It's judged like old-style classes for foxhunters—by the way of going, equitation, and turnout. The appointments like your sandwich case are scrutinized. I wore my great grandfather's top hat.

When I first started hunting, my dad would take me out on a lead line. My very first hunt was on Christmas Eve, and the whole experience was so exciting, as exciting as Christmas Day. Even more thrilling was the first time I hunted first flight with Keswick. I was on my uncle's horse, Dream. It was like a dream come true. That mare gave me more confidence than all the other horses and ponies I'd ever ridden put together. I think the most fun I've ever had on her was when Keswick went up to hunt with Middleburg. I rode with my uncle, whipping-in, so Dream was happy to be with her pasture mate, and I felt like we could go anywhere and do anything together. When I get to whip-in with my uncle or my dad, I just love it because my horse isn't worrying about the horses in front and behind, and I can hear what the hounds are up to much better when I'm not charging along in a large group. One time, our huntsman Tony Gammell asked me to ride with him, and that was amazing because you're right with the pack the whole way and can see what they're up to. It still amazes me how he can tell all those hounds apart. I'm not there yet, but it's something to aspire to. I'm hoping I'll be able to go out with the staff on horseback in August for early cubbing because being in college this fall will make it harder for me to get out during the regular season. My dad and I got a young horse off the track, and early cubbing is a good way to get him started hunting.

You learn so much about hunting when you get to ride with a whip. My dad has been doing it for so long, no matter where we are, he always has some story about when he was there before. Half the time when hounds jump a fox, my dad will have a pretty good sense of where the fox is going to go. Most foxes seem to have their patterns for running, and he's been hunting the same territory for so long, he gets to know their behavior pretty well. You can ride in the field for a long time and

*Lizzie in her great grandfather's top hat, on the day she won the Corinthian Class in Warrington Horse at Hunt Night 2012.*

not get that knowledge because you're so busy paying attention to the horses in front of and behind you.

One day, if I'm able to get out hunting a lot, I'd love to whip-in like my dad and uncle. But I've got a long road ahead of me before I get to that point because I want to go to vet school and become an equine veterinarian. I've been working with Old Dominion Vet since I was a sophomore in high school, and I've really loved assisting the vets. When I'm finally done with school, I want to have a job that keeps me involved with horses and foxhunting. 🐎

# Sally Lamb

FOXHUNTING FOR OVER FIFTY YEARS, HER GREATEST JOY IS
PASSING ON HER KNOWLEDGE TO YOUNGER GENERATIONS.

I always loved horses for as long as I can remember. I jumped on every Shetland pony I could find. My parents knew nothing about horses, and there weren't really riding lessons in the area. You just found a pony or horse to take out hunting, and there were people around to help you out. In the 1950s, there were real horsemen like Ennis Jenkins, who had a way of getting you to settle on a horse. Jack Payne and Oliver Durant always had their eye out for any kid that wanted to learn. Delmar Twyman scared the heck out of me, but he was always right! Jim Bill Fletcher was one of the Masters of the Rappahannock Hunt and was one of the biggest land-owners in the Culpeper area, but he always made you feel welcome when you were out hunting. He was Mrs. Randolph's lawyer and was as tough as she was, but he was an inspiration to me as a kid. I kept my eye on him and learned by example. There was a lot of competition and cooperation between Mrs. Randolph's Piedmont and Mr. Fletcher's Rappahannock back in the day. Rappahannock territory was so mountainous, I never realized there was a piece of flat land in America! The footing was tough, and so were we. We felt like we were on easy street when we hunted the gently rolling groomed hills of Piedmont.

I think the biggest influence on me growing up foxhunting was a colored groom named Moody. He worked for Jim Bill Fletcher and was always out with Rappahannock. Although his primary job was Fletcher's horses, he always kept an eye on the kids. He made sure everyone had fun and got the job done. He's the reason I love leading the hilltoppers today. There's nothing like sharing what you love to do with others. Now Mrs. Randolph wasn't so encouraging to children out hunting. I'll never forget

*I'm definitely of the tradition that after keeping your eye on the hounds, the most worthwhile thing you can do out foxhunting is make sure someone else is having as much fun as you are! I've been so fortunate to have so many great people in my life that have opened my eyes to this wonderful sport, and there's nothing I enjoy more than doing the same for others.*

showing up one day at Piedmont with a new bridle, and she told me to go home and come back when my tack looks used. She said, "If it's not dark leather, I don't want it on my hunt field." I left in tears and swore to myself that when I was a grown-up, I'd never do that to a kid.

Jim Bill Fletcher did an ingenious thing years ago when he went to all the county supervisors in Culpeper and surrounding counties and got them to pass a bill where it is illegal to shoot a fox unless you can prove it's causing damage to your livestock. That's one of the reasons all those Northern Virginia hunts have so many fox in their territory today—that and the fact that there aren't any fox pens in the area that will pays trappers for live fox.

When I was growing up, the warhorses were a big part of Virginia's horse business. Dunnie Eastham and his brother Tommy had farms on opposite sides of Ben Venue Road. They were the go-to guys for the best field hunters around. There was a military stable in Front Royal that had been breeding strong bombproof horses since the Civil War. They were American warm bloods that could go all day. In 1955, the army disposed of most of their horses, and Dunnie herded them down to his place in Flint

Hill, where they became the field hunters for the Northern Virginia hunts. The American foxhound comes from the same area in Culpeper County. There was a family named Bywaters that bred for speed and nose, and that breeding is the backbone of the American foxhound today. It's a smaller, lighter hound that can navigate the steep rocky terrain of the Rappahannock Mountains. That breeding is deeply entrenched in the Keswick hounds, where I've been hunting since the early eighties, when we moved down from Culpeper.

Even though I had always ridden in the first flight, it was a natural fit for me to start leading the hilltoppers at Keswick when the position needed filling because at Rappahannock, we always went from hill to hill to follow the hounds because our territory was too steep and rough to follow right behind them. I've always looked at my job here as the best way to get newcomers in the sport hunting safely and knowledgably. If I do my job well, a lot of them will move up to the first flight. At the beginning of the season, I have all the green horses and riders, but as it gets later in the season, many of them will move on and leave room for others coming along. The hilltoppers will always be the biggest field in early cubbing and the smallest by the end of the year. I'm a big believer in everyone having fun and newcomers feeling welcome. I want people to love hunting, but I want them to respect the traditions, which are there for good reasons. If someone is invited to wear the colors of a hunt club, it should mean that they have a true understanding of the sport and have earned the right to wear them. If you follow hounds on horseback, you need to make it your business to learn the huntsman's horn calls so you can know what they're up to if you can't see them. I'm sorry so few huntsmen carry a cow horn any more. Oh my God, what a beautiful sound. The Poe brothers could blow a horn like no one else. Jake Carle also could make calls on a hunt horn that you'd never forget.

It's hard to believe I've been hunting well over fifty years. I still love it like that little girl on her pony Pee-wee. I'm definitely of the tradition that after keeping your eye on the hounds, the most worthwhile thing you can do out foxhunting is make sure someone else is having as much fun as you are! I've been so fortunate to have so many great people in my life that have opened my eyes to this wonderful sport, and there's nothing I enjoy more than doing the same for others. When I was young, people like Oliver and Charlie Brown's daddy, Elzy, always had something for me to ride

and the time to help me become a better rider. If you love foxhunting as much as I do, you don't have a choice as to whether you do it or not. I've never had a lot of money, but where there's a will, there's a way, and there are folks that can see your shared enthusiasm and help

*Rappahannock Hunt in late 1950's. Ollie Dodson, huntsman, in the foreground and the three Masters, Wade Massey on the right, Jim Bill Fletcher in the center, and Oliver Durant on the left.*
MARSHALL HAWKINS

you make it happen. Today, I try to do the same for kids coming along.

When I think back on my lifetime of hunting, the thing that stands out for me is all the people that helped me along the way. You'll remember a handful of great days, but it's the people that form your fondest memories and the reason why I'm still out there doing what I love. Because people helped me, I want to do the same for others. I always tell the kids riding with me that they need to pass on their riding knowledge as soon as they acquire it. It builds a foundation for the sport to continue. Nowadays, most kids are taught to ride by people who don't foxhunt or even ride cross country. I get kids all the time who think they can ride but are afraid to venture outside of the ring. I insist that they do, and you've never heard such whining and fussing in your life until they get the hang of it. But when they do, they are ready to follow the hounds, and the real fun begins. It's a lot harder nowadays to get kids to love riding cross country. I think there's so many other distractions, like

SALLY LAMB    199

team sports, and their parents are carting their kids from one game to the next instead of going out riding as a family. It used to be that most of our landowners in Keswick were also foxhunters. Not so anymore. Our club is making a concerted effort to get young families to join—parents who have young children they'll bring along with them out hunting. We have thousands of acres in preservation easement and one of the greatest packs of hounds anywhere, but we always have to remember to encourage the next generation to enjoy our sport. They are the future.

I laughingly say I'm addicted, but it's a wholesome life of being outdoors in nature and sharing your great adventures with other people. The true magic of the sport, for me, is watching the teamwork of the hounds. You'll never see a group of human beings get along that well! Strike, hit, go, and they're off like a well-organized machine. One of the reasons I always bring food to enjoy after the hunt is I love to listen to all the stories people bring back to the trailers at the end of the day. They get bigger and better every time they're recounted! I think I know what I saw, but by the time several people tell me what they experienced riding right next to me, I have to wonder. Maybe it doesn't really matter. Everyone has their own interpretation of experience. 🐾

# Andrew Barclay

NOW IN HIS SIXTIES, HE WHIPPED-IN FOR LES GRIMES
BEFORE BECOMING HUNTSMAN HIMSELF OF GREEN SPRING
VALLEY HOUNDS IN MARYLAND. HE NOW LEADS THE
MFHA'S PROFESSIONAL DEVELOPMENT PROGRAM AND IS
THE AUTHOR OF *LETTERS TO A YOUNG HUNTSMAN*. LIKE
HIS MENTOR LES GRIMES, HE WAS INDUCTED INTO THE
HUNTSMAN HALL OF FAME AT THE MUSEUM OF HOUNDS
AND HUNTING AT MORVEN PARK.

I couldn't start foxhunting until I was old enough to drive because my family just had a one-horse trailer and no one was going to haul me to the meet and wait around until I was done. My background is very much backyard horses on a shoestring budget. When I was sixteen, I was able to work at an event yard in England. When I got back home, I got my driver's license and started hunting with Rose Tree in Pennsylvania for my last two years in high school. After graduation, I was an exercise rider on the track, and, believe it or not, I rode dressage in a traveling show. I taught lessons at a riding school and started working for a very crooked horse dealer who worked there with me. He was ripping off the people at the riding school. I saw all I needed to see and then some and got away from that situation. I saw an ad for a whipper-in at Green Spring and was amazed when I got the job. I was twenty years old in 1974 and didn't realize that taking that position would be a lifelong path for me. I thought I was headed toward being a jockey, but I had so much damn fun whipping for Les Grimes that time just kept going by. Les was everything to me. He taught me everything I know about foxhunting and life in general. He was the old-fashioned Virginia

*I've broken just about every bone in my body, but I wouldn't trade those years for anything. Over the course of my career, I've probably had at least twelve concussions. As I tell my wife, when I wake up in the morning with a chronic headache, "Look at the fun I had getting this way!"*

huntsman who hunted hounds from the time he could walk. It was in his blood, and I was the fortunate recipient of that knowledge.

The Green Spring Valley Hounds Masters Sheila Jackson, Kitty Jenkins, and Fife Symington were also big influences on my way of hunting hounds. Kitty was my harshest critic and biggest supporter, and her influence can't be underestimated. Like Les, her knowledge of horses—and animals in general—was extensive. My third season as a whip, Les got hurt, and I started carrying the horn while he recovered. I realized that was what I wanted to do eventually, but instead of looking for a huntsman position elsewhere, I continued to whip for Les with the understanding that when he retired, I would take his place. His were big shoes to fill. He was a wonderful horseman who could ride anything and make it look good. He had a deep understanding of nature and the order of things—not just dogs but game in general. Even though he didn't have much education, he was one of the smartest men I've ever met because he really understood what was going on. Like the Poe brothers, his family worked for rich people and knew much more than their employers. Their learning came from experience, not books. When Les retired, I inherited a magnificent pack of hounds, beautiful countryside, and great Masters. He'd taught me a lot about hound breeding, so I had a pretty good idea of how to crossbreed the American and English hounds with a dash of Penn Marydel. For the first seven or eight seasons, I'd work with Kitty Jenkins on breeding decisions, and after she retired, Duck Martin and I would work together on our breeding program. I had twenty really good seasons of hunting hounds until my body had had enough. Even though I always knew how fortunate I was at Green Spring Valley, sometimes I couldn't help but think about what it must have been like here years earlier, when men were back from World War II and wanted to make up for lost time, when men like Fife Symington were in their prime and hunting hell-bent. I think my best years as huntsman were probably between my tenth to my twentieth season. It took a decade to really come into my own, and ten years later, injuries started really taking their toll.

After I retired, I got involved in the MFHA's professional development program, and I realized that I had some ideas that weren't available in print, so I was inspired to write *Letters to a Young Huntsman*. While I was huntsman, it never occurred to me to write a book, but once I had more time, I started writing articles for *Covertside*, and I thought I'd pass on to the next generation what had been passed on to me. The MFHA professional program is never going to make someone a good huntsman if they don't have the innate potential, but the old tradition of going from second whip to first whip to huntsman was a ten- to fifteen-year apprenticeship, and nowadays, kids don't get that background before they are expected to carry the horn. So Dennis Foster, Tony Leahy, and Mason Lampton all got to thinking one night and came up with this idea and asked me to help them get it organized and keep it running. I think the program has done a lot of good for the sport. It's a yearlong course that starts at the Virginia Hound Show, where the first thing they do is spend the day in the ring with judges. It's a great opportunity to learn about breeding and confirmation from the best there is on the subject. The next day is spent at the MFHA office learning about hound registration, and they are given a very impressive library of books. I give them assignments every month, and then they are tested on what they've read. During the season, we send the students to hunt with packs throughout the country so they can get a different perspective from what they are used to. I try to get around and hunt with each of them throughout the

*Andrew carrying the horn for Green Spring Valley Hounds at a joint meet with Piedmont in the mid-1990's. Ned Halle was Joint Master at the time and is whipping-in.* DOUGLAS LEE

season. Probably the best thing I have to offer the students is that they can call me whenever they have any questions or concerns. With my experience, I can look at situations from a lot of different angles and hopefully be a help. The standards of the sport, from turnout to breeding, need to be established and maintained. There's no longer enough old-school people like Kitty Jenkins and Les Grimes to go around, and this program hopefully helps bridge that gap. Huntsman is not just a job, it's a way of living. It becomes your whole world, and that's better than okay if you love it as much as I did.

My son is just about to go into hunt service, and it's with very mixed emotions that I'm sending him off on that path. I'm proud of his commitment, but it's a hard life, and I can't help but feel protective. I've broken just about every bone in my body, but I wouldn't trade those years for anything. Over the course of my career, I've probably had at least twelve concussions. As I tell my wife when I wake up in the morning with a chronic headache, "Look at the fun I had getting this way!" I lived the dream for twenty-seven years. I can't think of anything I would have rather done. Hell, I'd still love to be doing it if I was physically able to ride like I used to. My wife has had to be the one to pick up the pieces every time I was injured, and she's understandably concerned about our son following in my footsteps. In fact, my concern for her was one of the main reasons I retired—that and the fact that my balance is no longer reliable. My son is the same age I was when I started working at Green Spring. I feel like he's going into the profession for the right reason. He's doing it because he loves hounds. He's had his own foot pack for years and is dedicated to the sport. 🐾

# Ned Halle

In his mid-sixties, he continues to whip-in at Green
Spring Valley now that he's retired MFH. His law
practice focuses on land conservation.

My grandfather had a farm, and I started riding when I was five years old. These were backyard horses kept in barbed-wire paddocks, and of course, in my memory, they were never unsound, and everything was fine all the time. We'd curry the mud off the top and just go! The first thing my grandfather got me was a burro named Jim. I had a red western saddle, and he'd tie a rope around his waist and tie it to Jim's halter to keep me tethered next to him. He was a bit overprotective because my older cousin was almost killed when riding with my grandfather. He got run away with and dragged with his foot through the stirrup. Of course, my mother was less than supportive of me riding anything after that accident. I'll never forget bringing that old burro back to our barn. My grandfather hobbled him and threw him in the back of the station wagon. I thought Jim was grand. My mother saw how much I loved riding, so she sent me to get some lessons. When I was thirteen, they sent me to a riding camp, and that was when I got my first pony. Little Oakie was one of those ponies who might run away with you, but I just loved him because I knew he was always game to go. When I heard that anyone could go out with the hunt club on Thanksgiving that fall, I showed up on Oakie with an unpulled mane, jacked-up stirrups, and no saddle pad. I had no trouble going over whatever obstacle came up. It was just a question of whether I could get him stopped.

My first hunt was a deep muddy day with a huge field. At that time, Green Spring Valley didn't have a second flight. At the second four-foot post and rail at an in and out, Oakie's legs hit the rail, and I fell off in the mud. Of course, he ran off without me, but I was able to eventually get back on and go on with the program. Les Grimes was hunting the hounds back then, and I thought the whole thing was the best fun I'd ever had. I was hooked. I was only fourteen years old, so I didn't have a truck or trailer. My friends and I would ride cross country in hopes of running into the hunt. They were less than welcoming when we tried to join in, but that never deterred me from wanting to join as soon as I had the means to do so. When I eventually went off to college, I missed riding so much that I found a stable and hunt club. I met a woman who let me ride this wonderful horse named The Count. About a year or two after I graduated, she called me and said he was for sale. By then, I was back in Maryland, working at the Green Spring Hunt barn. That horse was the best crossbred in the valley. I'd hunt him in a six-inch shank, and just like Oakie, he pulled like a freight train. But I didn't care because he had enough heart for the both of us. Kitty Jenkins was Joint Master at the time, and she was always blasting me for not staying with the field. From day one, I wanted to be with the hounds, and I had a hard time always following the Field Master. I respected the heck out Mrs. Jenkins. She and Sheila Jackson ran a great show. In hindsight, I realize Kitty and Big Sheila were schooling me to be Master, and their lessons were rigorous. I saved every dime I could and bought this farm in 1974 and have been here ever since.

When I first started hunting, I'd show up late and wasn't well turned out, but Mrs. Jenkins and Mrs. Jackson whipped me into shape. I hunted for I don't know how many years as a landowner before I was invited to be a member of GSVH. Eventually, I think they realized that no matter how they treated me, I wasn't going away! I was fortunate enough to get my hands on some good horses and rode timber races as well. I was owner and trainer too—probably because I wasn't a good enough rider to ride other people's horses! I was late coming into racing. I didn't ride the Maryland Hunt Cup until I was forty. Unlike my parents, who were clueless about horses, my wife is a horse person and very supportive. Our first child was born two days after the 1991 Hunt Cup race, and I never felt any pressure not to keep my eyes on that goal. We had the number of the taxicab company taped on the icebox in case I couldn't get her to the hospital. Later on, she hunted that racehorse. All my hunt horses came from the

*Ex–timber horses are absolutely the best field hunters. My favorite part of the sport of foxhunting is to get a horse off the track and give it a whole new life as a field hunter. The good ones love it as much as I do, and you really become a team.*

racetrack. They're all rejects for some reason or another, but they don't feel that way once they're out hunting. Ex–timber horses are absolutely the best field hunters. My favorite part of the sport of foxhunting is to get a horse off the track and give it a whole new life as a field hunter. The good ones love it as much as I do, and you really become a team.

I was invited to whip-in about ten years after hunting regularly, around 1984. Andrew Barclay was huntsman then, and he said since they could never get me to stay with the field anyway, I might as well do something useful! One of the biggest pleasures of being a whip is inviting young people to ride with me so they can really learn about foxhunting. To me, they are the future, and we should always encourage them to keep the sport we love alive. It's a team sport with a lot of moving parts. And here I am, more than thirty years later, still whipping-in. Even when I was Master in the early nineties, I kept that job. The Mastership wasn't a position I was jockeying for, but I felt like I couldn't really turn down the position because of my involvement in the club. I'm a big believer in new blood coming through leadership positions as well as having the continuity of long-term leadership. Duck Martin has been Joint Master for as long as I've been whipping-in, and his experience counts for a lot. I always looked at him as an MFH mentor. Although I'm eternally grateful to the tough love Mrs. Jenkins and Mrs. Jackson gave me when I was first starting out, Duck's quiet way of making things happen without confrontation has been my example. After sixteen years of being Joint Master, I felt like I had accomplished what I set out to do and it was time to step aside and let someone new take my place. You don't want to have this encrustation at the top and have members who want to come up to leadership positions be turned away. There needs to be circulation of fresh blood. You don't want the club to become sclerotic. Anything that's alive needs to be open to change at the same time that traditions need to be upheld.

Although I continued to whip-in before, during, and after being Master, it took a while to get used to no longer being in charge, especially out hunting. Even when you're more than ready to let go of the reins, it's still an adjustment to get off the pedestal. I must say I'm quite comfortable now with no longer being in charge. The responsibility of where you meet and when you meet was something that wears on you over time. You're just sick if you lose permission to hunt somewhere. You feel responsible for the loss. Being a whip is enough responsibility for me. It's a challenge to keep up with this fast pack of hounds. You have to process a lot of information all at once. I still won't carry a radio, even though the rest of the staff does now. For me, I feel like it diminishes my venery. A radio or cell phone is too easy to rely on, and as a result, it weakens my hunting skill. You no longer trust your eyes, ears, and instincts in the same way. Sometimes when you're whipping, you need to go where you can't hear a thing, just in case the hounds do turn that way. I know a radio would save my horse a lot of running around, but I'm afraid of becoming too reliant on the damn thing to the detriment of my senses. Part of the allure of foxhunting is the anachronistic nature of the sport. If you rely on the radio, you're not using your senses to the best of your ability. That's a big part of the fun, and I don't want to lose that relationship with the fox and hounds.

As a lawyer, my practice has evolved through the years so that land conservation is over 50 percent of the work I do. Through hunting, I naturally got involved as these programs were formed. As Master, I had to know all the landowners, and as a lawyer, I knew all the benefits and

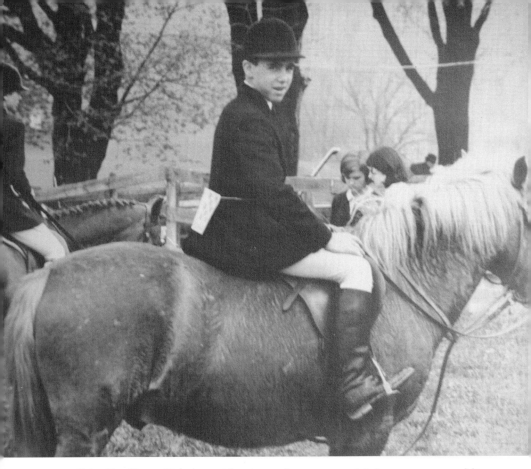

*Ned at 14 on his pony, Little Oakie—often showing up at Green Spring uninvited, but never deterred!*

ramifications of easements. It's been a great melding of my interests and abilities. Through the statewide Rural Legacy Program, we've been able to buy up development rights in our hunting territory and conserve the land. It's a pool of money put aside by the state for land preservation, and any area can apply. The funds buy development rights so the property can stay rural, thus protecting the environment. Sometimes I pull out the hunt directory and appeal to landowners and members to buy the development rights themselves so a golf course or development can be stopped. Say what you will about foxhunting people, they'll put their money where their mouth is when it comes to preserving the countryside.

The funny thing is, when I retired from being Master, I thought I'd pull back and not hunt so much. But as I've gotten older, I realize that I won't be able to do this forever, and my desire to get out there every chance I get is stronger than ever. So what if the weather is terrible? I'm going if it's possible to get down the driveway. There's nothing else I'd rather be doing. I've always felt that way, but now that I'm in my sixties, it's even more so. I was so used to being the young whippersnapper for so long, and now I see the old-timers on foot at the meets, and I realize that I won't be able to keep up with the hounds forever, so I appreciate every opportunity to do what I love best. My motto has always been, if you can go, go. Don't look for excuses to hold back because they'll always be there to get in the way of what you really want to do if you let them. ❧

# Sheila Jackson Brown

LIKE HER MOTHER BEFORE HER, SHE IS MASTER
OF GREEN SPRING VALLEY HOUNDS IN MARYLAND.

We grew up with horses, of course starting with ponies. We had a very badly behaved Shetland named Dusty and later on two perfect Welsh ponies who would jump anything. They taught I don't know how many generations of kids to ride after we outgrew them. We would follow Mummy ("Big" Sheila Jackson) out hunting until she became Master of Green Spring Valley foxhounds in 1965, a position she accepted under the condition that Stuart Janney would let us kids follow him so we would be looked after out in the hunt field. He had the most fabulous fox sense and gave us a terrific education in the sport. By the time we were ready for large ponies, my sister Cappy and I were ready to hunt on our own without adult supervision. We did pony club as well. My brother stopped riding when he got older, but Cappy and I still have a life-long love of the sport. I moved to Rhode Island when I got married. I took a horse with me and started doing a lot of eventing.

I'd still come back a couple of times a year to get some hunting time in with Green Spring. Back then, it was not so unusual to hunt your event horses, but you don't see that so much anymore, which is a shame because I think it's good for a horse's mind to do different things. The MCTA (Maryland Combined Training Association) and my family ran a training and prelim event here on this farm for thirty years. In 1995, we moved back to my family's farm when my mother got to the point where she shouldn't live alone. It was so wonderful to get back home and be able to hunt three days a week. Even though my mother was too fragile to ride, she wanted to hear exactly, blow by blow, everything that went on out hunting. Sometimes we'd bring the hounds to her bedroom balcony so she

*I think to be a good Field Master, you have to have a little bit of a fox sense—to have a feeling of what's going to happen next. The importance of hearing can't be overestimated. It's not just following the huntsman; you have to listen to the hounds' voices and make split-second decisions.*

could see them. After a lifetime of riding to the hounds, in her old age, she loved the sport through her children and grandchildren, and that was something important to us all. I still wear her hunting coats and have her whip. I have her shamrock stock pin that I wear on St. Patrick's Day.

After I returned home, I started taking the field more and more regularly because I had great horses and knew the territory from growing up here. Walter Brewster asked me to be Master in the spring of 1996, and here I still am. The biggest thing for any Master is the landowner relationships and keeping the country open to hunting. It's challenging and very time consuming, but I love it. Luckily, I have three Joint Masters, so we can kind of divide and conquer. I usually do the fixture card, and probably because I'm the only woman Master, most of the social stuff is left to me—not because I'm good at it, but at least I think to do it! Duck Martin does the hound show stuff, and George Mahoney is great dealing with the staff and horses. Whit Foster really keeps his eye on the grounds, staff, and stables at the hunt club and was instrumental on the planning and raising of funds for our new kennels. We have more landowners now to work with than in my mother's day because the big landholdings have been sold off into smaller parcels of land. Each different owner has different criteria from where and when you can go through their property. Another big difference from when my mother was Master here is that nowadays, most of the landowners don't foxhunt. You have to spend more time getting them on board to support what we do. Years ago, I think hunt clubs had more of a sense of entitlement. That's not the case today. We come with our hat in our hand to ask permission to clear trails and invite them to landowner events to acknowledge our debt to their generosity. Even though Ned Halle has retired from being Master, I still consult him on things concerning landowners because he's great at working with all types of people. Our main goal is to stay out of trouble. He's a lawyer, so both the hunt and the landowners rely on his expertise. Ned is also a great whip—he has always whipped-in, even before becoming MFH.

For me, leading the field is the most fun part of my job as Master. I see my role as keeping the field as close to the action as we can be without interfering. It's fun to share my knowledge of what's going on at any given time with anyone who's interested. I think the more you know, the more you'll enjoy the sport. I think to be a good Field Master, you have to have a little bit of a fox sense—to have a feeling of what's going to happen next. The importance of hearing can't be overestimated. It's not just following the huntsman—you have to listen to the hounds' voices and make split-second decisions. Our huntsman Sam Clifton hunts a covert quick and quiet, so you have to rely on the hound's cry. He doesn't lose me often, but I know he's always trying! Kidding aside, we have a good rapport and work well together. I know where all the jumps are and which way the best route between two points lies, even where most of the holes are, but that doesn't make it boring for me. Quite the contrary—that knowledge allows me to focus on following the hounds. I know my field wants to run and jump every chance they get, so it's my job to keep them happy and as close to the hound work as possible without getting in the way. One thing I've given up on is trying to second-guess scent. Every time I think I know, I'm proven wrong. When all the conditions are supposedly right, it can be a nothing day. Or, if it's blowing like stink, they can still hold a line. It's a mystery that keeps it exciting.

Until I became Master, Green Spring only had one field. Anyone who showed up was expected to run and jump. There were people spread out all over because they or their horses couldn't keep up. Now with a second Field Master, we can keep the slower group together and go through gates, and I don't have to worry about stragglers. One thing that has changed since Mummy was Master is we don't socialize after the hunts like we used to. There used to always be a tea back at the clubhouse on Saturdays when I was a kid, but now most people have other obligations after hunting. Life is so much busier with so many other options than when I was growing up. My sister Cappy, Sally Janney, and I would spend hours at the clubhouse and the staff apartments after hunting while the grown-ups had cocktails. All my friends foxhunted. We went straight to our ponies and horses after school, and that was our weekend activity. We were fearless. My mother always said, "You have to eat a peck of dirt before you die," and every time you fell off, there was no hesitation to getting right back on again. Of course, tears were not acceptable. My sister and I had a great rivalry riding together growing up. To this day, we love hunting together.

It takes a special horse to do my job as Field Master, and I've been really lucky to have some wonderful horses over the years. They have to be brave to be the lead horse. You can't have a horse refusing when there's twenty people riding behind you. Most have been timber horses, so they have good jumping basics as well as a good sense of self-preservation. I love doing clinics every chance I get because the cross-training is so important. These horses are responsible for carrying us through some difficult situations, and every now and then, you get in a spot where all you can do is trust the horse to see you through. I can hear Jimmy Wofford sitting on my shoulder telling me what to do, and sometimes that's just sitting up and letting the horse do it. That's why lessons are just as important for the horse as they are for the rider. I'm often in the saddle for five hours, and that takes a toll on their backs as well as mine, so I have to take care of us both. Thoroughbreds get a bad rep, which is often undeserved. I think they are so smart and brave and athletic. They can spoil you for anything else. Nowadays, you'll see more crossbreds than thoroughbreds in our field, but for heart, endurance, and athleticism, you can't beat a thoroughbred. Jack Fisher and Ann Stuart take all their racehorses out hunting with us for the great education that riding to hounds cross country can give you. They're schooling their horses, but there's nothing wrong with having fun while you're at it. I can't tell you how many great foxhunters there are who have won the Maryland Hunt Cup. Almost all of our staff horses are cast-off racehorses. We're in the middle of a lot of tracks and steeplechase courses and are the lucky recipients of some wonderful retired racehorses.

*Richard and Sheila Jackson, with Sheila and her sister Cappy on their ponies and their brother Richard standing with the family Labradors.*

Like just about every place else now, coyote have encroached on our territory, though so far, we still have plenty of foxes to run. Coyote will kill a fox if they have the opportunity because they rely on the same food sources. The way they slink around does not make me admire them like I do the fox. I love the way the foxes run, with their thick fluffy brush straight out behind them, using their smarts to outwit the hounds. Now I can't say that our hounds would never run a coyote, but they don't like to change scent lines once they're running, and they'll run right over a coyote line to stay on the initial fox scent. One thing I don't like about running coyote is I always feel like I'm chasing the tail hounds. You're flying and flying and flying and are always behind, always playing catch-up. You don't really get to keep your eye on the hounds the way I like. I do like visiting the other hunts to run coyote from time to time, but I'm always so happy to come home. At the end of the season, you go through withdrawal, and this year will be even worse because we didn't get out as much as we usually do, so it's hard to feel like we're done. But we have to let those vixens raise their kits so there will be plenty of foxes once cubbing season rolls around. 🪝

# Colin Smith

STILL IN GRADE SCHOOL, HE'S BEEN HUNTING SINCE
HE WAS IN DIAPERS. HIS MOTHER IS A PROFESSIONAL
TRAINER AND WHIPPER-IN AND HIS FATHER A PROFESSIONAL
HUNTSMAN, SO HE SAYS, "I WAS BORN INTO THIS LIFE."

I've been sitting on a horse since I was a baby. I can't remember the first time I rode by myself, but I can certainly remember my first pony, Paintbrush. He was the sweetest thing. He carried me everywhere, no problem. He was such a nice pony, I didn't even need to have a lead line by the time I was six. I moved up to slightly larger and faster ponies, started popping over logs, and now at ten, I have moved up to my pony Jackie. She's such a good, brave jumper that I've started first flight on her. She can be a handful, but she's worth it. She can jump the moon. I remember looking at the field flying by and thinking how fun it looked to run and jump like that. And you know what—it is! Of course, when I would watch the first flight fly by when I was younger, it didn't seem that scary, but I didn't realize that the pony you're riding is just as important as your riding skills. You've got to have a brave pony to follow hounds, no matter how well you ride. A good pony or horse underneath you can really build up your courage and make you a braver rider.

My mom gives riding lessons to me and my friends, who also like to foxhunt. She's always reminding me to watch out for my chicken wings— when I hold my elbows out to the side while going over a jump. She's always giving me pointers that help me in my riding. After a big day out hunting, I'll groom my pony and think I'm done, and my mom will point out that I missed a cut that needs to be cleaned. There are a lot of boarders in our barn, and I help mom out when I'm not in school. She was a professional whip for many years, so she pretty much knows everything you need

*You've got to have a brave pony to follow hounds, no matter how well you ride. A good pony or horse underneath you can really build up your courage and make you a better rider.*

to know about foxhunting. My dad, Adrien Smith, is a huntsman, so I was born into this life. Santa brought me my own hunt whip last Christmas, and now I can crack it as loud as anyone, though I'm not so good at blowing the horn. I'd really love to start whipping-in when I get a little older. My mom's teaching me how to crack my whip over the crest of my pony's neck because she says it's best use your whip over the horse's neck instead of away from their side. I've been lucky because I've always had my mom next to me, telling me what's going on when we're out hunting. It makes it a lot more fun when you know what the huntsman and hounds are up to. You really need to use your eyes and ears. She doesn't need to tell me to be quiet as much as she used to. When I first started foxhunting, I used to always be asking my mom, "What are they doing?" but now I know to be quiet—just look and listen. That's the best way to learn what is going on. I love to smell that skunky smell. You know a fox is around, and the hounds will probably be running soon.

I'm really excited about doing some races on Bailey, the fastest pony we have on this farm. He's kinda a pain to ride sometimes because he'll want to run away with you—but when you're racing, that's not necessarily a problem! Bailey's trainer is Elizabeth Scully, and even though she's only fourteen, she has about the best hands around and is fearless over jumps. She certainly doesn't have any problem getting Bailey to do whatever she wants. Elizabeth loves to hunt, even though she's a show rider too. Lots of horse show people aren't too comfortable riding outside of a ring, where you can't control what's going to happen next. Of course, for me, that's the most fun part! Another thing I really love about foxhunting is all the different animals you get to see when you're riding cross country. The other day out hunting, I saw three red-tail hawks squealing and swirling. I love seeing the plant life up close and the views far away. It's all so beautiful. All different times of year are beautiful for different reasons. The green turns to red and yellow, then to bare trees and snow. It's all gorgeous, but Jackie does not like snowballs in her hooves.

After waiting so long through the summer to start hunting again, I think cubbing is my favorite time of year—just because you're so happy to finally get to hunt again! The first thing I think about when hunting season is over is going fishing. Another thing I love to do is go rabbit hunting on foot with the basset pack. To look at them, you'd never think bassets could be so fast, but they can really get going—floppy ears and

*Colin in the saddle with his mother, Mimi Schmitz.*

all. Right now, I sometimes have the opportunity to whip-in with the beagle foot pack, and that's great experience for me to get ready to whip for Green Spring Valley when I get a little older. In the summertime, my favorite thing to do is ride bareback and swim with the horses. You can just hold on to the mane and float over the back. As long as you have a good pony or a good hound, there's always something fun to do.

# Connor Hankin

A COLLEGE STUDENT WHO WHIPS-IN FOR TWO HUNTS
AND RIDES IN THE GOLD CUP AND THE GRAND NATIONAL
STEEPLECHASE RACES, HIS FIRST LOVE IS THE
THOROUGHBRED HORSE.

I've lived on a farm my entire life, and my older sister and dad always rode, so they had me mounted up while I was still in diapers. Honestly, for a long time, I wasn't really hooked on the sport of foxhunting. My dad would take me out when I was a little kid, but I had the typical ponies that would stop and throw me off, and I wasn't in love with it until I had a pony named Scooby Doo in middle school. By then, he'd been passed around to every kid in Baltimore County, and he taught us all to love foxhunting. He was the horse that got me hooked for life. He's still around today and even has his own Facebook page. I was fortunate enough to learn the ropes of whipping-in from Ned Halle, our retired Master who now whips-in. He took me along with him, and he taught me so much about hound work at the same time Scooby was teaching me how to ride.

At the same time I was whipping-in for Green Spring Valley on Scooby, my family had a racehorse named Bug River that won the Maryland Hunt Cup in 2004 and 2006. That experience got me hooked on thoroughbreds, and I started pony races on Scooby, and the first year, we'd lose by a nose every single time, and I was convinced he didn't want to pass the lead horse. But the next year, I was determined not to let that happen again, and we won every single race we entered. That was a ton of fun. The trainer Charlie Fenwick was a good friend of my family and became my mentor. He had me come ride a horse named Buck Jakes, who was a big gray nineteen-year-old who had won a ton of races and would run off with me every time I galloped him. Mr. Fenwick would just be standing there

*We really believe that foxhunting is a great education for a steeplechase horse. We ride them in the back and jog the fences to teach them to be careful and really use themselves. It teaches them to pay attention. What you encounter out foxhunting is a lot trappier and uneven than on a racecourse.*

laughing, saying he's been doing that with everyone who rides him. I was probably fifteen at the time, and the horse sure had a lot more experience than I did! Mr. Fenwick saw my love for the sport and encouraged me to get my jockey's license as soon as I turned sixteen. My first race was at the Elkridge-Harford Point to Point on a horse named Make Your Own—and we won. Mr. Fenwick continued to give me good horses to race, and we hunted together over in Ireland as well as at Green Springs, becoming good friends along the way. We really believe that foxhunting is a great education for a steeplechase horse. We have these two racehorses over at Jack Fisher's right now that we want to run over timber this spring, so we're hunting them this season to get them ready. We ride them in the back and jog the fences to teach them to be careful and really use themselves. It teaches them to pay attention. What you encounter out foxhunting is a lot trappier and uneven than on a racecourse.

I've been so fortunate to have men like Ned Halle, Charlie Fenwick, and Jack Fisher in my life, but I'd have to say that the person who showed me the way is my dad. He is a major influence in so many ways. He gave me every opportunity and was such a good example. If I'm talking about influences in my life, then our Field Master Sheila Brown and a past whipper-in, Lissa Green, were great inspirations for my love of foxhunting. When I entered University of Virginia last year, I brought a retired racehorse with me so I could hunt, and I'm doing the same thing this year. Farmington Hunt has me whipping-in some this year, and my horse is a lot happier out by himself than with the field. Since I don't really know the territory yet, I just follow the hounds and listen for the huntsman's instructions. I've been racing for Jack Fisher this fall and hope to do so again this spring, though as a full-time undergraduate, I obviously can't catch as many rides as I'd like to. I don't have Friday classes, but it's still a tough schedule. As an amateur jockey, I do it for the love of the sport and the opportunity to ride in the Maryland Hunt Cup and the Grand National, which are for amateurs only. Every weekend I race, I'm competing against professionals that get to spend a lot more time in the saddle than I do. During racing season, I'll ride before classes three or four times a week. I have an equisizer that imitates a horse's movements, especially nearing the finish line. I run a lot as well for endurance training and do core conditioning for strength. I foxhunt every chance I get because I love it, not just to keep me racing fit. When I get home for Thanksgiving, I'll hunt Thursday, Friday, Saturday, and Sunday.

For me, the hound work is what foxhunting is about. That's why I so enjoy whipping-in because it keeps me even more connected to the pack than I would be if I was riding with the field. Riding by yourself, you encounter a lot more fox than you'd ever see in the field. The tricky part is knowing whether that's the fox the huntsman wants the hounds to chase. You certainly don't want the pack to split, and that can be a real possibility if there are a lot of fox moving about. I always contact the huntsman on my radio before I tally ho. A fox is a worthy opponent. I love to watch them outfox us! A foxhound has been bred for hundreds of years to pursue his game to the death, but the fox has skills that are admirable and almost always gets away. When hounds perform well and do what you want them to do, it's tremendously satisfying. There's nothing better than when they are running hot on the scent and everyone is riding flat out behind them to keep up. The thrill of the chase is really a thrill.

This last summer, I didn't get to walk out the hounds as much as I would have liked because I was riding racehorses every day for Jack Fisher. Both have early start times, so I could only do one. I'm hoping to get one more go on Battle Op at the Hunt Cup this spring, but I won't be hunting him after he retires. I tried it once, and it was pretty tough. After a few hours he gets so strong, it's no fun for either one of us. A thoroughbred horse needs to move on and stay busy out hunting, or he can get himself so worked up that he comes undone. GSVH hounds are keen and swift, so you'll see quite a few racehorses in the field because they have the stamina and speed you need for our kind of hunting. Like the hounds and the fox, they are marvelous creatures. I'll never forget one opening meet when we jumped sixty-eight fences. On a joint meet with Elkridge-Harford, I

was on a great Hunt Cup horse, and the hounds ran through this field where the only way to follow them was over this big line board fence into someone's backyard. There were about a hundred and twenty people in the field. The Field Master, Liz McNight, turned toward that stiff fence, and I looked at my dad, who wasn't as well mounted, and said, "See ya!" About half the field followed Liz by picking their spot along the fence line. My horse just sailed effortlessly, and by the time we landed, I was laughing hysterically because it was so much fun.

Before the Maryland Hunt Cup, I run the four-mile course to get a sense of what my horse and I will be up against. You don't get that option when you're out foxhunting. That's one of the things that makes it so fun—the thrill of the unknown. I love to hunt a thoroughbred horse because they are so light on their feet and come off the ground so much faster when it's time to jump. I love their balance. The relationship between horse and rider is a two-way street. You reach an understanding together that is intuitive. Both steeplechasing and foxhunting are sports that can't really be fully appreciated unless you experience them yourself. When I hunted in Ireland with Charlie Fenwick, we hunted five days in a row, four or five hours a day, and we were ready to go out again as soon as we got back to the States.

I know when I graduate from college, I'll have to move to a city to establish my career, but I'd eventually like to live somewhere in Maryland or Virginia where I can hunt on weekends and be involved in some aspect of steeplechasing. My dad works in Baltimore but is still able to do horse activities on the weekends.

I have a very different schedule than most college students. They are usually still asleep when I get back from riding. They probably don't even realize I've been gone! The sleep deprivation and exercise isn't as tough as making weight. Come January first, I'll need to lose twenty pounds before the spring races. They say a horse loses a length a mile for every extra pound of weight. I don't get fined like professional jockeys, but I want to win both for myself, the trainer, and the owner. 🐎

# Rita Mae Brown

A PROLIFIC AND SUCCESSFUL AUTHOR, SHE GREW UP
FOXHUNTING AND TWENTY YEARS AGO FOUNDED OAKRIDGE
HUNT, WHERE SHE IS HUNTSMAN AND MASTER.

My earliest memories of foxhunting were of being on foot with my grandfather, George Harmon, and his brother Bob. Both were veterans of World War I. The founder of Green Spring Valley Hounds, Redmond Stewart was considered too old for combat in the Great War, and he always had a soft spot for foxhunters who served in the war. He hired my great Uncle Bob to be his kennelman. My grandfather George came back from military service a shattered man who couldn't hold a job because of his drinking. He made his spending money with hounds that Mr. Stewart gave him by competing in hunting contests. They'd put numbers on their hindquarters and bet on whose hounds would hunt the best in the pack. When I was growing up, everyone I knew foxhunted. My mother hunted with both Green Spring and Radnor. My cousin Julia Brown, who was like a mother to me, had the best eye for horses of anyone, except Kenny Wheeler, that I have ever known. When I was a small child, she'd take me to the shed rows of the racetracks, and I loved talking to the black grooms who were veritable encyclopedias of all things equine. They'd give me insider information on the horses running that day, and I'd run back to cousin Julia, who I called Mother, and she'd place a bet on their advice and make a killing. Equine sports has been the great equalizer between men and woman for years and even more so today. The exciting thing for me is to see more women Masters and huntsmen through the years. Rich and poor, men and women, black and white— everyone hunted, drank, and danced back when I was growing up. African American culture is steeped in foxhunting. George Washington's huntsman

*Hunting with hounds has been part of man's history since history was recorded. I think language started when we began to hunt cooperatively. And believe me, the females didn't stay home waiting for the males to bring home dinner. Women hunted right alongside the men just as female fox and hounds do. It's a deep current that runs in all animals, including humans.*

was black, as was the great Casanova huntsman Cash Blue. During slavery, the good huntsmen were like rock stars. Some could buy their family's freedom if they successfully hunted their Master's hounds.

I followed my grandfather and great uncle on foot out night hunting or in hound competitions and rode the draft horses bareback on the farm as they plowed, but I never had a riding lesson until I was thirty-two years old. Julia, who raised me, never let me foxhunt. I think she was afraid I'd turn out like my natural mother. Our family is mixed up like a dog's breakfast. Julia was raised by my natural mother's mother, and I was raised by Julia instead of my birth mother. I was raised to be seen and not heard, which turned out to be perfect for becoming a writer. My strict southern upbringing taught me to be an observer and have a curiosity for the world around me. You could not ask for a better gift as a writer than to be forced to shut up and listen to the adults.

When I moved to Albemarle County and met Herbie Jones, he told me if I wanted to start foxhunting on horseback, I had to learn to ride in a saddle. He introduced me to Farmington's Field Master at the time,

Gloria Fennel, who sent me to Muffin Barnes, who has taught generations of foxhunters how to ride. She made sure I had a leg that would stay put when riding cross country. Farmington MFH Jill Summers was one of the great hound breeders, and after seven years or so, she warmed up to me, and I learned a lot from her. Because I spent so much time with hounds as a child, I don't even know what I know. As a kid, my idea of heaven was spending time with the hounds, and to this day, I feel the same way. Hunting hounds is instinct and experience. One of my mentors as a huntsman was Fred Duncan, who told me, "You hunt your hounds and don't look back." A good huntsman always puts his hounds first. You work with your hands and your heart. It's a calling. There's not enough money in the world to pay you to do the 24/7 responsibility of hunting hounds unless you love it. There's deep emotional magic involved. I have had the joy of watching and learning from a great line of huntsmen. My grandfather Harmon hunted with Dickie Bywaters, and I was taught by Fred Duncan, who whipped-in to Dickie Bywaters. Traditions are passed on and live on long after we're gone.

I'm from the school that believes hounds hunt better out of trust than fear. There's times when a smack is in order, but you don't start there. I was perfectly happy following Herb Jones in the hilltoppers, but when he lost that position through the usual machinations of hunt club politics, he was broken hearted and I thought, "What am I waiting for? I've always wanted to carry the horn and hunt hounds. I'll do this for both myself and Herbie and he'll have a purpose because it'll be such a mess and he just loves messes!" He went to the Farmington Master, Jill Summers, and begged her for some hounds for me to start my own pack. I knew her hounds had Bywaters blood, and that's what I wanted. She was good to me and gave me six couple. Many years later, she told me she didn't think I'd stick with it, but I did and did a good job with the hounds. That was one of the proudest moments of my life. Her approval meant the world to me.

There's a real tradition of folks passing down their knowledge so the sport can continue and thrive. Ginny Moss of Southern Pines poured all her knowledge of foxhunting into me over the years. People can be so generous when they know you love the same things they do. Mrs. Moss and Fred Duncan were my mentors with the hounds. Dr. Jones was not a hound man, but he got me riding and was invaluable teaching me everything about riding to hounds. He was with me every step of the way when I started opening up land in Nelson County for hunting. He'd go to the county courthouse and get the maps so we could figure out who we needed to approach. Herb loved to solve problems and was good at it too. It's hard to believe Oakridge Hunt is now in its twentieth year. There's still lots I want to do. I'd really like to pick up the pace a bit. We certainly have the territory to support more speed. One of the farms out here is thirty thousand acres. My smallest fixture is a thousand acres. The people here are real straightforward, so my job as Master is pretty simple because they either like you or they don't. God bless Virginia. They still have laws on the books protecting a huntsman's rights to follow his hounds through private property. Virginians are passionate about their property rights, but they don't trump a hound's right to chase his quarry.

Right now I have thirty-two couple in the kennels. Over the years, I've crossbred my Bywaters hounds with Skinker hounds from Orange County. Mrs. Summers probably wouldn't approve, but it works for me. Hound breeding is an intuitive science. I'd like to enlarge their number because our territory is large and rough. It's not manicured and groomed like Orange and Piedmont. Never will be, but that's okay because we've got a great thing going on up in these hills. My hounds are the joy of my life. That and literature make my world go 'round. I studied classics in college, and it's worth the effort to learn Greek and Latin. They are the framework of our culture. *Arrian on Hunting*, written in 200 AD, holds as true today as it did then. The Greek soldier Xenophon wrote the foundation treatises of horsemanship and hunting with hounds four hundred years before Christ, and his observations are as right as the day they were written. The first hunting treatise in English was written by the Second Duke of York in the Middle Ages. Hunting with hounds has been part of man's history since history was recorded. I think language started when we began to hunt cooperatively. We needed to work together to bring down a mastodon, and we needed to communicate to do that. And believe me, the females didn't stay home waiting for the males to bring home dinner. Women hunted right alongside the men just as female fox and hounds do. It's a deep current that runs in all animals, including humans.

The great thing about foxhunting—if you give it your heart and soul, if you give it time—is that you begin to see how everything fits together and you begin to cherish this Earth in a way you would never do otherwise. It makes you feel a part of something bigger than yourself. My grand-

*Rita Mae's mentor, Fred Duncan, hunting the Warrington hounds in the late 1960's.*

father and mother taught me to listen to the birds and pay attention to all the clues around us that are filled with information. If you hear crows, you know the fox is probably traveling in that direction because crows hate fox and will pester them to leave the territory. If you see goldfinch in the covert, you can be pretty sure it was at least a half an hour since a fox passed through. If you see a raptor, he's often shadowing a fox because they eat the same things. Over time, you learn to look and listen, and you see the connections between all living creatures. Something happens to you when the hounds open up and you hear that music. My heart starts to race, and it's thrilling—the best feeling in the world. All thoughts go out of my head, and I'm just present.

I started the *Sister Jane* series of books because I wanted to get the word out to the nonhunting public about this way of life. I remember when the first book came out and I had a reading in San Francisco. I was sure I was going to get clobbered, but the audience asked the best questions and were fascinated with the concept that, like hounds and foxes, we're born to hunt. There's no need to apologize for who we are. To hunt is to be human. That's why your eyes are in the center of your face. Of course, all the gay men wanted to talk about was the clothes, which they absolutely loved!

# Maureen Britell

AS KEEN AND ENTHUSIASTIC ABOUT THE SPORT AS ANYONE

YOU'LL EVER MEET, SHE LOVES THE ROMANTIC LOOK

OF RIDING SIDESADDLE.

I've always loved horses for as long as I can remember, but I never competed in horse shows or foxhunted as a child. I just rode for fun and then, when I was older, taught riding at children's camps. After I got married and had kids, we moved to Maryland and were invited to attend the opening meet of De La Brooke Foxhounds. I was thrilled because I'd have an opportunity to be around horses again. That was *it* for me. I was overwhelmed by the beauty of the sport and was overcome with a desire to participate, even though I hadn't been on a horse for ten or fifteen years. It was like love at first sight. I got my kids into pony club and got myself a bombproof horse. Moe was terrific because he was so fearless. He gave me courage, and I could spend my time out hunting—watching the hounds instead of fiddling with the horse. I now see how lucky I was to find the right horse to build my confidence. I've since seen so many people be scared away from foxhunting because they are on a scared horse.

I'm very drawn to the traditions and the history of the sport and why we do what we do when out following the hounds. Foxhunting is very much wrapped up in early American history. When George Washington was being defeated by the British at the Battle of Harlem Heights, the Brits blew "Gone Away" on their horn when he started retreating, and that made him so mad, he turned back in anger at the insult and had his first field battle win against the English. In the early 1800s in Washington, DC, the hunt used to run right by the Congress. There's a great story about the hounds running in full cry by the Capitol building and the members of Congress jumping on their horses and following the chase. Our stock ties

*Like most sidesaddle riders, we have the whole Jane Austen thing going on. We're true romantics at heart. Ladies riding sideways have no problem keeping up with the guys, and we look really good while doing it!*

make sense because they not only protect your neck, but they can be used as a bandage or sling. Now maybe my top hat doesn't make a lot of practical sense, but it looks damn good. Now the veil—that makes a lot of sense because it hides a multitude of sins! Sidesaddle went out of fashion once it was permissible for women to wear pants so they could ride astride. Something romantic and beautiful was lost in the change, and I think it should not be gone and forgotten. There was a woman named Freddie Foxwell at De La Brooke who rode sidesaddle, and the first time I saw her in the field, it took my breath away. Like most sidesaddle riders, we have the whole Jane Austen thing going on. We're true romantics at heart. The secret to jumping sidesaddle is to have a horse that jumps long and flat, like a steeplechase horse. I started taking lessons from Sandy Hoyer, and she warned me not to have an opinion about sidesaddle until I'd had at least five lessons. Until you find your spot, where your hips and the horse's shoulders are in line, you can't find your rhythm. Now I feel more secure sidesaddle than I do astride. I'm so much higher on the withers, and I feel like my horses are more responsive as a result. Their backs are freed up. They are aware of your spine movement, and that's your aid more than your leg or hands.

I'm always in awe of the beauty of our hunt territory. To watch the hounds work is a privilege, and that's not the only thing that's going on out there. I've seen bald eagles mating and fox walk right next to my horse and scratch his ears. Combine the beauty of nature with the thrill of the chase, and it is easy to get addicted. What I love about the sport is you never know what's coming next. There's always the edge of the unknown. We get to gallop across hundreds of acres. Instead of reading a book or watching a movie about exciting adventures, we're having exciting adventures of our own. Foxhunters have been accused of being adrenaline junkies, but the excitement of a fast run is only a part of it. Following the hounds, we get to not only see the wonders of nature but also feel a part of it.

I'm a weekend warrior. I work all week and can't walk out hounds and learn their names. I'm in awe of the huntsman and whips and their relationship with the pack. I'm so grateful for the effort they put in during all the days when I can't hunt. I look at both the staff and the hounds as top-notch athletes. I have total respect for their dedication and discipline. Almost without exception, the entire field is so grateful when we're out there hunting, and nothing feels better than gratitude. No matter how different your backgrounds, when you meet a fellow foxhunter, you have a common bond that overshadows your differences. I have so many friends that I probably wouldn't get to know if we didn't foxhunt together. I know foxhunters sometimes have a reputation of being unfriendly, but I've never felt that at all. Both at De La Brooke and now at Middleburg, I've never felt anything but included. The same goes when I travel to other hunts. Riding sideways always elicits a double take, but I always feel welcome.

Both of my kids have stuck with the horses. My daughter loves to foxhunt as much as I do, and my son is involved in the grand prix show jumping world. My husband, a former fighter pilot and commercial pilot, will get on a horse and ride, but he's not drawn to it. I tell him, "Sweetheart, there's women in tight pants, wearing tall leather boots and carrying whips, and there's alcohol and speed involved. You'd love foxhunting." He agrees it sounds like nothing not to like, but he refuses to wear riding pants! He loves to follow the hunt on foot or car top, but he's just not a horse person.

I've been fortunate enough to get to hunt in Ireland. I've gotten some great hunt horses from there. This was my first year of riding sideways over there. The livery horses had no trouble with the tack, and now I'm a

*Maureen "riding sideways" behind the Stonehall Harriers in Ireland.* EQUUS PIX

true believer on both sides of the Atlantic! We're organizing a Diana of the Chase event in England in honor of the old sidesaddle steeplechase races. There's a group of ladies who ride sidesaddle that will be going back to Ireland next year after the race and maybe do one there as well. There were about twenty of us out with Limerick this year, and forty of us showed up for Stonehall the next day. The first day, we hunted five and a half hours. Of course, there are parties at night. I was so sore that when I finally got into the bathtub, I had to roll over on my stomach because my backside was raw. That didn't stop me from going out the next day with Stonehall Harriers. I was looking sharp in my full regalia, but I was so sore, I could barely move as the forty of us sidesaddle ladies gathered in front of the castle before the hounds were cast. After the first three fences and a couple of sips on a flask, I was better than fine and had the time of my life.

Back in the States, I'm usually the only one riding sideways, except at Middleburg, where there are a few of us. It was great to be surrounded by so many like-minded women across the pond. Those Irish ladies are a scream. They are so beautifully turned out at the same time they're smoking cigarettes through their veils and swilling whiskey on the run. Hacking back to the trailers, the guys insist on giving our sidesaddles a try. One thing you can say about the Irish—they sure know how to have fun! That trip last November turned the tide for me, and I suspect I'll always hunt sidesaddle from now on. Once you find your flow, there's no going back. I only hunted sideways in preparation for the Ireland trip, and now I realize I have more fun sidesaddle because I feel so secure. I don't feel like I'm coming out of that saddle if something goes wrong. Of course, sometimes you might need to get out of the way if the horse falls down, so that could be pretty bad if you can't bail out in time. I think it's a fair trade-off. Ladies riding sideways have no problem keeping up with the guys, and we look really good while doing it! I hope to be kickin' on indefinitely, even if I have to get hoisted up into the saddle. 🐎

# Lynn Lloyd

A HORSE-CRAZY GIRL FROM PENNSYLVANIA WHO HAD A DREAM
TO GO WEST AND HUNT COYOTE WITH FOXHOUNDS, SHE HAS
BEEN LIVING THAT DREAM FOR OVER THIRTY-FIVE YEARS.

Growing up in the countryside of Pennsylvania, there were five kids and very little money to go around. I think I was born wanting a horse. My parents knew nothing about horses and didn't have the slightest interest. I remember being in the milk house of a neighboring dairy farm, and there was a wall calendar with pictures of Dale Evans and Roy Rogers on it. I knew that horses and the West had to be in my future. From the time I could walk and talk, I kept badgering my parents to get me a pony, and when I was four or five, they ordered a Shetland pony from the Sears and Roebuck catalog. He came not only with a red western saddle and bridle but also with his testicles! I guess a stallion was cheaper than a mare or gelding. A stud yearling is probably not the best choice for a child's first pony, but what did we know? Needless to say, when they placed me on his back, I came off pretty darn quick! I scared the poor little thing to death, but I was not deterred. I was determined—no helmet, no lessons—just trial and error.

When I got older, I got odd jobs and saved up my money for a horse. I found a neighbor who had a barn, and I mucked the stalls in exchange for board. I understood that my parents didn't have the money to support a horse, so I figured out how to take care of it myself. It did me a lot of good. I know when I face the day, I can take care of myself. As a teenager, I saved up enough money to go to a riding school in England after I graduated high school. That was an eye-opener. I'd never had a riding lesson and knew nothing about body clipping and pulled manes. In three months, they had me posting and jumping well enough that I got a teacher's certificate.

*Cowboys make great whips because they know how to wrangle without pushing too hard. My job as MFH is to encourage, not discourage. If you can't afford all the proper gear when you get started with us, I don't worry about it. If you like it enough to keep coming back, I know you'll fall in line and want to support the traditions.*

I could now give lessons myself. Better still, I was exposed to foxhunting. While riding cross country with my fellow students, I heard hounds in full cry, and oh my God, a switch went off in me that I didn't even know I had. Once I heard that music, I knew that was something I wanted to be involved with. Because I needed to work to make enough money for the trip back to the States, I got a job as a groom to a woman who foxhunted regularly. Mrs. Marlor introduced me to the folks who hunted the farmer packs and let me use her retired horse to go out with them. That horse was amazing and could do absolutely anything that needed to be done—a real confidence builder. Mrs. Marlor told me that she'd had many grooms over the years, but since I arrived, her horses had never been so fit, and her tack had never looked so bad. As wonderful as she was as an employer, I knew I'd never want to stay in England because I'd never be comfortable with the class distinction that colors everything.

When I came home and got a job as a riding instructor at St. Lawrence College, I used take the students across to Canada to hunt. After England, I knew foxhunting was something I wanted to do for the rest of my life, but I still carried around a longing to head West. As a child, every time I'd be riding around in the backseat of my family's car, I'd be looking out the window and imagining riding through all the land on both sides of the road. One of my earliest goals was to ride across the United States—a westward adventure. In 1973, at twenty-three, I realized if I was going to really do my great adventure, I'd better get moving. My thoroughbred horse died when I was riding in a steeplechase, but I was not deterred. A friend of mine offered me her Anglo-Arab that was a complete runaway on the hunt field, and she thought the three-thousand-mile ride would do him good. As soon as we took off, he ran away with me, and I just sat there and said, "Go right ahead. We're heading West." Well, it didn't take him too long to learn he'd better conserve his energy. After about a week, he'd completely changed his tune and was so quiet that I was able to ride him in a halter so he could eat along the way. I just let him eat the grass alongside the road, and at night, I'd tie him to a longline, just like I did my Sears Roebuck pony. I picked up money to feed myself along the way by stopping at farms and offering to do barn chores. I met so many great people on my travels. I only had to steal once. When there was no water to be had anywhere, I jumped a slow-moving train and tossed the large water jugs from the engines down on the ground so I could water my livestock and myself. I tell you what—robbing a train is good old-fashioned fun! I traveled with a water bucket tied to my tack so whenever I came to a water source, I could give my horse and dog a drink. I finally made it to California, where my sister was living. I sold the horse and got a job at a tack shop to make enough cash to drive back East with my sister, Carol.

When I got back to my home state of Pennsylvania, I opened a boarding and training barn, and I started a farm pack. Buster Chadwell at Essex was more than generous in helping me put a pack together. He taught me so much, I'll be eternally grateful. He drafted me some terrific American hounds. He knew what I needed, even if I didn't. Because I knew all the farmers from riding through the area as a child, I had so much land to hunt. Those old farmers taught me everything I needed to know about life—that there are no guarantees and that you get to decide every morning when you wake up if you want to be happy or sad. I feel so fortunate because I've always been appreciative for any help I've gotten along the way. I'm one of those fortunate people whose dreams have come true, and I'm very grateful for it because I know they didn't have to. Buster Chadwell used to come across the river from New Jersey and hunt with me a lot when I was in my mid-twenties. He saw how much I loved foxhunting, and I think he really enjoyed seeing my curiosity and enthusiasm. I know today I feel the same way about people who are just entering the sport. When I'd go hunt with Essex, he'd always let me hunt right beside him. What an education. I modeled my relationship with my hounds on how I saw him behave with his. His son Roddy was whipping-in to him, and I kept my eye on him too. Those were some wonderful years with horses and hounds, but by 1980, my personal life was a mess, so I decided to take a geographical cure and loaded up two good horses in my trailer and once again headed West. I drove until I ran out of gas and money and ended up right here, right outside of Reno.

I got a job working for the hunter/jumper trainer Julie Winkle. Every time I got paid, I put gas in the truck and went exploring, looking for a place to start another training/boarding barn and hunt. I got my first piece of land for two thousand down. It had well and septic and an old ramshackle barn. There was no telephone or mail service out here back then. The roads weren't paved. It was very challenging to get contractors out here to get things done. Every time I taught a lesson, I'd buy another two-by-four. I'd gotten a trailer to live in while I was building the barn and kennel. I about froze to death that first winter. I got my first hounds from Los Altos because a whip from Essex was now the huntsman there. So off I went, in search of coyote. I built up my field with the people who would come by my barn and take lessons. It didn't take me long to realize that this Nevada high-desert territory is way too big and dry for English hounds. A fellow name Walter Epps had two Walker hounds for hunting mountain lion, and he was about to shoot them because he couldn't get them off coyote. They were just what I needed to get a good pack of foxhounds that will run coyote. Scott Tepper started hunting with me and became my Joint Master. As a lawyer, he was invaluable helping me register my pack and getting the Red Rock hounds recognized. He sent me to New York to meet the MFHA folks. I never could have jumped all those hoops without him. Walker hounds weren't recognized as foxhounds back then, but Scott found a loophole that if the Walkers had been hunting fox for at least three generations, they could be recognized. Well, I didn't hunt fox because they were pretty scarce in Nevada. So the MFHA changed the language to include whatever quarry was available. In thirty-five years of

*Newspaper photo from an article about Lynn's cross country adventure in 1973.*

hunting here, I've chased two fox. The coyote had taken over, and now that wolves have been brought back from extinction, the coyotes are breeding with them, and they are moving into places where they haven't been seen in hundreds of years. Coyotes will breed with feral dogs. They are so adaptable that they'll continue to thrive. Red Rock was registered in 1983 and recognized in 1987.

One of the most unusual things about Red Rock is we have millions of acres to hunt. The US government owns 87 percent of the state and opens it up to hunters. Of course, the sheep and cattle ranchers love to see us make the coyotes feel unwelcome. There's no trees to trim or paths to groom. Everything is pretty much sand and sagebrush among the rocks. All I have to do is build jumps over the wire fence, but the fences are few and far between. Thirty-five years after I first arrived, I have close to a hundred and fifty hounds in our kennel. You need a lot of hounds to hunt three days a week in this large, rough, steep country, and you need a large pack so they can rest between hunts. When I'm on road trips and we hunt several days in a row, I'll take only my prime hounds, between about five and eight couple, so they can run together and not get strung out. Also, they are in better condition than the older or younger hounds. I also will travel only with boys and the neutered or girls and the neutered so I don't have bitches coming into season and dogfights on my hands.

Because of the size and steepness of our country, I have to rely on my whips to be in the right place at the right time. They need to travel high so they can keep an eye on things when the pack takes off running. Sometimes they'll carry a horn so they can hunt the hounds until I can get to them. Cowboys make great whips because they know how to wrangle without pushing too hard. When I started hunting here, I quickly learned that riding with my hounds wasn't always the best place to be. Once they're locked on a line, you might be better off riding on the ridge where the whips aren't so they can't disappear over a mountain. Those hounds don't need my help once they're running coyote. I just need to keep up and keep out of the way. I know better than to blow my horn if I'm riding behind the pack while they're running a line. I've got to get in front of them if I want to pull them off.

My job as MFH is to encourage, not discourage. If you can't afford all the proper gear when you get started with us, I don't worry about it. If you like it enough to keep coming back, I know you'll fall in line and want to support the traditions. I encourage children to hunt with us by not charging a cap fee. I just ask that they bring whatever they can afford to pay in dog food. I want them to understand why we're here and why there's a membership fee. I have a real soft spot in my heart for kids that love fox-hunting because it reminds me of my own childhood. Of course, I never saw a foxhunt until my late teens, but I believe I knew it was out there for me before I even knew what it was. 🐾

# Robin Keith

AFRAID OF HORSES ALL HER LIFE, ROBIN DECIDED IN HER
LATE SIXTIES TO JOIN HER DAUGHTER AND GRANDDAUGHTER
AND TAKE UP FOXHUNTING. SHE GOT HER COLORS WITH RED
ROCK HOUNDS ON HER SEVENTIETH BIRTHDAY.

I have two daughters, and my youngest, Amy, has always been a pony girl. She was in love with horses from the first time she looked at one and, like a lot of little girls, was always begging for one of her own. After we saw her commitment to her riding lessons, we got her one, and she rode her every chance she could. I was always afraid of horses my whole life. I fell off as a child the first time I sat on one, and I never wanted to have anything to do with them after that.

Of course, when your child has a horse that lives on your place, there's no way you can avoid dealing with it. I swear that horse knew I was afraid and used to hide when she saw me timidly look out in the pasture before I walked through the gate. She'd wait until I got out in the middle of the field, and then she'd come galloping out of nowhere— straight at me—and scare me to death. I'd just stand there thinking, *Amy said she wouldn't run over me. I can do this, I can do this.* That mare really reinforced my fear of horses. After Amy grew up and had kids, she started foxhunting. She loved it so much, she kept telling me I had to join her, that it was so much fun. She knew I loved being outdoors in nature, but the horse factor was something that seemed insurmountable. When I was in my mid-sixties, Amy gave me horseback riding lessons as a birthday present. I tried to forget about it, but she kept pestering me—or maybe I should call it "relentless encouragement." Just to get her off my back, I finally went to take the darn lesson. They put me on a giant but saintly horse named Einstein that tried his best to keep me on his back.

*Foxhunting is like life itself—it's the journey, not the destination. I'm so grateful to be on this path. It's given me the community, the challenge, and the fun I needed in my life.*

He knew I was scared to death, but I could feel his patience and concern. Still, he was a horse, and I was petrified. One day, dogs were making a ruckus by the ring, and Einstein looked over in that direction, and I went right over his shoulder. I was amazed that I didn't die, that I didn't even get hurt. Once I realized that falling off isn't the worst thing in the world, a lot of my anxiety fell away. After that, I started taking riding lessons for myself and not just to humor my daughter.

About that time, I was getting ready to retire, and I was thinking about the things I needed after retirement to stay engaged and continue to grow. The first was a sense of community. The second was a challenge, tackling something new. And the third was fun. No matter how old you are, I think it's important to never lose that sense of wonder and excitement—to have fun. My daughter Amy is a whipper-in for Red Rock Hounds, and her daughter Sidney has been hunting with them since she was about eight years old. I saw what Amy and Sidney were sharing together at Red Rock Hounds, and I decided that if I was lucky enough to have a daughter and granddaughter who wanted to share their passion with me, it was time for me to join them. Every Sunday at dinner, Amy and Sidney would regale me with the wonderful adventures they had on the hunt, and it eventually dawned on me that the only thing holding me back from living my life on a fuller level was myself, so I had to get out of my own way. They convinced me to come with them on an away hunt and follow on a quad (four-wheeler), and I was struck by the exciting beauty of the hunt. I started taking lessons from Red Rock's Master and huntsman, Lynn Lloyd, and that's where I learned the difference between being scared and being terrified! I can hear her now: "Come on, honey, you can do it!" Riding is like breathing to her. She doesn't realize some of us have to think about it. But her enthusiasm is infectious, and I thank goodness that I caught it. Her fearlessness made me rise to the occasion.

My first year with Red Rock was mainly about overcoming my own fear. But I was determined because I saw the joy that was available to me if I could just relax. A voice in my head would sometimes say, "Be reasonable, you can't afford to break a hip," and another voice would say, "Life is for the living, and you should grab on to fun when you find it." That first year out hunting was about learning how to ride well enough that I could let my eyes go somewhere besides between my horses ears. I might hear the horn and think *Gee, they're out there somewhere* but not really have a clue what

*Robin, with her dual inspirations—
her granddaughter Sidney and her
daughter Amy.*

was going on. Once I was able to ride by feel instead of by thought, I could open my eyes to the sights and sounds around me. Folks in the hunt club were so supportive that it really helped me build up my confidence. I found that sense of community that I was looking for and eventually transitioned from fear to enjoyment.

By my second year of hunting, I was able to actually watch the hounds work and enjoy nature's wonders all around me. Our territory is rocky and steep. It's a whole different ballgame than riding in a ring. Once I got my own horse, I began to develop a bond, and now that we have gotten to know and trust each other, it's like I know what he's going to do the moment before he does it, and I think he feels the same way about me. Riding with Pat Hodges has taught me so much about the sport and art of foxhunting. If the hounds are running north, she knows to head east to catch up with them on the next ridge. These mountains and valleys in Nevada make you have to sharpen your geometry skills. She also has great knowledge of local history, so she has all these wonderful stories to share as we go along. One of my favorite things about the sport is that no two days are alike. The weather, the terrain, the pace of the hunting, your horse's mood, and the mood of the people around you are always a unique experience. This year, our huntsman invited me to ride in her pocket. I was simultaneously terrified and thrilled at the prospect, but there's no way I could refuse such an honor. We usually work hard to keep our hounds from running up a mountain range called the Dogskins, which is very steep and rocky. As fate would have it, the day I'm riding with Lynn, the hounds fly up the Dogskins without looking back. So off we went up this very steep ascent, and I was terrified. But once we reached the summit and I looked out over those mountain ranges, I was thrilled and thought, *Wow—I might be a badass!*

I turned seventy this year and just got my colors today. I'm probably the oldest person to get their colors, but that's all right. Better late than never! I'm so glad I was so determined to overcome my fear because I'm now enjoying such a wonderful sense of accomplishment. Now I'm just finishing my third season with Red Rock, and I can honestly say, I've never had more fun in my life. I know plenty of people who are so bored in retirement, always thinking back on the good old days. Well, for me, these are the good old days! I've found how to be thrilled without being terrified. I feel centered and balanced, and I'm not afraid. As I get to know my horse and the hounds and learn the countryside, I just get more and more invested in this wonderful sport. I can even discern between a coyote and a jackrabbit when the hounds start to speak. I can now understand what Lynn is doing with the hounds by the sounds she makes on her hunt horn. This year, Lynn has even trusted me to lead the second flight from time to time, and I've had enough confidence to enjoy doing it. I remember people saying to me, it only gets better and better, but that's hard to understand unless you experience it. Foxhunting is like life itself—it's the journey, not the destination. I'm so grateful to be on this path. It's given me the community, the challenge, and the fun I needed in my life. 🪶

# Hunting Terms

Note: This glossary originally appeared in *Introduction to Foxhunting* (5th edition) and is reprinted with permission from Dennis Foster of the MFHA.

**Autumn Hunting** Very early in the year when hounds first start hunting. Young hounds are learning to hunt; older hounds are getting conditioned; young foxes are learning to evade hounds; and horses and riders are getting in shape. It is a time when hunt attire is rat catcher and the hunt usually doesn't stay out as long for fear of exhausting young hounds. Autumn used to be called cub hunting or cubbing.

**Away** When the quarry has left a cover and gone away; the hounds are gone away.

**Babbling** When hounds are giving voice or barking for no good reason. It could be nothing or the faint scent of the quarry too long gone to run. It is not good because it distracts other hounds from working to find the prey.

**Back** When the quarry heads back to where it came from, Tally-ho back; if the hounds come out going the wrong way, the term is "hark back."

**Biddability** The hounds' desire to please and willingness to be controlled.

**Billet** The excrement of the fox, which is distinguished from all other, by the fur of rabbits, which is nearly always to be seen in it. It is always very dark.

**Blooding** A tradition going back to ancient times where the blood of an animal that was killed is smeared on a person's forehead and cheeks. The practice was done only on people who experienced their first kill on a hunt. It is significant to honor the dead animal. Some hunts still blood people who request it. The MFHA does not recommend it because too many people don't understand why it's done. It does not, however, forbid it.

**Blue Bird Day** Thought to be a bad scenting day with blue skies and no clouds.

**Blue Haze** Thought to be a bad scenting day when a blue haze or fog is present.

**Breast high** Also a burning scent, when hounds run at utmost speed because of breast-high scent. They do not stoop their heads, and go a racing pace.

**Brush** The tail of a fox or coyote. Awarded upon a kill by the Master.

**Bumping the line** Refers to hounds finding and losing the scent or line of the quarry over and over.

**Burning scent** The English definition is when hounds run almost mute, owing to the strength of the scent. An American definition is when scent is where hounds can carry the line without putting their noses down and the cry turns to a roar as they gain on their quarry.

**Burst** The first part of a run out of cover, if quick, is called a sharp burst.

**Burst him** A term used when a fox is killed, owing to a sharp burst.

**Buttons** Hunt buttons are awarded with hunt colors. Each button has the logo of the hunt engraved on it. Hunt buttons are only worn with formal attire.

**Capping** When a fox is killed, it is the custom in some countries to cap (give a tip) for the huntsman; some man takes around a cap or glove, and men are expected to drop a tip into it. It also means when a man takes off his hat or cap and waves it to bring the huntsman to a view. Capping is when you visit a hunt that you are not a member of. You pay a capping fee to the Secretary of the Hunt before you leave the meet.

**Carries** After a frost, the ground adheres to the quarry's feet, then the ground carries.

**Carry a good head** When hounds run well together owing to the scent being good, and spread out so that they extend wide enough in the front for almost the whole pack to smell the line. But it most frequently happens that the scent is good only on a narrow line for a few hounds to get it so that the back hounds have less scent to lead them on and do not get to head so as to be all abreast.

**Cast**  When the huntsman sends hounds into a cover or brings them together and then sends them another direction, he is said to be casting his hounds.

**Challenge**  When drawing for a fox, the first hound which throws his tongue is a challenge.

**Changed**  When hounds have left their hunted fox and changed to another.

**Check**  When hounds in chase stop for want of scent or have overrun it.

**Cheering**  When hounds are encouraged by a horn or halloo.

**Chop't the quarry**  When the quarry is killed as soon as found. There is no run; it usually happens with very sick, wounded, or hurt quarry caught napping in open areas.

**Cold-hunting or Trailing**  When hounds can scarcely smell a scent and pick it out with difficulty. Hounds speak intermittently when cold-hunting.

**Colors**  Every hunt has their particular color. This color is worn on their collar and lapel when wearing scarlet. When hunting in formal attire riders have either scarlet or black coats, but the colors on their collar are always the same. Only members who have been awarded colors can wear that color on their coats. Members without colors must wear a plain black coat. When a member has been awarded their colors, it is considered an honor acknowledging them as full status members of the hunt. Once awarded colors they must wear hunt buttons on any coat with colors.

**Couple**  You count mounted hunting hounds by twos, the number of couples.

**Cover**  Any somewhat thick place that will hold the quarry.

**Covert**  The cover where the hounds look for the quarry. It can be heavy brush, thick grass, woods, or anything that requires the hounds to search through it.

**Crash**  When hounds are running in cover, and it appears that everyone is there, it is called a good crash.

**Cub**  A young fox or coyote.

**Cubbing or Cub Hunting (also Autumn Hunting)** Hunting early in the season. A period where hounds go out very early. Young hounds learn to chase the quarry, and young quarry learn to get away from hounds. Usually very short early morning hunts in informal attire. In the early days in England, it referred to a time they would try to cull young fox populations early in the season.

**Dew on spiderwebs** Said to indicate bad scenting conditions.

**Downwind** When hounds are running with the wind behind them.

**Draft** When you get a hound from another Hunt.

**Drafted** When hounds are given to another Hunt, they are drafted.

**Drag** The scent left by the footsteps of the fox or coyote. Also, the scent left from a lure dragged on the ground for hounds to follow simulating a live fox in a drag hunt.

**Drain** Underground where foxes or coyote often run to. Often, it is a man-made culvert or pipe.

**Drawing** When hounds are working a covert or an area, they are said to be drawing it.

**Dwelling** A hound that gives tongue but does not move on. When hounds do not get on to the huntsman's halloo, probably feeling a stale scent sometimes, till moved by the whipper-in; also, a slow huntsman is apt to dwell.

**Earth Stopping** Refers to the old days in England when before the hunt, fox dens were plugged up to prevent the fox from an early retreat and to have a longer chase. The MFHA considers it absolutely unsporting. It is against the rules both in the USA and now in England.

**Eloo back** When hounds come out, to turn them back.

**Excitement Riot or Mettle in England** When hounds are very fresh and fly for a short distance on no scent.

**Eye to hounds** A person is said to have a good eye to hounds, whose eyes in the chase are always fixed on the leading hound or hounds, by which he has a great advantage over others as he turns his horse's head whichever way the leading hound goes immediately. This person is a menace if he is riding too forward or close, resulting in turning the game.

**Feeling a scent**  A termed used when any hounds smells the scent; when bad, it is said they can scarcely feel the scent.

**Field Secretary**  The person a hunt designates who, when people arrive at the meet, collects caps, gets waivers signed, and directs parking is sometimes called the field secretary.

**Flighty**  A hound which is not a steady hunter is called flighty; also, when the scent changes from good to bad repeatedly, it is called flighty scent.

**Foil**  When the quarry runs the ground over which he has been before, it is called running his foil; sometimes a reason for hounds not being able to hunt it where they have been before. It also includes the quarry running through farm animals, like sheep or cattle, to foil the scent or spread manure. Whatever causes a good scenting line to no longer be smelled.

**Forward**  A halloo implies to get on or that the hounds are running ahead of you.

**Full cry**  When the whole pack is running hard after the quarry and throwing or giving tongue.

**Going to cover**  Going to the place where the quarry is likely to be found in order to draw.

**Gone to Ground**  When a fox or coyote goes into natural earth, a hole, or a drain.

**Handles a pack**  A term used when speaking of a huntsman who, sensing that hounds are at an irretrievable loss, picks them up to cast in the direction he thinks the game has gone.

**Hark! Halloa!**  When a person hears a halloo at a distance and the huntsman does not, he should halloa, "Hark! Halloo!" and point with his whip if in sight of him.

**Headed**  When the quarry is going away but is headed, that is, turned back the way he came or away from its intended path. Usually used to refer to a person/persons or horses that headed the quarry.

**Heel**  The hounds are said to be running heel when they get on the scent of the quarry and run it back the way the quarry came from instead of the way it went.

**Hit**  When hounds are at check and recover the scent, it is hitting it off. Or the first hound that smells the scent is said to have made a good hit.

**Hold hard**  A huntsman's or Field Master's verbal command to quickly stop for whatever reason, usually when the pack checks to keep from riding over the line. When overzealous or eager riders are pressing hounds too closely.

**Hold them on**  For huntsmen to take the hounds forward and try to regain the scent.

**Holding scent**  When the scent is just good enough to hunt the quarry a fair pace but not enough to press him.

**Hooi**  The view halloo, if tally-ho is not heard; or when hounds are at a check and it is desirable to get them on.

**Hunt Breakfast**  A brunch after a hunt. Normal attire is your hunt coat or a change to a sport coat. Spurs should be removed and boots cleaned before entering.

**Hunting whip**  Consists of a crop and lash specifically for mounted hunting. Only staff are allowed to use one around hounds, and it is seldom if ever used to hit them. It can be cracked to get hounds heads-up or shown to get a hound to move in a particular direction. Field members can carry a hunting whip, but it is only used if they are asked to help whip-in, to open gates or pick up something that has dropped.

**Laid up**  When a vixen fox or coyote bitch has had cubs or pups, she is said to have laid up.

**Laying**  That part of a covert in which quarry is generally found.

**Left-handed**  Such hounds are called left-handed which are not always right but apt to be too wide and fly without a scent; the sooner they are drafted, the better, although they frequently have some excellent qualities.

**Lieu in**  Get in place; get in there (originally came from the French).

**Lifting**  When hounds are scarcely able to hunt a scent across bad scenting ground, the huntsman is induced to take them off it and move them forward where he thinks he may hit off the scent, probably to a halloo. Some sportsmen condemn the practice, preferring the hounds find the line on their own. Others believe it is good as long as it isn't done too often to make up ground on the quarry. Particularly in country where scent is bad, an example would be high desert.

**Line hunters**  Any good hounds which will not go a yard beyond the scent and keep the pack right (invaluable hounds); by some called ploughholders because they can smell and hold the line on ploughed ground.

**Litter**  Young foxes or coyotes or the cubs or pups belonging to a fox or coyote. Young foxhounds with the same dam and sire are also called a litter.

**Lure**  The formula of the scent used on a dragline. The lure is dispersed on a rag or some type of disperser and drug on a dragline. It can also be dropped as a liquid directly to the ground. It can be fox or coyote urine or a mixture of fox or coyote urine mixed or diluted with water, anisette, or anything that will make it last longer or give it the desired results of simulating a pack chasing a quarry.

**Main earths**  Large earths in which foxes generally breed.

**Mask**  The head of the fox or coyote. Awarded upon a kill by the Master and then mounted by a taxidermist.

**Moving scent**  When hounds get on a scent that is fresher than a drag, that is, the scent of the quarry which has been disturbed while traveling.

**Mute**  Hounds run silent or mute when the scent is so good that the pace they go prevents their giving/throwing tongue, but if a hound always runs mute, it is an unpardonable fault, even if in every other respect he is the best hound in the pack. The better he is, the more harm he does.

**Noisy**  When a hound gives his tongue without a scent. This is also called babbling. It is a bad trait and distracts other hounds from hunting.

**Open**  When a hound gives tongue, he is said to open on the scent.

**Open Bitches**  Unspayed bitches that can be bred.

**Over it**  When hounds have gone beyond their scent in chase, it is said they are over it.

**Owning a scent**  When hounds give tongue on the scent, they own the line.

**Pad**  The foot of a fox or coyote. Also can be awarded by a Master upon a kill.

**Padding a fox**  Finding the print of a fox's foot.

**Pinks**  A term used to describe the red or scarlet hunt coat. Originated from a fable of a tailor whose last name was Mr. Pinque, who supposedly made the first red hunt coats. People started calling red coats pinks after the tailor, and it caught on. Maybe this came about because some red coats bleach out to pink after enough use, or it was a name-dropping trend for those in the know. The correct term is red or scarlet.

**Point-to-Point**  The distance of a run on a map by a straight line. Also the name of a race used by Hunts to make money for the Hunt. The races usually involve jumping, simulating what is required from horses that hunt.

**Rabbit earth or spout**  Where a fox sometimes gets into when pressed: meant to imply that it is not a regular fox earth.

**Rat Catcher**  The clothing worn before the formal season begins or on days designated by the hunt. Also called informal attire.

**Rate**  You rate a hound when you change its behavior. You can do this with you or your horse's body language, your eyes, your voice, a lash, or any other means used to stop it and get it to do what is expected.

**Reaching**  Reaching means hounds reach forward well ahead of the huntsman, looking for their fox. The term can also be used when describing hounds' action at a check. Once hounds have lost at the check, they should fan out and reach well forward, covering large areas.

**Riot**  When hounds hunt anything besides intended quarry it is called riot; the rate used is "Ware riot."

**Roading Hounds**  Anytime you have the pack packed up, moving alongside a road.

**Scarlets** Formal function attire. Individual hunt colors are worn on the collar and lapel. Scarlets are traditionally a swallowtail. It is traditional that ladies wear black or white gowns at formal hunt functions, like a ball or dinner.

**Sinking** The quarry is said to be sinking when it is nearly beaten.

**Sinking the wind** When people go downwind to hear the cry, it is called sinking the wind of the hounds.

**Skirter** A hound which is generally too wide of the pack and not running the actual line. Hounds do this to get an unfair advantage getting to the front. Usually involves avoiding the thick places; skirters break a pack's heart and should be culled.

**Slack** When the scent is bad, hounds are apt to be indifferent and will scarcely try to hunt their quarry, and are said to be slack.

**Speaks** When a hound smells the scent, it is sometimes said that such a hound speaks to it.

**Stained** Also called foil; when the ground has been passed over by cattle, sheep, other livestock, and/or the hounds or the field before.

**Steady** When a hound will not run trash or deer, he is considered steady.

**Stern** A hound's tail.

**Stopping** When hounds will not hunt, it is said they will not stoop to the scent, that is, will not put their noses to the ground.

**Streaming** When hounds go over or across an open country like a flock of pigeons, it is called streaming away.

**Stroke of a fox** Is when hounds are drawing, it is evident from their manner that they feel the scent of a fox, although they do not own it.

**Tally ho** The halloo when anyone sees the quarry, and only then; if desirable to halloa it loudly. Field members do not use tally ho or halloa when riding the field. They report the sighting to the Masters.

**Tally ho back** When the fox comes out and heads back again.

**Throwing tongue** When a hound barks or gives voice.

**Throw up**  The exact spot where the hounds lost the scent in a chase is known by their throwing up their heads, and it is said they threw up here.

**Ticklish scent**  When the scent varies from good to bad and, at times, scarcely any in the chase, although just before it was very good.

**Tight in his tongue**  When a hound seldom throws his tongue, though not quite mute, it is said he is tight in his tongue.

**Tipping**  It is appropriate and traditional to tip the professional huntsman when given a special kennel visit or an unusually good day hunting. It is also appropriate to tip the professional huntsman when a hunt drafts you a hound.

**Trash**  Refers to hounds chasing something they shouldn't be chasing.

**View Halloo**  A loud rebel yell or scream used when viewing the quarry. Usually only whippers-in and huntsmen are allowed to use it. It is never used if hounds have opened on the quarry, only when hounds have not found and the quarry is viewed by a whipper-in. Also called holloa, hooi, or rebel yell. Others would use the term "tally ho" when the quarry is viewed but never while in the field of riders.

**Ware**  Shortened form of beware. To take note of something you need to avoid. Usually ware hound, ware wire, ware hole.

**White whip**  A white crop and lash (the normal color is brown) only used by huntsmen on special formal days.

**Whoop**  The death halloo.

# Acknowledgments

J ust as Masters of hunt clubs are fond of saying, "Thanks first and foremost to the landowners because without their generosity, there would be no foxhunting," my first and foremost thanks goes to the people in these pages because without their willingness to share their personal experiences and introduce me to others who had wonderful stories to share, there would be no book. The generosity of my fellow foxhunters in this book kept my enthusiasm and determination alive through the years it took to compile this collection. I was given a place to stay and a horse to hunt at hunt clubs across the country. I send a special thank-you to Vicky Collins at Green Spring Valley, Mason and Mary Lu Lampton at Midlands, Bobby and Susie Ashcom, Lynn Lloyd at Red Rock, John Coles with Orange County, Al Schreck at Los Altos, Tot Goodwin at Green Creek, and Marty and Daphne Wood with Live Oak for hospitable accommodations and a suitable mount. Every place I went, I felt welcomed and encouraged.

Lee Gildea's whimsical line drawings are a much appreciated contribution to this book. He read every interview and drew it as he saw it. I'm also indebted to the encouragement that Norman Fine has given me since I first started working on *Foxhunters Speak*. He brought my manuscript to Jed Lyons at Rowman & Littlefield, who passed it on to Emily Tyler with the Derrydale Press Foxhunters Library. I am also grateful to Dennis Foster for his generous contribution of the glossary of terms from *Introduction to Foxhunting*.

The two people who have been my biggest support system and to whom I'm eternally grateful are my son Hugh and my husband David. Hugh had the patience of Job teaching me all things digital. I literally couldn't have done it without him. David was my North Star, who planted the seed of this book and gave me the nurturance to ensure its growth and full flowering.

# Index

Italicized page numbers indicate photographs and illustrations.

injuries, 58, 65–66, 77, 86, 183, 204–5

*Mary Motley Kalergis*

# About the Author

Mary's photography has been exhibited in museums and galleries internationally, including the Smithsonian Institution, the Chrysler Museum of Art, the San Antonio Museum of Art, the International Center of Photography, the Virginia Museum of Fine Arts, the Southeast Museum of Photography, the Diaframa Kodak Gallery (Milan, Italy), and Museum Fur Photographie (Germany).

Her documentary photography books include *Giving Birth* (Harper-Collins), *Mother: A Collective Portrait* ( Dutton), *Home of the Brave* (Dutton), *With This Ring* (Chrysler Museum of Art), *Seen and Heard: Teenagers Talk About Their Lives* (Stewart, Tabori and Chang), *Charlottesville Portrait* (Howell Press), *Love in Black and White* (Kensington Press), and *Considering Adoption* (Atelerix Press).

In addition to these eight published monographs, her photographs have been published in numerous anthologies and collections, including Aperture's *Mothers and Daughters*; Pantheon's *Generations*; Stemmle's *In Their Mother's Eyes*; National Geographic's *Star Spangled Banner*; Fawcett's *In Celebration of Babies*; Andrew McMeel's *Waiting for Baby*, *Reflections*, and *The Enduring Circle of Love*; Ballentine's *Preparation for Birth*; and McGraw-Hill's *New Parenthood*.

Photographs by Mary have appeared in numerous newspapers and magazines, including *The Guardian* (London), *Camera Manichi* (Japan), the *New York Times*, *People*, *Time*, *Newsweek*, *Glamour*, *Marie Claire*, *Ladies Home Journal*, *Seventeen*, and *Sports Illustrated*. She has served on the faculty of the International Center of Photography and has been a "special stills" photographer on movie sets. Mary lives in Charlottesville, Virginia, with her husband David. They have four children and six grandchildren. Visit her website at www.mmkphoto.com.